Dominican Cultures
The Making of a Caribbean Society

Dominican Cultures
The Making of a Caribbean Society

CONTRIBUTORS

José del Castillo Pichardo
Carlos Esteban Deive
Carlos Dobal
Frank Moya Pons
Ernesto Sagás
Rubén Silié
Bernardo Vega
Marcio Veloz Maggiolo

TRANSLATED FROM SPANISH
BY CHRISTINE AYORINDE

Markus Wiener Publishers
Princeton

For information write to: Markus Wiener Publishers
231 Nassau Street, Princeton, NJ 08542
www.markuswiener.com

Library of Congress Cataloging-in-Publication Data

Ensayos sobre cultura dominicana. English
   Dominican cultures : the making of a Caribbean society / contributors,
   Jose del Castillo Pichardo ... [et al.] ; translated from Spanish by Christine
   Ayorinde. — 1st ed.
   Translation of lectures presented at Museo del Hombre Dominicano, 1979-1981.
   Includes bibliographical references.
   ISBN-13: 978-1-55876-434-7 (hardcover : alk. paper)
   ISBN-10: 1-55876-434-8 (hardcover : alk. paper)
   ISBN-13: 978-1-55876-435-4 (paperback : alk. paper)
   ISBN-10: 1-55876-435-6 (paperback : alk. paper)
   1. Dominican Republic--Civilization. I. Castillo Pichardo, Jose del. II. Title.
F1935.E5713 2007
972.93—dc22
                                    2007007969

Contents

LEMBA

BARTOLOME DE LAS CASAS

ENRIQUILLO

Preface to This Edition

In 1981 when I was asked to put together this book of essays in my capacity as director of the Museo del Hombre Dominicano, we were in the process of remodeling the fourth floor of the building in order to offer a museographic representation of the three main facets of Dominican cultural heritage—Taino, African and Spanish—and of the subsequent processes of hybridization and mixing. The information in these essays gave our museologists a clearer idea of the task before them. At that time, we also put up the three statues that adorn the entrance of the museum, each one reflecting the struggle for freedom. They were of Enriquillo, one of the island's original inhabitants; Lemba, an African slave; and Fray Bartolomé de las Casas, a Spaniard. The volume was a great success and became a university textbook that has run to six editions.

Today, a sizeable proportion of the population of the Dominican Republic as well as of the other Caribbean islands lives outside the country, particularly in North America. For this reason it is time to sponsor an English edition which will undoubtedly enable people in the Dominican diaspora to better understand both their own culture and that of their forebears. It can also be used as a school and university text in the English-speaking world.

Bernardo Vega
President
Fundación Cultural Dominicana
Santo Domingo, July 2006

vii

Publisher's Note

Ensayos sobre Cultura Dominicana, the original collection of lectures on which this translation is based, became a classic in Dominican Republic historical studies when it was published in 1981. Even though the Trujillo dictatorship had fallen twenty years earlier, the book still caused a sensation among students and the general public alike. For the first time, the leading scholars and personalities of the Dominican Republic explored the multicultural dimensions of Dominican society.

This English translation now makes those original lectures available to the countless numbers of Dominicans and individuals of Dominican heritage living abroad. Like the book from which it is translated, it reproduces the lectures as closely as possible. Because they were not necessarily accompanied by full documentation when they were presented, the documentation in this edition is, in some places, inevitably inconsistent or even missing. There are occasional references to works that are not included in the chapter reference lists or Selected Bibliography. References that *are* included may not be accompanied by full documentation.

The urgency of publishing a book of such distinction more than offsets, we believe, those instances where there are gaps in the documentation, and we are confident that, despite those few gaps, readers will appreciate and gain from the exceptional scholarship encompassed by this collection of essays.

CHAPTER ONE

The Indigenous Inheritance in Dominican Culture

BERNARDO VEGA

Introduction

The aim of this collection of essays is to analyze the main features of the culture of the Dominican Republic, or *dominicanidad* (Dominican-ness) by studying the different ethnic groups and the political and economic phenomena that both form part of and have shaped the national historical process. This project fits perfectly with the objectives of its sponsoring institution, the Museo del Hombre Dominicano, an anthropological museum. Among these objectives are the rescue, preservation, presentation and study of all the archaeological and ethnographic components of our cultural heritage.

The Appropriate Context

Intensive contact between Spaniards, enslaved Blacks and indigenous peoples lasted for no more than fifty years on our islands. This of itself is a factor which inevitably limited the impact of the indigenous culture on Dominican culture, howev-

1

er developed the culture might have been at that time. (However, it was not as developed as Meso-American and Inca cultures, for example.) Although we must acknowledge that the Dominican culture reached a higher level of development in the Greater Antilles compared to its place of origin in the tropical rainforests in the northeast of the South American continent.

I believe these preliminary comments are necessary to locate the indigenous influence in its right and proper context. This avoids making the same mistake as those who, inspired by a well-intentioned but unscholarly romanticism, have exaggerated this influence as a—perhaps unconscious—way of vindicating the exterminated race, or worse still, of downplaying the African influence on account of prejudice.

The indigenous component of the Dominican culture should not be overemphasized. Genetic factors alone explain why European and African cultures have played a more prominent role in the evolution of our culture. Nevertheless, what we can rightly defend is the persistence of certain indigenous cultural legacies despite the brief period of contact. Having established the frame of reference for this analysis, let us now begin.

The Economic Base

Within the economic sphere, the most enduring influence of aboriginal culture can be observed. Although this influence has naturally diminished over time, it still persists to a greater extent than is generally assumed. This assertion is not motivated by my own professional bias but rather an objective analysis of the survival of certain prehistoric agricultural practices. In a predominantly agricultural country, such as the Dominican Republic still is, and with traditional forms of agriculture, the importance of *roza* (cleared ground) and *conuco* (small-holding) cultivation cannot be underestimated. Both are indigenous legacies.

Roza and *Conuco* Cultivation

The Arawaks brought roza cultivation, that is, "tumba y quema (slash and burn)" agriculture from the South American tropical forest. Anyone wishing to observe its present-day survival needs only to fly over the Dominican Republic's mountains and plains, especially during the months of March, April and August, to see the columns of smoke rising from the fresh "*tumbas* (cleared ground)" or "*claros* (forest clearings)" made by rural inhabitants. This nomadic form of cultivation entails periodic moving of the family home. First it involves the felling or "tumba" of the trees, clearing the undergrowth, cutting the tree trunks into small pieces and then setting fire to everything. This clears the ground and fertilizes the soil with a rich layer of ash. During the burning, all the lost fertilizers are retuned to the soil and others already in the earth are released.

For anyone who has seen an agricultural "tumba" in the Orinoco-Amazon region, its resemblance to those of the Dominican Republic is clear, resolving any possible doubts about a greater African influence on this practice, which is also common on the African continent but has variations that distinguish it from the South American way.

The *conuco* (a Taino word) is characterized by the simultaneous cultivation of various crops within the same area. This reduces the need for trade as it makes the farmer more self-sufficient, especially when sowing is carried out so that the different plantings ripen one after the other. Food can thus be harvested throughout the year. The fact that conuco production is centered on tubercles such as *yuca* (cassava or manioc), *batata* (sweet potato) and *mapuey* (*Dioscorea trifida* L.) has the added advantage that roots can be left in the soil until required, thus eliminating the problem of storage and surplus perishables.

The agricultural combination of *roza-conuco*, which was inherited from the Taino, has been the most widely-used farming technique throughout the entire history of the country. The *montero* (hunter), the *hatero* and the owners of the short-lived plantations of the sixteenth century used other forms of cultivation. However, these practices never became as important as those of the small family property. The chronicler Oviedo states that the Tainos: "Beside their villages had their farms and *conucos,* which was what they called their inheritances of corn fields and *yuca* and groves of fruit trees."

The roza method of cultivation causes extensive damage because it is based on a false premise: an unlimited supply of forest for cutting down. In our modern society, the indiscriminate use of this method leads to deforestation and erosion.

Montones and *Coa*

Another important pre-Columbian farming technique, which survived until the end of the sixteenth century, is the cultivation of manioc on *montones*.[1] The chroniclers recalled that when the city of Santo Domingo was still located on the eastern bank of the Ozama River, the whole west bank (the present-day colonial part) was a large area of montones on which manioc was grown.

In *El Pleito Ovando-Tapia,* Rodríguez Demorizi explains that: "On the same site where the city of Santo Domingo stands, Cristóbal de Tapia had a hacienda with 38,000 thousand *montones* of *yuca* and chili. At that time a thousand *montones* of manioc was worth fifty *castellanos*[2] of gold."

The montones system was so widespread that the Spaniards

4

used it as the basis for the system of land measurement employed in the Antilles. Thus, in 1513, the king of Spain instructed Pedrarias Dávila:

> You should give and point out to the *escudero* (squire) and the person who has served and may serve us, and who may take up residence there, lands for distribution in which he may put and mark out two hundred thousand *montones*, and this is called a *cavallería* of land, and to the peon at the rate of a hundred thousand *montones,* which is a *peonía.[3]*

On the other hand, the *coa* (digging stick) is the only surviving pre-Columbian farming tool in Dominican agriculture.

Las Casas recalled a *cacique* (chief) who: "Of his own volition brings 4,000 to 5,000 men, unarmed except for their *coas*, which are scorched sticks that they use as hoes, and asks the Governor where he would like him to make a large farm of *casabi* bread."

Casabe

Turning now from production techniques to specific crops, there is no doubt that *yuca* and its processed version *casabe[4]* are the most important contributions of Taino agriculture to the Dominican diet.

Casabe was not only the Tainos' main food crop; in the early period, the conquistadors would literally have died of hunger without a non-perishable product like casabe. The need for it reached such extremes that, while demanding gold in tribute from the indigenous peoples, the conquistadors demanded casabe from others, curbing their avarice to survive. Then, when the indigenous peoples looked for ways to defeat the Spaniards, they chose to live in the mountains so that no one would tend the montones of manioc, in the hope that the Spaniards would die from lack of food. All the ships departing from Santo Domingo to discover new lands carried casabe as essential food for the crew.

In his play *La Villana de Vallecas,* Tirso de Molina mentions *Jabjao* which was a fine casabe reserved for *caciques.*

The importance of casabe in the Dominican diet at the beginning of the seventeenth century is evident from the 1606 census since out of the 9,648 slaves, only 888 worked in the sugar mills and domestic service. The rest worked mainly on *estancias* (farms, estates) where they produced ginger, casabe and corn.

In the Spanish attack on the pirates of Tortuga in 1653, the booty obtained was eleven vessels laden with artillery, salt, "cazabe, yuca and other cultivated products," since the pirates on "the coasts of the northern strip, make their settlements and farms of tobacco, ginger and cazabe."

In 1672, a hurricane "damaged the *conucos* of *yuca* and plantains which the inhabitants used to feed themselves." According to the *Real Audiencia,* in a letter written in the same year, "economic activity in the entire colony was limited to subsistence labor following the collapse of cocoa, and people now concentrated on making *casabe,* which became the most productive activity, since [casabe] was the daily bread of the population."

Casabe continued to be important in the seventeenth century. Moreau de Saint-Méry visited the Dominican Republic in 1783 and said that: "Plantains, corn and casabe are what serve them as bread." In the same century, popular poetry illustrated the importance of casabe. Maese Mónica declared:

No es ningun asunto grave
en el que os vengo a ocupar
pues sólo vengo a buscar
una torta de casabe.
En lo posible no cabe
el que de ti yo me valga;
y para que con bien salga,
si tu amistad me remedia,
dame de una torta, media,
que yo no busco una carga.

It is no serious matter
With which I come to bother you
As I have only come to ask for
A casabe pancake.
Within the realms of possibility does not fit
What I might avail of from you;
And so it may turn out well,
If your friendship oblige me,
Give me of a pancake, the half,
For I'm not seeking a burden.

The importance of casabe was also mentioned in the nineteenth century. Randolph Keim travelled to the Dominican Republic in 1860 and noted that: "the bread of the country is made from the root of the *yuca* plant." He adds: "Arepa, a type of corn bread—is widely used and is not disagreeable to the palate—There is no difficulty in having *yuca* and corn available throughout the entire year."

To sum up, *yuca*, corn, *casabe*, the *arepa* and *catibia*[5] (all Taino words) have continued to be an essential part of the

Dominican diet. Today, *casabe* is still produced in the same way it was by theTainos, and utensils still bear the same Taino names: *Guayo* (grater), *Guariquitén, Naiboa, Cuisa, Jibe* (sieves) etc. The importing of corn flour has declined, unlike in Haiti where sorghum and corn form an essential part of the diet.

In popular language there are sayings such as "hacer la yuca" and the *yuca* dance.[6]

Guáyiga

Guáyiga was another important indigenous crop adopted by the Dominicans for making "chola"[7] and *almidón* (starch paste). Its contemporary use has been well documented by Veloz Maggiolo. Las Casas explained how: "On the Coast of the Province of Higuey roots are grown which are not found on the whole of this island; these roots are called guayagas and from them they make the bread that the indios ate throughout this entire province."

In 1516 the Fathers of the Order of Saint Dominic wrote to Monsignor de Xevres that: "There were some people who, not having cazabí to give to their indios, took other roots called guiaros which are wild roots that are grated to make bread, in order that it can be eaten without killing anyone, it is necessary for it first to rot and become full of worms, and then it can be eaten without it killing anyone, and with this bread and nothing else, they feed their indios."

As livestock was "falling off," the virgin lands were turned over to pasture. Over time, knowledge of how to avoid being poisoned was lost. There is an interesting quote about how, when Santo Domingo was under siege in 1809, in order to avoid dying of hunger the inhabitants chose to eat guáyiga but with rather unpleasant results. L. H. Lemonnier De la Fosse explains how: "…they had nothing to give the exhausted men, who were for the most part incapable of moving and lacked the necessary strength for digging in the earth beneath the very walls of the city to uproot a plant, the guáyiga, whose root is a deadly poison, but when grated and washed five or six times it settles to form a nutritious paste. This paste produces a pap similar to our trays of pâté displayed in the grocers' shops of Paris. And it sold! And the poor were unable to buy it and had to make do with a type of bran extracted from the root which caused a swelling of the legs very similar to elephantiasis. Dropsy and death followed."

On the same subject, Gilbert Guillermin, wrote: "The roots of guáyiga, a poisonous plant whose preparation calls for the greatest care and whose use is dangerous, became the mainstay of the inhabitants for a second time. We took advantage of this time of peace to expedite the digging of the guáyiga, the gathering of which became more and more essential each day." (The quote about the swelling of the feet leads us to think that perhaps the swelling in both legs, commonly seen on so many urns—Taino artifacts—may well represent the effects of consuming guáyiga or yuca without having removed the toxins. This technique represented a major advancement since the pantheon of Taino gods mentions the first person who showed people how to eat *yuca* without being poisoned.)

Tobacco

Tobacco is the third important crop that survived the Conquest and then spread, becoming one of the major export commodities from the seventeenth to nineteenth centuries. It remains important today and is the fourth largest source of the country's foreign currency earnings.

The *Cohoba* (*piptadenia peregrine*) was used as a hallucino-genic in the ritual of the same name and should not be confused with tobacco which had a different use. Las Casas is very specific when he mentioned that: "In this island Hispaniola and in the neighboring islands they had another kind of herb similar to lettuce, and this they dried in the sun and on the fire, and made from some dried tree leaves a little roll such as when one makes a paper musket, and they put a little of that herb inside it and lit the roll at one end, and through the other inhaled or drew the smoke into their chest, which provoked drowsiness in the flesh and the whole body; so that they felt neither hunger or tiredness, and these rolls they called tobaccos, the second syllable being long."

Other Indigenous Foodstuffs

Other important indigenous foods that are still used today are *maíz* (corn), *yautía* (cocoyam, *Xanthosoma sagittifolium* L.), *maní* (groundnuts), *palmito* (palm hearts), cotton, *mapuey*, frijol beans, *batata* (sweet potato), *lerén* (potato-like tuber, *Calathea allonia* L.), *bija* (annatto; *Bixa orellana* L.) and *ají* (chilli). Not many people know, for example, that it was on the Dominican island that Europeans first saw corn and groundnuts, which are now very important worldwide. Oviedo provided an interesting description of corn:

> The type of bread of the indios is of two orders on this island (Hispaniola), very different and distinct from each other, and it is very common on most of the islands and even in part of Terra Firme; and so as not to repeat it later, we will note here what kind of thing is that bread which they call mahiz, and what is that

they call cazabi. The mahiz is a grain, and the cazabi
is made from a plant called yuca. The indios have this
order for sowing the mahiz. The mahiz grows on stalks
which sprout ears or corncobs a foot long; or larger or
smaller, and thick, like the wrist of the arm or less, and
full of thick grains like peas (but not completely
round); and when they wish to sow it, they cut down
the bush or the reedbed (because the land where only
grass grows is held to be fertile in these parts; like that
of the reedbeds and groves), and after that cutting or
clearing has been completed, they burn it, and the ash
from what has been cut down is left, leaving the land
as if it had been spread with manure...I mean that
these indios, although they are ignorant of such pre-
cepts, nature shows them what is advisable in this case,
and also the need to clear the land of the trees or reeds
and plants that grow there of their own accord, in
order that the indios may sow and make their fields;
and always whenever they sow is when the moon is
waxing, because they believe that, as it waxes, so does
the crop grow. And when they have to scatter the seed,
the land having been cleared, five or six indios (or
more or less) depending on the means of the farmer,
each a step away from the other, standing in rows, and
with sticks or clubs in their hands, and they strike a
blow on the ground, with the point of that stick, and
they move it about, so that it opens up the earth a bit
more, and then they take it out, and in the hole, they
throw with the left hand, four or five grains of mahiz
which he takes out of a small sack that he wears
around his waist or hanging from his neck crosswise

like a swordbelt, and then he uses his foot to close the hole containing the seeds, so that the parrots and other birds do not eat them; and then they take another step forward, and do the same thing. And in this way, in time and continuing in this fashion, in rows all those indios, they sow until they reach the end of the field or plot of land they are sowing, and in the same manner they go back to the opposite end, and turn round sowing, until they fill the whole field, and they stop sowing it…and because the mahiz is very dry or hard, so that it may grow more quickly, a day or two beforehand they leave it to soak, and sow it on the third day…In this island of Hispaniola and in the others they eat the grain roasted, or when it is tender without roasting it, when it is almost like milk; and when it is this soft they call it ector, about to curdle or recently curdled. Which is good and flavorsome, after Christians settled this island, they give it to the horses and beasts that they use, and it is a great source of nourishment, and they also give it to the black and indio slaves whom the Christians use.

In addition, the first grains of corn taken to Europe came from the Dominican island. In his letter to the kings about his third voyage, Columbus, wrote about: "corn, which is a seed that produces an ear like a corncob, which I took from there and already there is much in Castille."

With reference to groundnuts, Oviedo said: "The indios on this island Hispaniola have a fruit they call maní." Las Casas was more explicit, also referring to Hispaniola:

They had another fruit that they planted and which grew, or was formed, beneath the soil, which were not roots but the same as the inside of the hazelnuts of Castille; that is that they were similar to hazelnuts without the shell, and they had their shell or husk in which they grew and with which they were covered very different from hazelnuts, because they were like broad beans in their pods when they are on the vine, though the pod was neither green nor soft, but dry, almost like pea pods or the chick peas in Castile when they are ripe for picking: they were called *maní*, the final syllable being stressed and were so tasty that neither hazelnuts nor walnuts, nor any other nut from Castile, however tasty, could compare to it. And since they always ate a lot of these because they taste good, they then get a headache, but if not too many are eaten the head does not hurt nor are there any other ill effects; so that you are well aware, it is always eaten with bread made from cazabi or wheat, if there is any.

As regards fruit, the following are indigenous to the island and were eaten by the Tainos: pineapple, guava, *guanábana* (soursop), *lechoza*, whose indigenous name papaya is preserved in other areas but not by the Dominicans, *jagua*,[8] *caimito* (star apple, *Chrysophyllum cainito* L.), *jobo* (hog plum), *anon* (sugar apple), *hicaco* (cocoplum), *cherimoya* (custard apple), *mamón* (custard apple) and *mamey* (mammee apple, *Mammea americana* L.).

Other important non-edible agricultural products were cotton, henequen, calabash, and agave.

An estimate based on current statistics from the national

accounts shows that 5.3% of the total tonnage of agricultural products produced in the Dominican Republic today is made up of the products mentioned above, all of which aboriginal peoples cultivated and consumed. This should come as no surprise, since we frequently make the mistake of focusing attention on agricultural exports such as sugar, coffee, cocoa without considering that a high proportion of the national agricultural production is made up of goods consumed by their producers without passing through the hands of third parties. Any country person will say that he or she eats "provisions," that is, manioc, sweet potato, corn, *yautía*, and *mapuey*, the same tubercles that were eaten by the indigenous inhabitants. An interesting study would be to examine the likely pre-Columbian influence on *sancocho*,[9] which uses all these ingredients and is a common dish throughout the Antilles where it is also known as *ajiaco* and pepper pot. The word *ajiaco* is Taino and might be derived from *ají*, referring to the Taino custom of eating *cazabe* with *ají* in a type of soup.

In 1969 our Central Bank carried out a survey to ascertain how a typical family in the city of Santo Domingo spends its money. In the case of the city's poorest families, thirteen percent was still being spent on the indigenous agricultural products mentioned above. A similar survey was carried out recently in the rural areas but has not been published yet. Even so, one can assume that the proportion spent on these products is well above thirteen percent.

To sum up, the influence of basic products used by the Tainos on Dominican contemporary diet is surprisingly extensive. The Tainos left behind a variety of foods that are now staples in the Dominican diet. The great poet, Juan de Castellanos, master of the *octava,* was quite right when in 1589 in his *Elegías de*

Varones Ilustres de Indias (*Elegies of Illustrious Men of the Indies*) he placed the following poem in the mouths of the Antillean indigenous people who were confronting the Spanish presence:

Si son gentes de buenos pensamientos
A bien es recebilos, si son gratas,
Si vienen fatigados y hambrientos,
Darémosles comidas bien baratas;
Guamas, auyamas, yucas y batatas,
Darémosles cazabis y maices,
Con otros panes hechos de raíces.

Darémosles jutías con ajíes,
Darémosles pescados de los ríos,
Darémosles de gruesos manatíes;
Las ollas y los platos no vacíos;
También guariquinayes y coríes,
De que tenemos llenos los buhíos,
Y curaremos bien a los que enferman,
Colgándoles hamacas, en que duerman.

If they are people of good intentions
It is right to welcome them, if they are agreeable,
If they arrive tired and hungry,
We will give them very cheap meals;
We will give them of our foods
Guamas, auyamas, maniocs and batatas,

We will give them cazabis and corn,
Along with other breads made from roots.

15

We will give them jutías[10] with ají
We will give them fish from the rivers,
We will give them from the large manatees;
The pots and the plates not empty;
Also guariquinayes and corí,
With which our bohíos are full,
And we will cure well those who become ill,
Hanging hammocks for them, in which they may sleep.

Fishing

Different Taino methods of river and marine fishing have survived in the Dominican Republic.

First:

The system of weirs has been extensively documented in one
of my earlier works. Essentially it consists of a series of cane
posts or mangrove sticks set into the mud very close together
and interwoven with reeds. They cover all or almost all of the
river mouth or the wide part of a lagoon or calm sea inlet. These
aquatic stockades force all the fish to swim in a given direction
on account of its funnel shape, at the end of which is an area
shaped like a circle or double circle where the stockades and fish
converge and from which the fish cannot escape. Weirs of this
type are still found in the lagoons of Rincón, Redonda, Limón
and at the mouths of rivers such as the Yásica.

As Oviedo also explained: "They fished using channels of
fences made by hand, setting shafts in the reefs where the sea
swells on the shores." Even Las Casas added: "The fish were
trapped in the port as easily as in a fish tank, being corralled by
strips of wood and canes that were stuck into the bottom, very
close one to the other, forming a cage."

Second:

Poisoning the rivers with *barbasco*.[11] The Tainos used a plant called *baiguá*.

Third:

Use of traps (*nasas* – a Taino word) made from fibers that could be moved from one part of the sea to another. Nowadays these traps provide a magnificent example of native basketwork and are of Taino origin.

Fourth:

Use of *tarrayas* (nets). Las Casas mentioned that the Tainos fished in the sea and in the rivers using "very well-made nets." Archaeologists have found many examples of the weights used with nets.

Fifth:

Wading in chest-deep to gather *lambíes*, *burgaos* and other types of shells in the shallows. Taino techniques that have disappeared also include fishing with arrows, harpoons and the use of dams.

The majority of the fish that abound in the waters of the Dominican Republic still have Taino names: Carite, Menjúa, Cojinúa, Jurel, Dajao, Guábina, Macabí, Tiburón, Guatapaná, etc. The fish that should not be eaten are called "ciguatos."

Marine fauna also have Taino names: *Lambí* (queen conch), *Burgao* (citarium pica), *Carey* (hawksbill turtle), *Juey* (crab). River fauna are called *Hicotea* (turtle) and *Jaiba* (crab).

Hunting

The indigenous inheritance in this area is less obvious. In

some parts of the country, we have noted the survival of the technique of catching small birds using gum from the *copey* (*Clusia lanceolata* L.). Copey is put on the tops of trees so that the birds' feet get stuck and they are unable to escape. Las Casas mentioned this method. The hunting of crabs (and river fish) by "cuabeando," that is, dazing the fish with lighted torches, is also documented as being of Taino origin.

Some authors have suggested that preserving the meat of mammals such as *hutías* and iguanas, fish and birds by smoking is a Taino tradition and that the word "Bucán" (spit roasting) is also Taino, as is the word "Barbacoa," the device used for smoking the meat. Buccaneers and hunters lived off meat preserved in this way.

Before leaving the topic of food, it would be useful to mention two Taino legacies in the area of drink: *mabí* (Pru) and *cacheo*. The first is made from a reed that is actually called *indio* and the second from a palm.

Handicrafts and Domestic Furnishings

Ceramics

The survival of the tradition of making clay pots with pre-Columbian motifs and techniques in the area of Higuerito, near Moca, has been amply studied by García Arévalo It is likely that the traditional *tinaja* (large earthenware jar) found in every house or *bohío* before the advent of electricity reveals a Taino influence. The possible pre-Columbian origin of the typical clay *cachimbo* (pipe) of the Dominican peasant farmer is somewhat more debatable. Elpidio Ortega and Veloz Maggiolo have carefully investigated this topic.

Wood

The *batea* (a Taino word), used by the indigenous people to prospect for gold in the rivers, is still utilized for that purpose in the area of Miches and in the rivers of El Cibao. The *higuero* (a Taino word) was widely used in the Dominican Republic as a water container until very early in the twentieth century when the square kerosene and oil cans became more common. Las Casas noted that: "There is another very useful tree on this island (Hispaniola) and that is the one called higuero by the indios, the penultimate syllable being stressed; this produces gourds that are round like a ball – they used these as drinking glasses and plates and bowls." Their use for making the *güiro*, a musical instrument, appears to date back to the historical era, though the word is Taino.

The *canoa* (canoe) and the *cayuco* (a small canoe), both Taino words and forms of transportation used in the prehistoric era by the indigenous peoples to cross from South America to the Antilles, were used extensively in rivers and lagoons and are still in use today. They are still common in Sánchez in the bay of Samaná. Their size, appearance and construction are the same as those described by the chroniclers, as is the oar, which exactly matches the description by the chronicler Oviedo, who mentioned that they called them *Nahe*: "These nahes are like long paddles and the big end is like the crutch of a lame person or cripple." This type of oar is quite different from those used in the Amazon region, for example. The *Cuaba*, commonly used today for carrying charcoal, is a Taino word. Oviedo noted that: "The indios of this island of Hispaniola call this tree or pine cuaba and they make much use of this firewood in the sugar mills, for lighting or lamps which they use at night until the early morning."

As for the *bohío* (a Taino word), there are various types that are not of Taino origin in the country. This is the case in those made from adobe. African influences are also found in the *bohío*. Nevertheless, a glance at one of the two depicted by Oviedo illustrates the similarity. In El Atajadizo and Boca de Yuma, Veloz Maggiolo found a rural *bohío* with a rounded shape like the second one depicted by Oviedo.

The *yagua* (Taino word) was the main material used by the Taino for thatching the *bohío*. Las Casas says that: "with these (the yaguas) they can cover the huts, and, even the houses in the villages; in sum, they have many uses and for good things...The palm heart is very sweet in its entirety and 20 men or more can eat from it."

Elsewhere he added that: "They use the tenderest part of the shoots as a vegetable, the leaves for putting a roof over rooms and to make baskets, hats, and ropes; the bark for filtering, the oil from the rind of the fruit for lighting, that from the flesh for cooking and the liquor from the trunk as a remedy."

In addition, the *yagua* was used to make the *petaca* (indigenous word), a rustic box into which charcoal is placed for sale. There are photographs taken in the city of Santo Domingo in 1916, which show that charcoal was sold exclusively in *petacas* at that time.

Basketwork

The *hamaca* and the *macuto* (Taino words) are the two most important types of pre-Columbian basketwork that were passed down. Until very recently, it was very common for people to sleep in hammocks, and this was mentioned by the foreign travellers who visited the country in the seventeenth, eighteenth and nineteenth centuries. In his diary Columbus noted that: "There came to the ships on that day many rafts or canoes to sell items made from spun cotton and nets in which they slept, which are hammocks."

Guacal (Huacal) is a Taino word for a basket. The manufacture and use of a range of baskets, extractors, sieves, mats and halters continue in the Dominican small-scale rural industries. These are made from different types of textile fibers and hemp. Although they have not been studied fully up until now, they reveal a Taino influence.

With regard to the *Cabuya* and *Henequén*, both Taino words, Las Casas noted: "The indios make very good large nets and fish hooks out of bone and tortoiseshell, and, because they do not have iron, they cut them using threads of a certain type of hemp that is found in these Indies, which in this Hispaniola they call cabuya and another finer one, nequén."

The technique employed by Dominicans in order to make cloth from wild cotton has been reported in the rural area of San Juan de la Maguana, as has the use of the traditional "huso" (spindle whoal), which has been found in archaeological excavations. The Cotton Zemí illustrates how skillful the Tainos were at spinning. There is a need to study the extent of the Taino influence on the *tarrayas*, dragnets and *nasas* (Taino word) used by fishermen.

Leather

The only example of the use of leather in pre-Columbian tradition is the skin of certain types of fish which was used for grating tubercles.

Mining

The Tainos identified some important mines for the Spaniards and consequently for Dominicans, thus contributing

21

to the creation of the country's mineral wealth. This is the case of the world famous and controversial mine of Pueblo Viejo in Cotuí. Pedro Mártir explained:

> In Hispaniola there is another region with the same name of Cotoy, which divides the provinces of Uhabo and Cayabo. It has mountains and valleys and plains; but as it is barren has few inhabitants: There lies the greatest abundance of gold. There is the origin of gold. One does not collect little lumps or pieces; one finds solid, pure gold in porous stones and between the seams of the rocks: Breaking the rocks one follows the veins of gold.

The mines at La Buenaventura (on the Río Haina) and San Cristóbal, as well as those at Sal de Barahona, were also pointed out to the Spaniards by the indigenous people.

Siting of Cities

A few important cities were sited on indigenous settlements. The indigenous people knew how to locate their settlements close to water, avoiding insects and such. On the other hand, when discovering La Isabela, Columbus chose a part of the beach near the mouth of several rivers, an area that had mosquitoes, as time would reveal. Columbus said there had been an indigenous village there but research carried out in 1978 by archaeologists from the Museo del Hombre Dominicano confirmed that the indigenous area lay on top of a hill, near the river but far away from the mosquitoes. La Vega, for example, was founded beside the settlement of Guarionex; San Juan de la Maguana on the settlement of Caonabo (Niti), and Puerto Príncipe on the town of Anacaona and Bohechío.

Language

The Taino contribution to the Dominican language, Spanish, and even English and French has undoubtedly been significant. Don Emilio Tejera points out more than 700 indigenisms, and Julia Tavares illustrates how twenty of them have passed into the English language.

Let us look at just three examples. First, the names of Dominican rivers. With just three exceptions, all the country's major rivers retain their indigenous names. Starting at the northern coast: Yaque, Maimón, Bahabonico, Yásica, Sosúa, Charamico, Joba, Boba, Nagua, Yuna, Nisibón, Sanate and Anamuya. On the southern coast: Yuma, Chavón, Higuamo, Casuí, Soco, Cumayasa, Ozama, Haina, Baní, Ocoa, Nigua, Isa, Tábara, Jura, Vía, Nizao, Duey, Bahoruco. In the interior: Mijo, Amina, Bao, Manabao, Maguá, Chacuey, Yabacao, Guanuma, Guaiguí, Jimenoa, Nibaje, Tireo and Payabo. On the border: Macasia, Artibonito.

It is interesting that two of the three exceptions are rivers which demarcate borders: El Masacre, which was called the River Dajabón (Taino word) until the seventeenth century, and the Pedernales which, also interestingly, took its name from the large quantity of flint it carried—and which was used for this precise purpose by the indigenous people. Itwas in this river that one of the most ancient sites was found, dating from 2600 years BCE and belonging to a culture that worked mainly in flint. The third exception is the River Isabela.

As a second example, we take the names of woods: caoba (mahogany), cuaba, capá, ceiba, corozo (acronomia), copei (pitch apple), guano, guayacán (lignum vitae), guazábara, guayaba, guázuma (West Indian elm), guaconeco, guao (comogladia dentate), mangle (mangrove), manacle, maguey (agave), majagua, balata, búcara, jobobán, pitahaya (night blooming cereus) tuna (prickly pear), yagrumo (trumpet tree), yarey and samo. All these are indigenisms.

Let us look at the third example, fauna: cocuyo, comején, curí, guabá, guaraguao, guacamayo, jején, jutía, iguana, maye, mime, maco, manatí, nigua, the hicotea and its companion, the catuán.

Some words have changed their meaning. *Batey,* which originally referred to the ball game or the bustling area where it was played, now refers to the dismal living quarters of the canecutters.

Guácara originally referred to caves or specific places with caves. Today, it has the connotation of age: "De los tiempos de las guácaras (From the time of the guácaras)," which refers indirectly to the antiquity of the caves.

Mambí[12] and *manigua* (swamp, forest) are now more commonly used in Cuba than in our country. *Guaitiao* meant great friendship between two people and was adapted by the Mexicans to "cuate" (pal, buddy). Túbano (cigar), Enagua (slip), Sabana (savannah, plain), Totuma (gourd), Jíbaro (wild animal or person, maroon), Macana (stick used to hit people), and Fotuto (whistle made from conch) are all indigenisms, as is Maniel,[13] despite being linked to the maroons or runaway slaves.

(In order to avoid repetition, I will not mention all the indigenisms referred to in earlier sections of this essay.)

Impact on Dominican Arts and Letters

In the field of Dominican literature, various authors have written on indigenous themes, especially in the mid-nineteenth century when *indigenismo* was a continent-wide movement. It is sufficient to mention here Galván and his novel *Enriquillo,* Javier Angulo Guridi and his play *Iguaniona*; José Joaquín Pérez and his poem "Fantasías Indígenas" and in the twentieth century, the stories and novels of Juan Bosch, Fernández Simó and Marcio Veloz Maggiolo. They generally treated the indigenous peoples in a romantic fashion, without entering into a discussion about social or political issues. There is more in Dominican literature about this subject than about Africans.

In the field of music, the indigenous influence has, for obvious reasons, been almost nonexistent. The *maraca*, the *güiro* and the *fotuto de lambí* (wind instrument with a conch shell) are insignificant legacies. In the field of painting, the indigenous theme has been barely covered except in the murals of Vela Zanetti. Greater use has been made of indigenous themes in sculpture—for example, the work of Pratz Ventós—and especially in the 1950s when there was also an attempt to develop more traditional crafts. In the last century, Desangles sculpted his "Caonabo."

Popular Medicine

There is no doubt that an important Taino legacy remains to be studied in this field. The chroniclers, especially Oviedo, list the curative uses of various plants and woods by the indigenous people. In recent years, at least two writers have gathered examples of Dominican popular medicine used by the rural population. However, no one has compared the two listings to see how much they have in common.

Oral Tradition

Oral tradition is one of the most interesting ways of assessing the degree of transculturation. Despite the passage of time, legends of the Ciguapa, the Jupía and the India del Charco, all linked to the Taino, have survived among the Dominicans—in particular, the myths of the Cemí OPIYELGUOBIRAN and the *opías* or souls of the dead that wander about at night.[14] The legend of the Bienbienes[15] can also be linked to these myths as well as to the maroons.

Popular Religion

Even though the magico-religious beliefs, the pantheon of gods or the Cohoba ceremony[16] of the Tainos have not survived among Dominicans, it is still true that Dominican popular religion has syncretic elements that recall the history of the Conquest. Carlos Esteban Deive noted how, in Dominican *vodú*, among the *luás* (deities) are found Anacaona, Caonabo, Cayacoa, Enriquillo, Guarionex, Guacanagarix, Guaroa, Hatuey, Mencía, Tamayo and the "Indian woman from Agua Dulce," or "Agua Azul."

According to Deive, the *luás* belong to four divisions (water, earth, air and fire). The water division is also known as the "Indian" division. In *vodú* ceremonies, "túbanos" of tobacco are used, recalling the Cohoba ceremony. Furthermore, in Dominican *brujería*[17] it is common to place Taino objects, which are uually made of stone and painted blue, on the altars. Many *huaqueros*[18] find it difficult to buy pieces from the country people since they believe these items have magical powers. Throughout the Caribbean, the petaloid axe or thunderstone, as it is called by country folk, is believed to protect people from lightning and to keep water in the earthenware jars cool as well.

Genetic Inheritance

There have been almost no studies in the country to determine the proportion of indigenous blood still found among groups of Dominicans. In recent years, the Cubans have been able to locate isolated groups that still preserve indigenous racial characteristics. It is obvious that the indigenous cultural influence in countries such as Mexico, Guatemala, Ecuador, Peru and Bolivia, where a large proportion of the population has indigenous blood, must be much greater than in Venezuela or Brazil, for example, where large but isolated groups have survived or in the Antilles where, for historical reasons, they no longer exist.

In conclusion, the greatest and most widespread presence of the indigenous peoples in Dominican contemporary culture can be found where this presence was previously non-existent. A peculiar set of cultural values in the Dominican Republic has created a convenient illusion, using a sophism that attempts to conceal a national prejudice. In addition, a large proportion of the Dominican population demands to be classified as "indios" or "indias " instead of *mulatos* or *mulatas*, when they in fact possess no indigenous genes.

CHAPTER TWO

Commentary on "The Indigenous Inheritance in Dominican Culture"

MARCIO VELOZ MAGGIOLO

My comments on Bernardo Vega's essay are few. His brief synthesis has very effectively covered the most important indigenous cultural survivals. He rightly observes that the encounters between Spaniards and indigenous peoples—and later between Spaniards, Africans and indigenous peoples—are the bridges over which various traditions crossed to become permanent features of present-day Dominican life. It is obvious that the most utilitarian aspects of the indigenous culture survived the process of ethnic and racial hybridization on the island.

The first interesting point raised by Vega relates to the South American legacy of cleared-ground cultivation, or the slash-and-burn system of clearing the forest for planting. This is important because it is part of the heritage of the entire Antilles—a heritage that is disappearing today in Cuba, Puerto

Rico and Jamaica, and has already disappeared in the Lesser Antilles, where the small land areas let this technique, the most widespread one in the Orinoco and Amazon regions, fall into disuse.

In recent comments, I identified another surviving indigenous technique, that of cultivation in *jagüeyes* (sink holes). This is common in the systems of *conucos* (smallholdings) of the inhabitants of the coastal regions in the southeast of the country and is easily identifiable along the coastal strip stretching from the capital to San Pedro de Macorís. However, methods such as *várzea* cultivation, that is, agriculture in the muddy riverbeds, appeared to have died out at the very moment of the Conquest. Varzea cultivation was common among the Mellacoid groups of the Cibao Valley. Pattern of mounds have also been found in the region of Las Galeras, Samaná, but there is no evidence to suggest that it may have been left over from the indigenous culture.

The conuco was the basic unit of indigenous production during the agricultural period, but it is clear that it was not an isolated case of self-sufficiency. Its difference from the conuco of today should be pointed out. In the case of the indigenous family, roduction was collectivized and redistributed. There is evidence that collective conucos also existed, resulting from the farming activities of several families or clans, who contributed through a particular tributary model to accumulating resources in kind for common use. One must also remember that if the conuco of today is an isolated and typical family unit, then it is so because it has lost its ritual qualities. rituals made conuco a clan property involving a system of common lineages within the tribal group, as Pané noted when he specifically referred to the gods of the three points who, according to Pane, made the sown fields more fertile. Today relationships within production are fundamentally different.

With regard to *casabe,* Vega clearly illustrates its pre-eminence up until the nineteenth century. The importance of wheat and wheat flour for making bread using the Hispanic model resulted from the export-import phenomenon created at the end of the nineteenth century. In addition, settlers from the Canaries, for example, whose main foodstuff was wheat mixed with cornmeal and then roasted, changed their basic ingredient to the latter, thus creating an Antillean *gofío* which was mixed with cow's milk or liquids that were different from those used in the Canaries. Since we are on the subject of immigrants from the Canaries, we should mention the existence of another hybrid, *sancocho*, which had its origins in the Canary Islands, but which was adapted in the Antilles. In the Canaries, it is called *salcocho* and its main ingredients are various meats and provisions, just as in the Antilles, parts of Cuba and Venezuela, all of which experienced significant immigration from the Canaries. Nevertheless, Vega rightly points out that the word *ajiaco* remained current in Cuba and became the name given to a dish that, while initially foreign, became Creole when it incorporated ingredients from the indigenous and African traditions.

Casabe, the bread of the Conquest, was produced in industrial quantities in veritable factories established on the island of Mona, as can be confirmed by the documents of the Real Hacienda de Puerto Rico, which were uncovered by Aurelio Tanodi.

Throughout the Antilles, casabe and yuca are almost synonymous because they are both produced from a similar process. Vega points out that in everyday conversation, there are sayings such as "Hacer la yuca," and there is also the *yuca* dance.

However, according to experts like Ortiz, the yuca dance is of African origin, and the word *yuka* is spelt with a 'k'. Hence it has nothing to do with the Antillean tubercle.

The *guáyiga* (zamia debilis) is an important indigenous meal. During the early period of the Conquest, Las Casas reports its presence in all the upland areas southeast of the Dominican Republic. He considered it the main staple of the indigenous people living in an area stretching from Macao—located in the Altagracia province of today—to as far as the outskirts of what is today Santo Domingo. Like the fathers of the Order of Saint Dominic cited by Vega, Las Casas also noted that guáyiga was eaten when the dough was allowed to rot until worms were present. It was then mixed to make a type of *arepa* cooked on griddles or *burenes*. In addition, guáyiga is the oldest documented agricultural foodstuff about which we have information. Among the pre-Ceramic or pre-agricultural inhabitants of Cueva de Berna, on the outskirts of Boca de Yuma, guáyiga was used as a food around 1800 BCE. Along with other colleagues from the Museo del Hombre Dominicano, I managed to extract well-preserved traces of guáyiga leaves from blocks of compacted ash in excavations carried out. This led to the conclusion that the root was roasted or used in some way as a food item. At the El Porvenir site, within a period ranging between 905 and 1200 BCE, pollen analysis carried out by J. Nadal in Arizona also yielded high levels of guáyiga.

One may assume then that guáyiga is the oldest plant food used on the island. The arrival of Africans in Santo Domingo led to changes in the use of guáyiga; it became an important type of bread called *chola* made with ingredients such as coconut, as well as by-products such as the so-called *blancmange* and various types of Spanish-influenced puff pastry. Vega gives a concise but interesting account of the history of guáyiga. Joseph Peguero also provided the following information: various shipwrecked people in the Bay of Samaná, attempting to reach Santo Domingo by the cliffs, ate guáyiga and most of them were poisoned.

Tabaco is an indigenous word, as Vega points out. According to the Chronicle, it was also an instrument used for inhaling during the *cohoba* ritual, whose name was wrongly given to the plant.

Corn was present in the Antilles at the time of the Conquest, and the word *maíz* is Arawak. It became widespread before the term "elote" or the Andean term. The same is true of *maní*.

An important fact, which was recently uncovered, is that, in 1969, thirteen percent of the typical Dominican family diet consisted of indigenous crops.

Like cornflour, the canoe was extremely important from the fifteenth to the nineteenth centuries. During the harvest, rivers were important for transporting produce, especially in a country without roads. Hundreds of canoes lined up the beaches of the Ozama during the government of Ulises Heureaux (several periods in the 1880s) and even later. Thousands of *petacas* (wicker baskets), used for measuring charcoal as well as all kinds of produce were stacked up in various places—and the urban housewives and city shopkeepers helped themselves from them. Until the 1940s, charcoal, *cajuiles*,[1] cashews, mangos, and most kinds of fruit were sold in *petacas* at different prices.

As Vega rightly points out, *mabí* (*mauby*), the fermented product of the so-called *bejuco de indio* (*Colubrina reclinata*; the bark of the carob tree), is of pre-Columbian origin. This popular drink of past centuries has, along with casabe, been a long-standing component of the diet of many Dominicans. *Cacheo* is less common because the viniferous palm (*euterpes vinifera*) used to produce it is becoming extinct. This delicious, thick, refreshing brew has disappeared over the years, but it was common in the bars of Santo Domingo in the 1940s when cacheo was brought from the west of the island and the southwestern provinces.

The national toponymy is full of indigenisms. As Vega rightly points out, almost all rivers in the Dominican Republic have indigenous names. However, there are some ecological details that would be interesting to explore further. What traces of the indigenous people can be found in the landscape and environment of the Dominican Republic today? In some parts of the island, there are still examples of an ecology that does not appear to have been shaped by present-day man: forests of *bija orellana* (annatto, *Bixa orellana* L.) in the area of Arroyo Vuelta where there are magnificent petroglyphs; *jagua* forests on the plateaus of Escalera Arriba, near Altamira and in Puerto Plata province, close to caves with burial grounds; medlar plantations in the areas of El Soco and Punta de Garza and in San Pedro de Macorís.

All of these are connected to the former indigenous settlements. Have the plants outlived the humans? Are these the distant offspring of seeds which were planted by some indigenous hand long ago and have since become perennial? In a place called Villa de Taní, near Ponce in Puerto Rico, where various indigenous plants grow, a forest of centenarian fig trees surrounds what was once the country house of the indigenous inhabitants. When asked, the people who live there reply that "it has always been there." Renato Rímoli believes that there are survivals or possible survivals of this type that need to be studied. However, as Vega has said, romanticism can be found on the pages of the literature. I do not believe that the indigenous survivals are few. They may not be as important today, but in their time they were fundamental to the consolidation of local economies and the spreading of the Conquest. Agriculture, bread, gold and navigation were part of the colonizing activity and were swiftly primed for incipient capitalism. Historically mines would not have existed without indigenous labor; or sugar mills without casabe; or the Conquest of Mexico without smoked meat and yuca bread. Everything revolved around new ways of life and new ways of doing things. The tributary was an indigenous channel employed by the Spaniards for their early agricultural activities. The cultural modalities have changed—and over time they have disappeared. However, it is clear that before we understand what we are, why we are and where we are, we need to understand—and I mean understand fully—the past, which appears inconsequential and intangible.

CHAPTER THREE

The Spanish Inheritance in Dominican Culture

CARLOS DOBAL

I

In order for Dominicans to embark on the difficult path of understanding themselves better, they should start by accepting a number of easily proven facts: they are a mixed people of Spanish and African descent with a drop of indigenous blood as a distinguishing feature of their race.[1] This mixture should be a source of pride for, as Renato Grousset says, "racial mixture is a condition for the advancement of civilization" and the "pure races" stagnate and retrogress.[2] "Mestizos are often extremely intelligent; from their position as a despised minority they manage to gradually become a respected or admired sector," according to Laloup and Nelis.[3]

However, as the historian Frank Moya Pons notes, "The sense of Spanishness in the Dominican has been stronger than the actual presence of that race."[4] Although today, the poet Héctor Inchaústegui Cabral says that "anything considered as folklore, which in the past was claimed as Spanish, now appears

37

to be Black African. Meanwhile, the Spanish element has re-treated to await better times when the pendulum swings back."[5]

Researcher Carlos Esteban Deive rightly states "that the ethnic groups that contributed the most extensive and varied characteristics to the national culture are the Spaniards and the Africans; with a clear and undeniable dominance of the former. This contradicts the view of some sociologists and historians whose anti-Spanish stance leads them to understate the predominance of the Hispanic element in order to emphasize the influence of slaves from different African nationalities."[6] But until recently, scholars have tended to regard the Hispanic as the most important ingredient in the culture from the sixteenth century onwards. This importance, they believed, was the result not only of its cultural superiority in relation to the Taino and the African cultures over which it prevailed, but also of the Hispanic component's being the one most attuned to and best encapsulating the spirit of the sixteenth century, thus becoming the most permanent element. One has only to examine the spiritual resources employed by the Spaniards for transculturating the subjugated groups and guiding them, in varying degrees, towards western civilization to comprehend the extent of Spanish dominion over the island. In fact, the earliest expression of this dominion over the island, which was discovered on December 5, 1492, is the name with which it was christened by the conquistadors: "Española."[7]

Transculturation is a phenomenon of social exchange resulting from the encounter between two different cultures. Throughout history there has always been an initial destructive reaction, sometimes mutual, or one-sided if the differences are very great. A process of reconstruction during which what has been dismantled is reconstructed follows. After that there comes a process of compilation or incorporation, which is an old-fashioned way of describing integration.[8]

The Spaniards attempted to impose their way of life and the national characteristics which they had developed over the centuries: their language, beliefs and institutions of political control. When they embarked on conquest and colonization, the Spaniards relied on two mechanisms of cultural penetration and transculturation. These were education and evangelization.[9] The impact of these Hispanic values has prompted us, continually and conspicuously, to consider their positive as well as their negative aspects. As Juan Bosch says: "Spain gave us everything it possessed: its language, its architecture, its religion, its way of dressing and eating, its art of war and its legal and civil institutions; livestock and even dogs and hens."[10] The wheel, and along with it the wagon, reached us from Spain. Ships, farm equipment, bells, mirrors, anvil and forge also arrived.[11]

Sugarcane was imported from the beginning of the Spanish occupation of the island. According to Oviedo, it was brought from the Canary Islands as a curiosity and then planted in gardens and vegetable plots. It was cultivated with such care that, in under twenty-five years, as P. Valverde points out, in Santo Domingo there were "twenty rich and powerful running and crushing sugarmills, and another three that were ready to crush in the year of 1535."[12] Coffee was perhaps the second crop whose cultivation was remarkably well suited to Hispaniola. "There is on the island a village by the name of Moca, because the coffee in its district is, in the opinion of the most discerning, at least as good as the highly praised Arabian coffee," says Don Ramón González Tablas in his *Historia de la Dominación y Ultima Guerra de España en Santo Domingo*.[13]

II

From the beginning of this essay, it is extremely important to stress that although Spain transmitted a large part of its cultural values to Santo Domingo throughout the sixteenth century and the final years of the previous century, it is also true that in later stages of Dominican history, Spain revitalized its long-standing roots, more intensely in some eras than others. Over a period of time, cultures that are reunited with their sources tend to recover the energy of their original values. Thus, as Van Der Meer observes, "civilizations find, in different eras, sufficient energy to make up for their own lost original values."[14]

Dominican history reveals several instances of reconnection with Spanish culture. Sometimes this was the result of enforced political links, at other times, it was part of a spontaneous and natural process. In his excellent essay, "Raíces, Motivaciones y Fundamentos de la Raza Dominicana," Fabio Herrera Miniño notes that, "the migrations of the seventeenth century served to deliver the settlers from barbarism. Specifically, a number of customs that are nowadays easily discernible in various towns throughout the country could be restored. The Spanish immigration, coming mainly from the Canary Islands, laid the foundations of nationality. In the following century this would erupt into rebellion against Spanish domination in 1821. It is easy to establish that our traditions are derived from the customs of the last century and, if we look at the previous centuries, what has been preserved arrived here via the neighboring islands where the Spanish colonial system maintained traditional forms of social behaviour with greater purity. ... Many traditions that we accept as our own have come from Puerto Rico or Cuba."[15] When Herrera Miniño refers to the Hispanic traditions that reached Dominican shores via Puerto Rico and Cuba, he could be referring mainly to Hostos' influence on Dominican education. According to Hoetink, this emphasized Comte's positivism as interpreted by the Spanish Krausists who were Hostos's teachers.[16] As regards the Cubans, the distinguished author J. I. Jiménes Grullón in his work *La República Dominicana* rightly refers to the Cuban immigration as being "very positive for the development of the sugar industry."[17] Evaristo Heres Hernández and Javier López Muñoz also discuss the Cuban migration in the work, "Exposición sistemática en estilo biográfico de los principales emigrantes cubanos, en su mayoría medicos, pero también maestros, ingenieros, comerciantes y artistas."[18]

During the early period of Cuban immigration prompted by the war of 1868 called the *Guerra Grande* in Cuba, and especially, after Dominican independence in 1844, significant numbers of Sephardic Jews, almost all from Curaçao, arrived. Surnames such as Pardo, Maduro, Senior, de Marchena, de León, Curiel and others belong to families that fled the Inquisition in Spain or Portugal, reached Holland via other countries and then took off for the Dutch possessions in the western hemisphere.[19]

The Semitic-Hispanic values that these immigrants brought with them are still evident in different spheres of Dominican culture and art. However, the Dominicans would undoubtedly experience the most interesting re-encounter with the "lofty" values of Hispanicity through contact with the Spanish groups who came to the country after Franco's triumph in Spain. They lent a new dimension to our traditionalist society, and their immigration was extremely beneficial with results that may be seen in the education of the generation born during the War. The Spanish immigrants, made up of intellectuals, soon disagreed with the methods of Trujillo's supporters and many of them left for other places with greater freedoms. However, the seed had been sown and the leftist rebellions of Dominican youth were inspired by the discourse of those intellectuals, some of whom settled in the country and managed to establish successful textiles industries,[20] as Fabio Herrera Miniño notes in his essay. They include the sculptor Antonio Prats Ventós, the painters Francisco Rivero Gil and Joan Junyer, the musician and founder of the Santo Domingo Symphony Orchestra Casals Chapí, the criminologist Serrano Poncela, Constancio Bernaldo de Quiroz, the historian María Ugarte; José Ramón Estrella, Francisco Vásquez Díaz (Compostela), the sculptor Manolo Pascual, Leopoldo Malagón, Vicente Llorens, Laudelino Moreno, Fernando Sant-Ruiz, Amós Salvas, the bibliophile Luis Florén, Jesús de Galindez, José Almoina, Chu (Alfonso Vila), the recently deceased Don Pepe Jiménez and the great critic Manuel Valdiperes.[21]

In addition, the continuous arrival of numerous Spanish priests and members of religious orders from the time of the Conquest until the present day was extremely important for Dominican education. Their colleges and influential institutions have kept spiritual links with Spain alive and active. (From the Espanolísima Orden de Predicadores, who founded the first higher education institution in the New World in Santo Domingo, to the Order of Mercy which founded convents and colleges that are still functioning, and the Society of Jesus which now runs important centers for education, communication and social action.)

Some notable members of the Spanish regular clergy, based in Santo Domingo, have continued to contribute greatly, by means of their extensive and painstaking historical research, to provide a more complete picture of the Dominican past. Thus the names of Br. Cipriano de Utrera, OFMCap and Br. Vicente Rubio OP should be included here.

III

On one occasion, Don Federico de Onís said that "the first pro-independence campaigner was the Spaniard who decided to break his political ties with his country, cross the Atlantic and settle permanently in the lands of America." The Spaniard to whom Onís refers can be imagined as a free man, because, by the very act of emigrating permanently from Spain, he was freely expressing his opinion. In my opinion, this is precisely the most outstanding expression of freedom. As José Ignacio Rasco recalls in his *Integración Cultural de América Latina*, our common master, the great scholar José María Chacón y Calvo, continually stressed the need to highlight criticism as a fundamental value in Spain's early colonizing activity.[22] Hence, paradoxically, the Spaniards who took possession of the available lands of the Americas by rule of force, which was still widespread in the Late Middle Ages world from which they came, also carried the seed of the civil liberties that would germinate several centuries later.

In his *Historia Colonial de Santo Domingo*, Maya Pons explains the origin of the conquistadors' actions, tracing it back to the time of the Reconquest. As he puts it: "One of the consequences of the Reconquest was the establishment of *municipios* and villages in the regions seized from the Moors. Those towns generally grouped together free men who, during the course of the war, had been able to free themselves from the bonds that tied them to other masters. In the majority of the cases those towns obtained guarantees, sureties and privileges

from the Crown that legally and practically ratified their autonomy from any power beyond that of the community."[23] He adds:
"The municipal organization was able to establish itself in the
new environment of the Indies, adapting to the conditions of
each region. In Hispaniola municipal life would also have its
own characteristics."[24] La Isabela had a *municipio* with *alcaldes*
(mayors) and *regidores* (council members). When the town was
abandoned and replaced by Nueva Isabela (known as Santo
Domingo today) as the capital of the island in 1496, the first
municipio was transferred there. By 1501, the cities of Santo
Domingo, Concepción de la Vega and Santiago had their own
local authorities appointed by the inhabitants. This is the only
example of direct democracy and popular representation in
colonial government and it was almost the only sphere in which
the settlers of lower social status could hold political office.
However, in terms of power, the municipal independence was
more theoretical than real.[25] As Jiménez Grullón points out,
"Total submission to the Crown was partially compensated for
by the development of municipal autonomy as represented by
the cabildos."[26]

The *cabildo* was a seed of democracy. When colonization
began in the sixteenth century, the inhabitants organized themselves "to the sound of bells," especially in the case of "open"
cabildo, not the other type of cabildo which was "closed," and
which later degenerated and became dominated by oligarchies
who controlled it on account of their learning or wealth.[27]

The definitive framework for the administration of colonial
society would emerge in Hispaniola: the *municipio*, the *audiencia* and the *virreinato*.[28] Yet, in the *municipio* the first inhabitants
openly stated their views on issues relating to community interests. Manuel Machado Báez, the eminent researcher from Santi-

ago, states that "the delegates from Jacagua, who attended the Junta de Procuradores held in the city of Santo Domingo on April 26, 1518, are the first Santiago intellectuals." A document from the time reveals their petitions, which were presented to the Junta:

• That the tithes not be paid in money as was the case, but in agricultural products and that those from cotton, *cañafístola*[29] and sugar be 1/30 or 1/40 since, in the Canaries, they used to pay 1/20 on sugar.

• That they do not allow personal tithes, as applied for by the bishops

• That the tithes and fees levied on the church structures be handed over to a steward so that they may be cleaned; and

• That the *regidores* may not occupy permanent posts since they tyrannize the Republic.[30]

The legal framework of land tenure in Santo Domingo also has its origins in Spanish law.[31] As a result, problems arose when Franco-Haitian legislation was introduced in 1822 under Boyer. The historian Frank Moya Pons, in his book, *La Dominación Haitiana*, states that: "The Spanish property law in force in the eastern region for three centuries, as well as the system of land tenure, was radically different from Franco-Haitian legislation. In the Spanish zone, the predominant system was, at least from the mid-sixteenth century onwards, that of commonly held land which entailed multiple occupation. Determining land tenure in the eastern part could not be carried out immediately without antagonizing the class of landowners, who opposed the Haitian regime on account of their Spanish origin."[32]

But none of the first fruits, the product of the Hispanic spirit, in the Dominican Republic can equal the eternal honor that was gained from the sermon that Fray Antón de Monstesinos devoted to denouncing the exploitation of the Indians in 1511. From this point onwards, until Fray Bartolomé de las Casas brought the subject to the attention of the Spanish court, which widely circulated news on the case, the dispute over the legal situation of the Indians of Hispaniola prompted the renewal of Stoic-Christian theories of natural law and the creation of international law. It would thus presage the well-known doctrines of Grotius and Pufendorff which were directed against arbitrary absolutism.[33]

IV

The main obligation imposed by the Catholic Queen for the conquest of America was that Christianity be disseminated throughout the newly discovered territories. For this reason, as soon as the conquistadors arrived on Hispaniola, they began to organize Catholic worship according to the religious rubrics of their distant homeland. Thus they built churches and founded religious organizations in which everyone could participate equally. According to César Nicolás Penson, in 1503 Nicolás de Ovando founded the Brotherhood of Our Lady of the Conception, the first charitable association in America. This was followed by others formed by whites, mulattoes and slaves, which added ceremony and color to life in the Colony.[34] In July 1592, the Cofradía de Nuestra Señora de los Remedios del Carmen y Jesús Nazareño was founded in accordance with canonical law in the city of Santo Domingo and based in the hospital of San Andrés. The Cofradía del Carmen y Jesús Nazareño aimed "to honor and serve Our Lord God and his Most Blessed Mother."[35] Father Rafael Bello Peguero offers the following piece of information: "On the 2 of July of 1592, to the señores Julián Hernández, Luis de Peña, Cosme Sanchez and

Pedro Gómez, of *moreno*[36] color, is granted and appointed the space they request to establish the Chapel of the Cofradía de Nuestra Señora de los Remedios y Jesús Nazareño, at the entrance of the gate of the Hospital of San Andrés (today the Hospital Padre Billini) which lies opposite the well."[37] Not surprisingly blacks and mulattoes were present in these early Dominican religious brotherhoods. A study by the anthropologist Martha Ellen Davis, who has conducted a great deal of research, revealed that there were already Africans religious brotherhoods in Spain in the fourteenth century, that is, before the discovery of the New World. It is evident, says the researcher, "that the syncretism between the African and Spanish religions occurred in Spain itself." Davis' work is extremely interesting and elegantly phrased. As she notes:

> One can see that the European-African medley emerged not in the New World but in the Iberian Peninsula before the Conquest. There were colonies of Black slaves in Spain in the fourteenth century, long before the Conquest of America. They were found mainly in Andalusia, Seville, Malaga and other places, even Madrid. It is therefore not surprising that these slaves established *cofradías* in the New World as they had already founded religious brotherhoods in Spain since the end of the fourteenth century. I had read about a *cofradía* of Black Sevillans founded in the fourteenth century with the nickname "La Cofradía de los Negritos." I found the original sources in the library of the town council and I was exceedingly pleased to know that this *cofradía* still exists! I had read that after the Conquest of America and the trade

in black slaves that followed, the black neighborhood in Seville was somewhat depopulated; although I walked around a great deal, I did not find traces of the former neighborhood nor of the character and nature of its original inhabitants. I only discovered the name of one street—"'El Conde Negro." The Black Count was Juan de Valladolid, Master of the Royal Wardrobe to the Catholic Kings. He was appointed Juez and Mayoral of the Blacks in 1475.

On the history and current importance of the *cofradía*: it appears that the "export" of the black population of Seville had been so complete that almost no one remained. In the past century, others were allowed to become members so that the *cofradía* would not die out through lack of personnel. Nowadays, the only black members of the Cofradía de los Negritos are people from the New World; a Cuban family and even a North American Protestant who, while performing military service at a US base near to Seville, joined in order to affirm a Black identity far from his country. As a basis for my investigation I could put forward only one general hypothesis: there is some relationship between the present-day Afro-Dominican and Spanish *cofradías*. I eventually concluded that I could not obtain anything from the Sevillean *cofradías* that would help me to understand the parallel Dominican phenomenon, neither in terms of history nor social organization. It is very possible that in the fourteenth and fifteenth centuries there might have been; but now the Cofradía de los Negritos has assumed the same form as the other Sevillean *cofradías*.[38]

In his research into the Hermandad de San José de los Llanos, his former parish, Archbishop Hugo Eduardo Polanco Brito states that the oldest brotherhood in San José, that of Santo Domingo, dates back to 1660.[39] And César Nicolás Penson, the notable Dominican *costumbrista*[40] writer, dates the foundation of the Hermandad de las Animas in the church of St. Nicholas in the city of Santo Domingo to 1849. According to him, this unusual association occurred in the following manner: a group of people went on Monday nights to the St. Nicholas Church, making up the venerable "Hermandad de las Animas." The procedure was to leave there on the stroke of nine and proceed through the deserted streets. Carrying a crucifix and several lanterns and announced by a handbell rung by one of them, they paraded shouting: "One Our Father and one Hail Mary for the holy souls of Purgatory." And everyone immediately responded more quietly: "Our Father, etc...."[41]

However, for Dominicans of all eras the religious influence of Spain attains its greatest expression in the deep-rooted devotion to the Most Holy Virgin under two main advocations: Nuestra Señora de las Mercedes and Nuestra Señora de la Altagracia. The devotion to Nuestra Señora de las Mercedes apparently dates back to the time of the Discovery, as Father Arnaiz states that: "Nuestra Señora de las Mercedes was the virgin carried by Fray Juan Infante, confessor to Admiral Columbus, an image given to him by Queen Isabella herself."[42] And according to Tirso de Molina, the Nuestra Señora de las Mercedes was given to the religious of the Order by Queen Isabel the Catholic when the friars crossed the Ocean with the "fortunate and memorable Captain Don Cristóbal." Tirso de Molina insists that it was members of the Order "who introduced baptism on that immensity of land." When the religious reached the island, the image was placed in the monastery of the city of Santo Domingo. Tirso was distressed that, while the cult of Nuestra Señora de las Mercedes was in decline, another miraculous image, under the advocation of Nuestra Señora del Rosario and venerated in the church of the Dominican friars, "gained the affections of the entire city." It was for this Virgin that the parties, cheering, novenas and competitions were held in those times, in grateful recognition of her "gracious favors and miracles." The establishment of a *cofradía* of the faithful, under the title of the Dolores, rescued the image of Our Lady of Mercies from the oblivion and the low esteem into which she had been plunged for years. The "Pious Brotherhood," as named by Tirso de la Molina , decided to re-enact the episodes of the Passion, Death and Resurrection of Christ.[43]

In 1650, an early chronicler, Canon Alcócer, wrote an extremely interesting account of the Virgin of Altagracia which can be found in a document held in the Biblioteca Nacional in Madrid. Canon Alcócer says that: "The miraculous image of Our Lady of Altagracia is in the town of Higüey, some thirty leagues from this city of Santo Domingo; the mercies that Our Lord God has worked and each day works for those who devote themselves to this Holy Image are innumerable; it is known that it was brought to this Island by two *hidalgos*, natives of Plasencia in Extremadura, named Alonso and Antonio de Trexo who were the first settlers on this Island."[44]

The ancient religious traditions that reached the Dominican Republic from Spain are still flourishing in the rural communities despite the present materialistic times. Many "inland" families have small altars in their modest homes, where, amid oil lamps and silver ex votos, crude religious carvings made by their forebears are worshiped. These simple images are the so-called

Santos de Palo. The sculptors of these santos de palo were mostly anonymous peasants, descendants of Spanish families who settled on the island and worked as carpenters or cabinetmakers. Many of them took up the craftsmanship on their own accord or else inherited it from their parents.[45]

Other religious ceremonies that are still found today, especially in the interior of the country, are the rosaries celebrated among people in the urban areas. The celebration involves proceeding out of the church with a statue of Our Lady of Mercies, St. Anthony or St. Joseph and visiting a wayside shrine on the road leading out of town.[46]

The devout custom of burning the holy palms on Palm Sunday to calm storms and the celebration of the feast of the Most Holy Cross were also inherited from the Spaniards.

V

The word is at the beginning of everything because it is the finest instrument of human communication. It is a sign of approach, sharing and unity. For these reasons, the Spanish language is perhaps the most substantial element of Dominican nationality. Recalling Núñez de Cáceres, I will say "that language made into a flag and a sign of impossible submission are the first portents of Dominican freedom."

The notable Dominican historian Don Emilio Rodríguez Demorizi, while acknowledging "its dissolute vicissitudes," grants obvious days of splendor to the "reign of the language of Castile in Hispaniola," signaling the debut as preacher of the novice Fray Alonso de Cabrera, "a singular master of Prose." There are also native writers such as the highly acclaimed poets Eugenio de Salazar, Tirso de Molina and Bernardo de Balbuena.[47] (From the beginning of the colony, libraries, such as those built by the historian Fernando de Oviedo, contained some of the most important works of the period: the Chronicles of El Cid, the works of Fray Luis de León and the "Vocabulario y el Arte de la Lengua Castellana de Antonio de Nebrija.")

In this brief panoramic view of Dominican letters of the colonial period, the examples of Marcio Veloz Maggiolo (who writes on a wide range of subjects) should be considered extremely realistic ones. Professor Veloz Maggiolo says that "we have reports of numerous courtiers able to handle classical meter and rhyme." In his *Silva de Poesía,* Don Eugenio de Salazar y Alarcón refers to his own occupation as poet and that of two gentlewomen of the Colony who were also poets: Doña Elvira de Mendoza and Doña Leonor de Ovando. Other than a few sonnets and allusions, little of the poetic output from that period remains. Although the Mercedarian monk Tirso de Molina lived in Santo Domingo in the seventeenth century, little is known about him beyond his participation in the floral games honoring Nuestra Señora de las Mercedes. Several authors have speculated that Tirso de Molina may have written his famous play, *El Burlador de Sevilla*, the first in the series of Tenorios, on the island of Santo Domingo and during his seclusion with the Mercedarians.[48] Veloz Maggiolo then adds: "Since the time of the Colony all the poetic influences in Santo Domingo derive from the worst Spanish literature. There was infinite bad taste, and bombasticism and grandiloquence were considered fundamental to good literature. On the other hand, during the seventeenth and eighteenth centuries, poetry was regarded more as a popular pastime than a serious and sober activity. We can state without embarrassment that, from the days of Spanish colonialism up until the movements for national independence, no good poets emerged in Santo Domingo.

This enormous literary void extended not only to poetry but other branches of art and literature, with the exception of Don Antonio Sánchez Valverde, whose book, *Ideas del Valor de la Isla Española*, was the first attempt to assess our geographical and human potential. Other than this, there is nothing that can be deemed important for Dominican letters."[49] I will conclude my brief outline of the panorama of our poetry during the nineteenth and twentieth centuries with these words: "Dominican poetry of the nineteenth century did no more than follow the traditional model of neoclassical poetry represented in Spain by Manuel J. Quintana and by Gallegos. Our great poet of the nineteenth century, Salomé Ureña de Henríquez, considered an important voice by Menéndez Pelayo, employed neoclassical meter.[50]

Veloz Maggiolo concludes his well-informed study with this fitting remark: "The leap of Dominican poetry towards completely new forms occurred at the beginning of the twentieth century."[51] Referring to the development of free verse in Spanish, Pedro Henríquez Ureña gives the names Domingo Moreno Jiménez, Héctor Incháustegui Cabral and Andrés Avelino as Dominican examples (*Obras completas*, Vol. 4, chapter 5, Universidad Pedro Henríquez Ureña, 1978).

Within Dominican popular poetry, Spanish poetry is the highest and most enduring form of expression and communication. As Bruno Rosario Candelier says, "ballads and epic poems from Spanish folklore arrived in the country with the Spaniards, along with other examples of Spanish culture."[52] Thus the verse of Lázaro Bejarano, from the second half of the sixteenth century, may be regarded as the first known example of popular poetry in Santo Domingo.[53] The unforgettable authority Don Max Henríquez Ureña said: "Spain did not only bring the culture of letters and books; it also brought treasures of popular poetry in ballads and songs, dances and games, and treasures of folklore in the copious collection of proverbs."[54] And the poet Tomás Hernández Franco, in his notes on popular poetry, adds: "The Spanish deluge in the Antilles was—and this needs to be very much borne in mind—also a formidable deluge of songs. From this is derived almost all of our popular poetry: the *copla* (four line verse), the *tonada* (song), the *décima* (ten-line stanza), the lullaby, games and riddles, either adapted to the landscape or assimilated wholesale. Our innovation on this material is not especially brilliant but nor was there was a great need to innovate as Spain provided us with a song for every occasion."[55]

Although there are more cultural elements from the Haitian-African influence than many Hispanophile authors would care to acknowledge, it is noteworthy that, in a country with such a large black element in the population, the folklore, strictly speaking, is predominantly Spanish. Edna Garrido de Boggs, who collected some 400 popular songs, games, anecdotes, verses and riddles, discovered only a few Africanisms in the vocabulary and only three songs referring to black people.[56]

It is curious to note how black people in the Dominican Republic have always opted for purely Spanish expressions. José Manuel Andrade provides an amusing example: "In Higüey I heard an old black woman sing a popular Spanish song to the melody of the *décima*, starting each couplet with the refrain 'Morena ya lo ve (Mulatto woman now you see).' The Spanish version, which is quite old, is generally sung to the melody of the Aragonese *jota*."

The Dominican version differs slightly:
Morena ya lo ve

Ayel me ha dicho que hoy
Morena ya lo ve
Y hoy me dice que mañana
Morena ya le ve
Y mañana me dirá
Morena ya le ve
Que lalga son la semana!

Mulatto woman, now you see
Yesterday he told me today
Mulatto woman, now you see
And today he tells me tomorrow
Mulatto woman, now you see
And tomorrow he will tell me
Mulatto woman, now you see
How long the weeks are!

The Spanish song goes as follows:

Ayer me has dicho que hoy
Y hoy me dices que mañana
Y mañana me dirás
Qué de lo dicho no hay nada.[57]

Yesterday you told me today
And today you tell me tomorrow
And tomorrow you will tell me
That what you said means nothing.

The best-known popular poets in the Dominican Republic are possibly Meso Mónica and Juan Antonio Alix, who were both very much of their time. Meso Mónica became popular in the city of Santo Domingo de Guzmán in the eighteenth century. Rodríguez Demorizi compares him to Antón de Montoro, El Ropero de Cordoba, the Jewish tailor who was considered the King of Wit in the fifteenth century.[58] This extremely famous satire, which appears in the "museo Epigramático, Colección de Epigramas, Décimas y Sonetos Selectos," published in Madrid in the last century, is by the master Mónica:

Si el lego que sirve fiel
Al padre Soto tuviera
otro lego, y éste fuera
mucho más lego que aquél
y escribiera en un papel
de estraza manchado y roto
de toda ciencia remoto
un sermon; este sermon
sería sin comparación
major que el del Padre Soto.[59]

If the lay brother who faithfully serves
Father Soto had
Another lay brother, and that one was
Much more lay than he
And if he wrote on a piece
of stained and torn wrapping paper
a sermon lacking in any learning
This sermon would be
Incomparably better than that of Father Soto.

And Juan Goico Alix:

Como hoy la preocupación
más de a una gente abruma
emplearé mi débil pluma
para darle una lección.
Pues esto en nuestra nación
Ni buen resultado deja:
Eso era en la "España Vieja"
Según desde niño escucho,
Pero aquí abunda mucho
El negro tras de la oreja.[60]

Because today worry
Weighs down many people
I will employ my feeble pen
To teach them a lesson.
Since this in our nation
Does not give a good result:
That was in "Old Spain"
from what I have been hearing since I was a child,
But here is very common
The black behind the ear.

Don Emilio Rodríguez Demorizi, who out of necessity is cited frequently, refers to song as one of the most important and wholesome pastimes of the Dominicans. Dominicans are born to the sound of lullabies. They grow up to the tune of children's rhymes and singing games. They sing at work—their machete songs or their *conuco tonadas*. They sing prayers on the nights of religious vigils. In songs about human existence, the richest vein of Dominican folkloric poetry, one also "falls in love singing." For example, the anonymous *decima* begins:

> Yo te enamoro cantando
> prenda de mi corazón

> *I win your love by singing*
> *Darling of my heart*

The depth of the Spanish roots of Dominican folklore, particularly literary folklore, is revealed in the pure Spanish quality in folkloric poetry, as in the following verse:

> Ni contigo ni sin ti
> tienen mis penas remedio
> Contigo porque me matas
> y sin tí porque me muero.[61]

> *Neither with you or without you*
> *Will my troubles cease*
> *With you because you are killing me*
> *And without you because I will die.*

As an interesting example of how right the distinguished scholar is, I transcribe the verse that the neighbor's gardener is singing as I write this essay. It goes like this:

> Tú no pareces mujer
> Tú pareces una rosa
> Tú te me da un parecido
> a la Virgen Milagrosa.[62]

You do not appear a woman
You are like a rose
You to me are like
The Miraculous Virgin.

The poet Tomás Hernández Franco explains the ease with which the Dominican can improvise verses according to the tradition of Spanish metrics. He reminds us that the Antillean child, with his adaptable mulatto spirit, has not felt the need to delve too deeply into the mystery of the ancestral songs:

Mañana es domingo
de vara y pendón
se casa la reina
con Juan Barrigón
Quién es la madrina?
Doña Catalina

Tomorrow is Sunday
With pole and banner
The queen is marrying
Potbellied Juan
Who is the bridesmaid?
Doña Catalina

And many others:

Señora Santa Ana
Porqué llora el niño?
por una manzana
Que se le ha perdido…

Las cortinas del palacio
son de terciopelo azul,
y entre cortes y cortinas
se paseaba un andaluz...

Doña Ana no está aquí
ella está en el vergel
abriendo la rosa
y cerrando el clavel...

Mambrú se fue a la Guerra
Qué dolor, qué dolor que pena!
Mambrú se fue a la Guerra
¡y no sé cuándo vendrá!

Señora Santa Ana
Why is the child crying?
On account of an apple
That he has lost...

The curtains of the palace
Are of blue velvet
And amid courts and curtains
Walked an Andalusian

Doña Ana is not here
She is in the orchard
Opening the rose
And closing the carnation...

Mambrú went off to war
What grief, what grief and what sorrow!

Mambrú went off to war
And I don't know when he's coming back!

All of these verses refer to things that are far from common in their lives, but which, perhaps for that very reason, fulfill a childish longing for adventure, dreams, for the impossible and for poetry. Mothers or fathers know that they are things from "the time of Spain" and smile.[63]

I have a very interesting personal anecdote regarding the songs and themes of re-encounter with Spanish tradition, and how once re-established they are taken up again enthusiastically. In mid 1967, I organized a University *Tuna* (student music group) at the Universidad Católica Madre y Maestra in Santiago which was similar to those performed in Spain since the Middle Ages. It was the first attempt to do so in the Dominican Republic. It is unknown whether the students at the Universidad de Santo Domingo formed any tuna in the sixteenth century. Although no documentary evidence has been found, one can assume that there must have been at least one. On the other hand, the amorous musical dialogue used by country folk to court young women was known as a *media tuna*.[64] For one reason or another, the student *tuna* has taken off and there are about twenty in the country today.[65] Manuel Andrade describes the Dominican *media tuna*. It is a sung challenge. If the contest is between a man and a woman, the man generally sings "en queja" and the woman "a lo divino." The man usually complains about her disdain and the woman turns her nose up at the lover's suggestions. The following are typical examples of *media tuna* songs:

(Reto en queja)
Dime niña qué pretendes?

61

que ningún joven te agrada
Si pretendes algún rey
cuatro tiene la baraja

(Respuesta a lo divino)
No pretendo ningún rey;
Solo un joven de importancia
Y tú como no lo eres
A tí te dejo en balanza[66]

(*Challenge "en queja"*)
Tell me, miss what are you seeking?
As no young man pleases you
If you are hoping for a king
There are four in the pack

(*Reply "a lo divino"*)
I'm not hoping for a king;
Just a young man of importance
And since you are not
I'm leaving you in the balance

Finally, two popular Dominican literary genres come from Spanish forms. These are the proverb and the tale. Many proverbs, which are often repeated in our countryside, are Spanish such as: "Más vale un malo conocido que un bueno por conocer (Better the devil you know that the devil you don't)"; "a otro perro con ese hueso (tell that to the marines)."

In short, the style of the Dominican folkloric tales is less flowing, more schematic and less rich in detail than those collected in Spain. Most of the tales appear to be of European origin. One example is Pedro Animale and Juan Bobo—and it is possible that Animale is a corruption of Urdemales which appears frequently in the Spanish versions.[67]

In addition, a large variety of archaisms dating from the distant time of the Conquest can be found in the speech of Dominicans from the interior of the country. Thus they often use the word "asina" for "así"; "mesmo" instead of "mismo," etc.[68] They also use the traditional Spanish title "don" for respectable men and "doña" for married women, especially in the countryside.

The importance of place names of Spanish origin cannot be overlooked. The historian and academic Julio Genaro Campillo Pérez covers the subject at length in one of his important works, pointing out that: "As he discovered new lands the famous Admiral and Viceroy Don Cristóbal Colón frequently bestowed names of Spanish origin to the world of toponymy." The distinguished historian Emilio Rodríguez Demorizi notes that by doing so Don Cristóbal was "giving free rein to his affective attachments and expressions of gratitude." That is why he christened the island La Española to pay homage to Spain. The first city that he built he named La Isabela in honor of Queen Isabella the Catholic and he named the valley of La Vega Real in memory of La Vega in Granada. Similarly, some minor navigator called the island of Cuba Juana, in honor of Don Juan, the principal heir to the Catholic Kings, and the island of Jamaica Santiago to glorify the patron saint of Spain, Santiago or St. James.[69]

In some cases the toponymy turns out to be valuable for the historical researcher. Thus in his well-known work, Carlos Larrazabal Blanco, notes that the historian Oviedo mentions some plants introduced by the Spaniards such as orange, lemon, pomegranate and banana trees, sugar cane, quince trees, *cañafístola* and others. However, he fails to mention the humble mango and *cajuil*, for example; yet the toponymy reveals that the *cajuil* had already been introduced in the sixteenth century since the name was given to a place in the region of La Vega in 1589 (Col. BAGN, no. 23, 1942, p. 308).[70]

VI

One cannot discuss the Spanish influence on Dominican song without mentioning the common Hispanic origins of Dominican, Cuban, Puerto Rican dances and of most Dominican music. In her book *La Música en Santo Domingo y otro Ensayos,* Doña Flérida de Nolasco writes that "in 1597 they shipped a sizeable cargo of books and of sacred and profane music from Seville to Santo Domingo."[71]

On the other hand, the Dominicans' passion for dancing dates back to very remote times. Lemonnier-Delafosse, cited by Rodríguez Demorizi, says that "the pale Dominican Creole women, born to be queens, do not ask any of their dance partners for a rest." Another Frenchman, Pére Labat, was able to say that "dancing is the main passion in Santo Domingo and I do not believe there is in the world another people more fond of dancing."[72]

Fradique Lizardo, the tireless researcher into folklore, citing Rodríguez Demorizi, notes that the Cuadrilla, an elegant Dominican dance of long ago, is of Spanish origin.[73] Although using some reservation, Lizardo also ascribes an essentially Spanish origin to the Dominican *zapateo*. The distinguished folklorist says that "much has been said about the Dominican *zapateo* and its possible origin in the Spanish *zapateo*. The choreography of the Dominican *zapateos* is much more complex and varied, although the action of tapping the feet may be less accentuated and electrifying than in the Spanish *zapateo*. We ask ourselves: Why is it so different? Is it possible that they have different origins?"[74] The Dominican *zapateo* is known to have three different styles:

Sarambo - a lively dance with percussion and face-to-face *desafíos* (challenges);

Guarapo – which has more figures and livelier movements;

Callao - at a given moment, the music stops and it is only the sound of the dancers' feet that maintains the rhythm of the piece.

Fandango - at the end of the seventeenth century, Moreau de Saint Méry describes what he saw as *fandango* in the country. This description is repeated almost word for word by Pedro F. Bonó about a hundred years later. However, with the passage of time, the word *fandango* acquired the meaning of party and people have forgotten that there was a dance named after it.[75]

Doña Flérida de Nolasco states that the *Carabiné* is a Dominican rhythm inherited from the Spaniards, and it has been modified over time through contact with ordinary people. Its original name has been lost or forgotten until now.[76] The master Luis Alberti notes: "With apologies to some, I do not believe our most popular dance rhythm has anything to do with Negroid or Africanist rhythms. To me, the merengue seems more like a mixture of a Spanish form with our rural *tonadas* from the interior of the country and the same could be said of its melodic features."[77]

According to Fradique Lizardo, the Baile de las Cintas (Dance of the Ribbons) "most probably comes to us from Europe and directly from Spain; we offer this information with a degree of caution."[78] And according to the same author, (probably citing my work, "Lechones de Santiago," published in the *Boletín del Museo del Hombre Dominicano*, October 1973) "the *diablos* originated in the Middle Ages and were incorporated into the Corpus celebrations by the bull 'Trasitorus' issued by Pope Urban IV on September 8, 1264. They took part in the *autosacramentales*[79] and in mystery plays in Spain. In the second part of the Quixote, in chapter fifteen, a Diablo exactly like ours appears with his bladder and bells."[80]

A careful study of the Sarandunga reveals some Hispanic roots in its beautiful folkloric choreography. Fradique, citing Boggs, notes the following: "Many years ago (Boggs, in an article written in 1950, estimates between 125 and 150 years), Piovisco Martínez went to sell his livestock in Haiti. Someone offered to sell him a Saint (that is an image of St. John), with the drums and the duty of holding a celebration every 24 June, which is his feast day. Every year on the night of the 23 June the celebration begins with dancing in honor of the saint. At dawn they all go singing to the river and wait for the sun to come up before bathing. One of the members of the brotherhood, with a red processional banner or sometimes the *capitana*, who carries it, is the person who represents the saint. That is the first person to enter the water. We believe that the participation of the *capitana* was an essential element of the celebration of the Sarandunga."[81] And who was the *capitana*? "Apparently the niece of don N. Guante, captain of the armies of His Majesty the King of Spain and a Caballero Gran Cruz, was the *capitana* of the "Brotherhood of St. John" and the only person granted the honor of carrying the most noble banner of the White Cross of Malta."[82] César Nicolás Penson points this out, as quoted in Fradique's work.

VII

When the Spaniards arrived on the island, they began a building program. First they built the fort of Navidad from the remains of the caravelle *Santa María*. After Columbus' second voyage, they founded the first European-style towns. After founding La Isabela and in particular after Nueva Isabela or Santo Domingo was established, numerous *villas* or towns were also built: Santiago de los Caballeros, Bonao, La Concepción dela Vega, Higüey, Buenaventura, Montecristi, Puerto Plata, Yaguana, Villa Nueva de Jáquimo, Puerto Real or Bayajá, San Juan de la Maguana, Cotuí, Hincha, Santa Cruz de Hicayacao or El Seibo and Santa María del Puerto. The *villas* had town governments and were granted the use of a coat of arms by the Crown. Santo Domingo had the first stone buildings.[83]

On his second voyage, Columbus arrived with seventeen ships carrying 1,200 men. There were officials, soldiers, farmers, priests, doctors and artisans. Among the latter were the first Spanish construction workers to arrive in the Americas, according to Holger Escoto in his *Historia de la Arquitectura Dominicana*.[84]

Marcio Veloz Maggiolo provides an unusual detail: "The architecture of the colony is all imported and does not incorporate any native elements that could enrich or lend variety to the early colonial buildings. This architecture is not uniform and is represented by very different styles ranging from Gothic to high Baroque forms, mainly in churches and arcades."[85] And Roberto Cassá recalls that the only detail offered by Oviedo about the rectangular houses is that they had a better appearance and were more spacious with a porch, an entrance hall and a sloping roof on both sides. In addition, this type of dwelling consisted of only one room, with no internal divisions.[86] And Cassa concludes by citing Loven who attributes a markedly Spanish influence to the rectangular houses mentioned by Oviedo.

Most of the buildings erected by the Spaniards were intended for religious worship. Using a felicitous phrase by the expert Luis Escobal, one can say that wherever the Spaniards planted crosses churches grew.[87] These included the Iglesia de San Nicolás, the first stone church built in the Americas, the Convento de Santo Domingo (seat of the pontifical Universidad de Santo Tomás de Aquino); the Iglesia de la Madre de Dios (known as Iglesia de las Mercedes); the Iglesia de Santa Bárbara and the Cathedral of Santo Domingo, the most important religious monument of the sixteenth century.[88]

They also erected military and civil buildings such as the Torre del Homenaje, the Royal Dockyards, the Casas Reales and the Alcázar Virreinal inhabited by Don Diego Colón, his wife Doña María de Toledo and their courtiers.

In the city of Santo Domingo, these buildings are distinguished by their Isabeline style, derived from the late Gothic, which combines medieval European and *mudéjar* elements. It is characteristic of buildings dating from the era of the Catholic kings.

Introduced by *mudéjar* architecture, brick is the main material used in Isabeline buildings. The use of brick began in the sixteenth century, and it was widely revived in the nineteenth century by the well-known Dominican architect Don Onofre de Lora, a worthy successor to the colonial master-builders. Using brick in construction, mainly as an ornamental device, has become obligatory in the city of Santiago. The baked bricks used on old tiled roofs in El Cibao, which retain the imprint of our grandfathers' fingers, are sought after by today's architects in order to lend their new projects the traditional stamp of a city founded by legendary Spanish nobles. Thus the historian J.G. Campillo Pérez contemplated the great building erected by the Haché brothers for their company in the heart of Santiago. He writes in the *Listín Diario* of 28 March that "in general terms the work is rich in terms of its finish and detail and it has a lofty structure. It is functional in execution and has a certain nostalgic appearance, since the huge façade is completely covered in brick. The 'bricks of the vernacular style,' the bricks of the region, the material widely used for the better buildings of Santiago de los Caballeros. Lacking the stone provided by rocks it had to replace this with the clay used for making bricks. Bricks, made from Santiago clay! The ones used to build the pioneering church of Jacagua as well as the present day Catedral del Apóstol, not forgetting the parish church with a single tower that existed for several centuries up until the earthquake of 1842. The bricks used to construct the public buildings of the past and present such as the old Cabildo and the present day Courthouse. By using this material they have honored the traditions of the location by paying lasting homage to brick, brickworks and bricklayers, the cornerstone, business and occupation of Santiago de los Caballeros from the fifteenth to the twentieth century."[89]

The Dominican taste for Spanish-style buildings of this type was accommodated when the Spanish refugees of 1940, among them the architect Auñón, built many neo-colonial style houses in Santo Domingo.

VIII

The history of painting in Hispaniola began with Diego Pérez, the little-known painter who arrived with the ships of the Discovery. But this beginning does not acquire its own specific characteristic until the arrival of the first artists who were enticed by the churchmen to decorate the churches in the dawning of the Colony. Juan, a painter who lived in Santo Domingo around 1500; Diego López, a "painter of images" from Seville came to the island in 1501; J. Sánchez from Seville who died in Santo Domingo around 1510; Alonso de Arjona came to the island in November 1511; Alvaro González, a painter from Badajoz who came to Santo Domingo. In 1513 Juan de Mendoza arrived and in 1539 Pedro Calderón; Alonso Rodríguez, a master painter arrived in Santo Domingo in 1538; Ximón, a painter arrived in 1552 and Cristóbal Moreno in 1553; Diego del Valle came in 1557 and Marino de la Torre in 1548, Alonso Callejo and Francisco Fernández de Estrada arrived in 1585 and Juan de Salazar in 1586. In 1586 Alonso Dávila came to the island "to paint images of the churches demolished by the English" during Drake's invasion. In 1590 Tomás de Cosa arrived and in 1599, Bernardo de Albornoz. León Calcagno, a painter, came in 1601. Rodríguez de la Fé restored the venerated oil painting of the Altagracia virgin in Higüey in 1708. Along with all these names are, as has been mentioned, a large number of anonymous works, especially of a religious nature. Even the author of the oil painting of La Antigua is unknown; as is for whom or in what year the oil painting was made.[90] The information presented above is found at the beginning of the book by Don Emilio Rodríguez Demorizi titled *España y los Comienzos de la Pintura y Escultura en América*.

In their book *Visión General de la Historia Dominicana*,

Valentina Peguero and Danilo de los Santos examine the major cultural elements of each period in the country's history, mentioning painting specifically. They point out that: "Painting was important in Spain, and the collection of Diego Colón and María de Toledo was the first to be brought to Santo Domingo. The first painters were brought by churchmen to decorate the churches. These painters remained largely anonymous and most of their works disappeared during Drake's plunder. Some canvases such as that of La Altagracia from Higüey and the portrait of La Antigua survive as pictorial works from the sixteenth century, as well as the remains of murals and medallions."[91] The two historians mention the traces of decoration on the ceiling of the Capilla del Santísimo Sacramento of the Cathedral recently discovered by craftsmen; the silhouette of a saint was also discovered recently on a side wall by the entrance to the church of the former Dominican convent.

The Marqués de Lozoya, a grandee by dint of his ancestry, wisdom and modesty, to whom I am indebted and who died recently, said: "From the seventeenth and eighteenth centuries many paintings were undoubtedly taken from Spain to Santo Domingo. It is likely that modest local studios were set up which, as in other American countries, copied Italian, Spanish and Dutch prints onto canvas and colored them in."[92]

Inspired by Lozoya's suggestion about the possible existence of local painting studios where Spaniards and native Dominicans produced a colonial Baroque hagiography that was characteristic of a period of deep religiosity and local color, I set off, over ten years ago, to tour the Dominican countryside, acquiring some lovely small panels with delicately painted and attractive images of virgins and saints. An account of my experience appears in the book *Pintura Colonial Doméstica*

Cibaeña.[93] Based on my research and studies, and perhaps somewhat boldly, I would suggest that a domestic colonial school of painting existed in the Dominican Republic from the end of the seventeenth century or the beginning of the eighteenth—and it displays essentially Hispanic features.

In the nineteenth century, following the many historical and political transformations experienced in Santo Domingo, Dominican painting was once again linked to Spanish painting. At the beginning of 1883, the Spanish painter Juan Fernández Corredor y Cruz arrived on the island from the Escuela de Madrid. Upon seeing the city of Santo Domingo, he exclaimed: What a Spanish city! And he stayed on to live among us.[94] The Spanish artist found the Dominican Republic suitable for developing his talents and he established a drawing and painting class at the Sociedad Amigos de la Enseñanza.

The realist artistic period, which was a time when everything had to be rationalized and reduced to scientific principles, influenced genre painting. In his biographical sketch, Rodríguez Demorizi describes the work of those who trained the great Dominican painters: Desangles, and Abelardo; Grullón y Robiou, Frade y Cabra. Initiated into art by the distinguished Spanish master, these Dominican painters would later discover their own styles, influenced by different schools.[95]

In the twentieth century, the Spanish refugees offered a connection with Spain once more. The range of names and artistic expressions is very extensive: José Gausashs, Francisco Rivero Gil, Joan Junyer, Chu, Antonio Prats Ventós and Manolo Pascual, the latter being primarily sculptors and true masters of Dominican sculpture. Angel Botello Barros, Eugenio Fernández Gavell; José Vela Zaneti, the great muralist whose works adorn the church of San Cristóbal (1948–1950) and the interior rooms of the monument at Santiago de los Caballeros. There is also the artist Pellicer who painted the ceiling of the Panteón Nacional.

The links with Spanish pictorial art have not diminished in recent years. Today, the great Dominican painters remain connected in various ways to the old Hispanic plastic tradition that circulates in their blood and their idiosyncrasies. Darío Suro, in his work "Arte Dominicano," describes the work of the great Dominican painters Gilberto Hernández Ortega and Ada Balcácer y Lepe[96] as having a "deep sense of drama," being "outstanding and dramatic" and displaying the "tragic sense." This dramatic quality of their work recalls the Spanish tragic sentiment.

Some great Dominican artists, such as Fernando Peña Defilló, have incorporated Hispanic stylistic trends. Suro locates himself within "Spanish constructive informalism." And Suro says Elsa Núñez, "[…] recalls certain tragic aspects of Solana's painting on account of the vivid use of color in her work."[97]

Finally, many of the currently acclaimed young Dominican painters have studied in Spain, among them are Fernando Ureña Read, José Miura and Mario Villanueva.

Also, as with the earlier examples, the Hispanic influence on our plastic arts affected different types of Dominican traditional crafts. Thus in the course of my ongoing ethnographic research in the corners of the "interior," I found important traces of original Spanish handicrafts in the Valle de Cibao, a much-loved Dominican region with a rich and deep Hispanic tradition dating back to the sixteenth century. Regarding what I have termed "pure handicrafts" – essentially utilitarian – foundry, saddlery, pottery, basketmaking, and carpentry, these display markedly Hispano-Arabic features. Curiously, most of the craft items with these characteristics are scarcely a century old. However, their self-confident execution indicates the presence of a living tradition that is several centuries old. What I have termed "artistic crafts" with intrinsically Spanish features are very important in El Cibao though unfortunately not many are being produced now and are even less well-known. These include popular religious paintings, the popular *santos de palo* carvings and the making of the masks of the so-called *lechones*[98] for the famous Santiago carnival.[99]

IX

If, after this lengthy survey of the Hispanic influences in our culture, we were to ask ourselves to what extent the Spanish roots have shaped the Dominican personality, I would answer sincerely that they have shaped it almost entirely. And to prove this point, I will attempt to outline, with pertinent and impertinent generalizations, similarities between the behaviors of the Dominican people of long ago and today.

Three characteristics stand out prominently in the conduct of the Spanish conquistadors, and they are the same ones that later emerged in Dominican historical undertakings. They are individualism, ambition and pessimism. These intrinsically Hispanic characteristics have a fixed and ordered sequence. If actions driven by individualism fail to satisfy ambition, then pessimism follows. All the actions of a historical past and present, whether good or bad, positive or negative, proceeded among the Dominicans in a manner that seemed to be determined by these categories.

In fact, documents can be used to study the personalities of the Spanish conquistadors. This way we can evaluate and subsequently ameliorate, shift or counteract the burden, positive or negative, that we have inherited.

Let us begin with individualism. The authoritarian Spanish State appropriated the land, property, labor and even the persona of the indigenous people by means of force. The tenuous argument of religious conversion, which was used to justify the forceful appropriation, cannot be concealed and perhaps reveals even more clearly Spanish individualism, in a metaphysical sense. In fact, the individual egoism of the conquistador who wanted everything for himself manifested itself openly and even spurred him on to violence. As Roberto Cassá notes in his work "Los Taínos de la Española": "The appropriation of *indio* labor was not permitted. This naturally met with opposition from the Spaniards who had moved to the colony to form the dominant private class, a contradiction that resulted in the uprising against Colón's government led by the *alcalde mayor* Roldán.[100]

In the seventeenth century, the famous captain and *regidor* of the town council of Santo Domingo, Don Rodrigo Pimentel best exemplified the force of unbridled individual power that respected no limits. The researcher Doña María Ugarte describes him in biographical notes as: "An overbearing character...generous and lavish when it suited his interests...he ridicules prestigious people in order to win over the governor of the moment...arrested for his involvement in a criminal offence he manages to have the case taken before the military authority and to make them allow him to use the whole island as his jail...; while he was trying to arrange his entry into religious life in order to improve his relations with the prelates, he had the nerve to place his lover Isabel de Ledesma with the order of St Clare as a nun."

In her book *Días de la Colonia*, published in Santo Domingo in 1974, Doña Flérida de Nolasco, reproduces a letter sent by Archbishop Navarrete to the King about the activities of

Pimental, who managed to become the representative of the Dukes of Veragua, descendants of the Discoverer, in Santo Domingo. The letter says: "He was always a Gentleman, Father of the Country and a great Servant of His Majesty in whose royal chests he managed to place upwards of 50,000 pesos, loaned without any interest. Today he is missed. To his own rivals, of whom there were many, he was good, would that there were many Don Rodrigos!" In fact, the people loathed him and one night, during his ascendancy, this inscription appeared on the walls of the Casas Reales: "There is no other law and no other king than Don Rodrigo Pimentel."[101]

We have discovered a very distant precedent for the horrible blight of corruption. This has its most subtle expression in the egoistical pursuit of advantage, for the benefit of themselves or others, by those public figures who put themselves ahead in some important office. Corruption is a thousand-headed hydra that the Dominican people and government are struggling to eliminate today. This is the case of the resourceful treasurer Santa Clara, a great friend and protector of Ovando who ultimately had no other option than to act against him but who at the same time helped him when it was convenient. Father Vicente Rubio O. P., a researcher of Dominican colonial history, published the following account drawn from Fray Bartolomé de las Casas:

> The king sent a receiver of accounts, ordering that they be taken to Santa Clara, using whatever severe measures might be required. They collected the accounts which amounted to 80,000 pesos in gold; they valued all their *haciendas*. The Comendador Mayor ordered these to be sold at auction, which they

always attended; and they acted with such prudence and industry that they gave everything a much higher value than beforehand. He had a pineapple in his hand, which is a very excellent fruit and which at the time was beginning to be found on this island, and, announcing a lot of mares and other very valuable items, valuing them at 500 or 1,000 pesos; the Comendador Mayor said: "To whoever gives 1,500 I will give this pineapple." The person who was able to do so most promptly replied: "It's mine, sir, the pineapple," and there were many who said and were saying this, not on account of the items being auctioned, which perhaps were worth less than half of what they gave for them, nor for the pineapple, but because they knew that they pleased the Comendador Mayor and they bought his favor so that later on he would give them more *indios* or more benefits in addition to those which they had.[102]

So-called "machismo," a damaging behavior that is unfortunately quite widespread in the Dominican Republic, has a notable antecedent in the treasurer Miguel de Pasamonte, the famous intriguer and enemy of the colonizers. "In his time he was accused of having in his house eight or ten girls as concubines, and would not allow another man to sleep in the house on account of jealousy, although he kept in it all the King's gold." Ovando wrote of Pasamonte that he had never known a woman. This is ironic, states Palm.[103]

On the other hand, some rulers frequently abandoned or unscrupulously destroyed the plans or works of their predecessors, and this is precedent in the same Comendador Ovando, who changed the location of the towns founded by the Disco-verer, according to Oviedo because "new rulers always want to reform the works of the former ones."[104]

However, the Spanish legacy of individualism in the Domini-can character did not include only blemishes, deceitful conduct and bad habits. It also brought and transmitted outstanding virtues, lofty values and heroic achievements. Spain was the first colonial power that allowed its conquistadors, colonizers and writers to debate the very rights and powers of the projects they were carrying out, thus stimulating and promoting the Spanish critical tendency that is so deeply embedded in the national character on both sides of the Atlantic. This critical approach toward actions and theories often became a way of expressing contempt for Spanish endeavors throughout the empire and provided an important stimulus for all kinds of rebellion.[105] It is clear that Dominicans inherited the tendency to criticize and despise even themselves from Spain. For example, the Bartrina's epigram, written in the last century, noted the following:

Oyendo hablar a un hombre
Fácil es comprender dónde vió la luz del sol
Si habla bien de Inglaterra es ingles
Si habla mal de Alemania es francés
Si habla mal de España, es español.[106]

Hearing a man speak
It is easy to see where he first saw the light of day
If he speaks well of England he's English
If he speaks ill of Germany, he's French
And if he speaks ill of Spain, he's Spanish.

78

In "Situación de la Cultura Española," Francisco de Ayala argues that Spanish individualism is not based on the French concept of the "a priori" equality of all men, but on the strong sense that in social relations each individual should proclaim his own worth and reject the impersonal achievements of the masses. This explains the lack of solidarity between people, the disdain for the State, the strong sense of personal dignity, the easily-offended honor, the fanaticism of the truly human struggle and the horror of cynical and cold inhumanity."[107]

In the late Middle Ages, individualism awakened from its lengthy inertia and initiated the recovery of the *fueros*[108] and liberties of Catalonia. The Father of the Homeland was greatly impressed by this during his European tour. Joaquín Balaguer, in the *Cristo de la Libertad*, recounts a revealing episode in the life of Juan Pablo Duarte: "Among the people of standing who are enthusiastically celebrating Duarte's return, are the priest José Antonio Bonilla and the doctor Manuel María Valverde. The latter suddenly interrupted the friendly greetings of the visitors to ask Juan Pablo a question that did not in the least surprise any of those present: "And what was it that most impressed you on your travels through Europe?" While everyone, including the questioner was expecting a frivolous reply, Duarte answered, in a voice quivering with emotion but also resolution; "The *fueros* and liberties of Catalonia; *fueros* and liberties that I hope we will one day give to our country."[109]

These medieval Spanish liberties shaped the municipal administrations, seeds of individual liberties that were mentioned at the beginning of this essay and constituted the backbone of the legislation of western civilization. Spain sowed this seed in the Dominican Republic and harvested the fruit of its race's individualism with the Republic's independence.

Two values that are legitimate offsprings of our Spanish ancestry stand out in the Dominican personality: personal courage and honor. The eminent Gregorio Luperón says that the Dominican is: "as noble as he is brave; bold and fearful in combat, he is humane and compassionate in victory" and he adds that "nowhere else on earth have they produced so many heroes."[110] A distinguished Spanish military man, Don Ramón González Tablas, shares the opinion of the renowned Dominican general. In his *Historia de la Dominación y Ultima Guerra de España en Santo Domingo*, he states that "The Dominican officers are, for the most part, men of courage who are highly accredited in their wars and civil disagreements. The most outstanding quality in the country is bravery."[111] Let us consider the importance of this assertion by a Spanish military man who had fought in Santo Domingo as we recall the popular aphorism that states: "Here one may be anything but a coward." Personal courage and honor among Dominicans can be seen in exemplary figures such José Ramón López, the Dominican journalist and author of "La Alimentación y las Razas." A brave fighter, he poured all the fire and force of his temperament into polemics and struggle. On one occasion, he was arguing with Augusto Chotin, an opponent of the dictatorship of Ramón Cáceres, and he turned this incident into a demonstration of personal courage and a display of romantic and gentlemanly chivalry.[112] In his article Juan Daniel Balcácer, the young and noteworthy Dominican writer, recounts two anecdotes showing how Hispanic honor and courage flourished among the Dominicans who defied Spain itself. Both anecdotes refer to the final moments of the patriot, martyr and poet, Eugenio Perdomo. Balcácer recounts how on April 17, 1863, Eugenio Perdomo and several of his comrades were executed following the sentence pronounced by the Consejo de Guerra Permanente. According to tradition, when the Spanish authorities offered Perdomo a donkey, he rejected it saying: "no, when Dominicans go to heaven, they go on foot." Another tradition recalls the fact that the day before he was executed, Eugenio Perdomo asked for permission from the guard who was watching over his cell to visit Virginia Valdez. The guard agreed to the request, but on the undertaking that the prisoner would return before daybreak; and before dawn—as he had given his word of honor—the poet returned to the jail to face the invaders' bullets.[113]

The second most outstanding characteristic of the conquistadors is ambition, which, like individualism, is very evident in later historical events and in the present day.

In order to consider the scope of Spanish ambition, we need to bear in mind what the conquistadors, the first inhabitants of the villas founded on Hispaniola, represented in social terms. Frank Moya Pons, referring to the time of the Conquest in his *Historia Colonial de Santo Domingo*, says: "The bulk of the population was made up of skilled workers, artisans and urban laborers, among whom was a significant proportion of Moriscos and Mudéjars[114] and the main body of the rural population consisting of free peasants, among whom was also a good number of Moors who had been reduced to servitude during the Reconquest." He adds: "It was out of this mass of the Castilian population that the conquistadors and colonizers of the New World emerged, since, in order to encourage emigration to America, the Crown made lofty promises of tax exemptions.[115]

The number of nobles and *hidalgos* who came to the Americas was extremely small, and they too aspired to rise within their social class. This means that the "European blood arrived eager for glory and needing to climb the social ladder—of Spanish society."[116] The ambition to rise above one's class and status motivated the newly arrived Spaniards to enlist in the main enterprises of the conquest; to study at the universities of Santo Tomás de Aquino and Santiago de la Paz, following the curriculum of the University of Salamanca, which at the time was considered to be "the most important seat of classical learning in the whole of Europe"[117]; and even to request that coats of arms be granted to the cities and towns where they lived.[118]

This ancestral desire for social ascent remains alive in all our communities. Being as we are, a country of mixed-race people, we retain a tendency to "whiten ourselves." David Dixon Porter, in his *Diario de una Misión Secreta a Santo Domingo*, says: "I have attended solemn masses in the Cathedral and I have never seen such a large, respectable and devout congregation. The most surprising thing was to see so few blacks among them, as they were generally white or mulatto-colored, of a range of shades, from darker to lighter; evidently revealing a disposition by the population to become as white as possible, although I cannot say that they have achieved their goal to any great extent."[119]

In his book, *Las Clases Sociales de Santo Domingo*, Marcio Mejía Ricart points out that: "A certain family pride links the different parts of the countryside by means of 'regional surnames.' These provide people from a particular rural area with support and a degree of respect, even outside the boundaries of their region, in any area of the national territory. For example, it is known throughout the whole country that the Bencosmes are from Moca; the Goicos are from Seibo; the Morrobels from Luperón; the Minyettis from Ocoa; the Cids from Copey; the Camilos from Salcedo, etc."[120] And therefore, they became related to Dominicans with respected surnames by marrying members of old and distinguished families, something that overrides even skin color; this is an ideal secretly cherished by many locals.

Marriage to a white person, in particular, a blond foreigner who will supposedly pass on to their descendants the ethnic characteristics of the Spanish conquistadors, has been equally sought after. Sometimes advantageous connections are attained through the typical ties of *compadrazgo*, which cement a close and longstanding friendship. Rodríguez Demorizi says that, when seeking a godparent, "the Dominican chooses the people he holds in high regard, teaching their children to view them with respect and to greet them formally with the *besamanos*, a custom that formerly consisted of kissing the godfather's hand. It is a courtesy that is very typical of the Spanish people, from whom it derives its chivalrous character."[121]

The third characteristic, pessimism, appears to stand out most strongly in the conduct of the Spanish conquistadors and is also evident in the subsequent historical deeds of Dominicans.

Although they came mainly from the south of Spain, the Spanish conquistadors felt that their spiritual home was Castile. They could not escape the human condition that Miguel de Unamuno calls the "tragic sense of life," which is felt by Christians who cannot reconcile their beliefs and their deeds in practice. As Unamuno also noted, they lived "struggling continually against themselves and in constant agony, since struggle is the true meaning of the word agony." A religious people, predisposed by their race to mysticism, the conquistadors experienced the unsettling effect of a natural world like ours that directly stirs the senses and lulls the emotions. This contrast tormented their rough spirits and lasted until, weakened and feeling abandoned and lonely, they allowed themselves to be overcome by pessimism and sadness. The Dominican inherited the agonized nature of the conquistadors because, being as Luperón says, a profoundly religious people, they live in a turbulent and sensual environment that is unsuitable for developing a metaphysical side.

As a fatalist on account of the weight of historical factors and his ample quota of Semitic blood, the Spanish conquistador bequeathed his fatalism to us. This may be the origin of the tendency for so many to resign themselves to the deeds of the *caudillos*. The phrase, "what can we do about it," is extremely common.

According to Herrera Miniño, "Sadness emanates as if it were a fundamental aspect of the Dominican's inheritance. The social environment performed its work of shaping his mind. As a product of the solitude and abandonment in which the colony found itself to be plunged, sadness was a determining factor in establishing a pattern of behavior that has become an essential part of the Dominican life. In the seventeenth century and part of the eighteenth, the trait of sadness was gradually consolidated."[122] And Minino further notes that, "fearful of the supernatural on account of the mixture of African beliefs brought by the slaves and the accommodating interpretation of the Catholic religion, all of this produced distortions in the mental formation of those born here, and these are impossible to eradicate even today."[123] Thus the Dominican idleness and decision to engage in effort, work and activity only when it suits is the product of this ancestral pessimism.[124]

The following poem, which serves as a prologue to the delightful novel by Ricardo León, *Alcalá de los Zegríes*, and

which so aptly describes the Spaniard, is perfectly applicable to
the Dominican of yesterday, today and forever:

Lector:
Este es el pueblo peregrino,
que con su espada fatigó la tierra
y abrió un surco en el mar.
Pueblo de Guerra,
de casta mora y de blazon latino
Leyó, en los astros su caudal destino
ganó la cumbre, traspasó la sierra
Y aún salvó el alto término que cierra
De la humana ambicón todo camino
Pueblo orgulloso, apasionado y fuerte
o trabaja, y lucha sin medida,
o se abandona a la pereza inerte
nunca acertó a vivir es un suicida
que abrasado en las fiebres de la vida
para saciar su sed, busca la muerte.

Reader:
This is the wandering people,
Which vexed the land with its sword
And opened a furrow in the sea.
A Warlike People,
Of Moorish race and Latin coat of arms,
It read its caudal destiny in the stars
It reached the summit, crossed over the mountain
And even overcame the lofty boundary that closes off
All paths to human ambition
A proud people, passionate and strong

Either he works and fights excessively,
Or he gives in to inert idleness
He never succeeded in living, he is a suicide
Who, consumed by the fevers of life
In order to quench his thirst, seeks death.

X

Essentially documented by the works of well-known and talented researchers and authors, this essay argues that the framework of Dominican culture today is fundamentally Spanish. The black contribution is, in some of its aspects, considered marginal and not as essential. But the Spaniards in fact bequeathed to Dominicans for centuries many of the negative characteristics, such as aggressiveness, sadness and laziness, typically attributed to the black element or the Taino element of Dominican idiosyncrasy.

However, it is fair to acknowledge that the black and indigenous peoples, who are present in Dominican blood, have orientated many of Dominican values in the formation of a national culture that is integrated into the society and ecology of the Dominican Republic.

As stated at the beginning, the Dominicans are a mixed people. Africa and America have dominated many of our somatic features, and Spain dominated the basic composition of our temperament and our way of seeing things.

In conclusion, I embrace the words of the exemplary Dominican, Gregorio Luperón: "Let whoever is interested in knowing know this: Spain today does not have enemies in the nations that were its American colonies but only emancipated children, who are true brothers for the Spaniards."

CHAPTER FOUR

The African Inheritance in Dominican Culture

CARLOS ESTEBAN DEIVE

Dominican Hispanophiles rarely speak of black people, show any interest in them, or study their native cultures and contributions to the Creole culture. In Santo Domingo, black people have lacked apologists until today mainly because their color recalls atavisms and phenotypes better consigned to the attic of oblivion. Quite a few Caucasians, with ancestors whose originally soft and white skin was more intensely tanned by the relentless tropical sun than they could stand, believe it is not in their interest to "degrade" the race but to "improve it." To support their views, they refer to "sensual" and "dark" Africa, teeming with "witch doctors" and "howling savages." This is an attitude that in no way flatters the native destinations.

The cloak-and-dagger Africanologists are no less extreme; as intellectuals, they reveal an anticolonial frenzy that makes them move away from anything reeking of Spain, as if anything Spanish were a plague. The eagerness of these intellectuals to vindicate black people—an eagerness that is legitimate but which should be controlled—has led them to fall into the most exaggerated historicist Manicheanism when discussing the subject of black people in Dominican culture. This tendency, which surfaced in 1973 after the First Colloquium on the African Presence in the Antilles at the Universidad Autónoma de Santo Domingo, has since spread like wildfire—especially among the most dyed-in-the-wool and orthodox Marxists who argue that Santo Domingo is merely a copy of black Africa, while any Hispanic elements in our culture should be regarded merely as something marginal and not essential.

This dangerous antagonism to which each faction is so fiercely and furiously devoted tends to support a process that destroys the image of Santo Domingo as a cultural entity. Its deforming and minimizing effects can be observed in a type of cogitative insistence, loaded with incidental, changeable or even superfluous topics. Instead of delving into the Dominican *ethos*, its historical and social particularity, or the concept of what identifies Dominicans as a race and the traits that distinguish them from others, the sociologizing efforts of the two tendencies outlined have lapsed into excessive triviality. This interpretative astigmatism has a distorting effect, making the cultural entity already referred to unrecognizable. This is highly dangerous.

A reasonably reliable and insightful attempt to undo the distortions in order to bring into the open, free from contamination, the anthropological elements that make up contemporary Dominican culture is necessary. However, to clear up any possible conceptual deviations, it is important to understand the Dominican culture as a way of life that is not common, or as a set of behaviors that distinguish them as a people with certain peculiarities, a people formed as part of a process—much of it spectacularly tragic—of historical osmosis. Different ethnic groups have participated in this process, with varying degrees of prominence, producing the "we-ness" that shapes the collective consciousness.

The topic in the title of this essay is not only controversial but also extremely perplexing on account of its elusive quality. In my humble opinion, there is nothing more difficult to pin down in phenomenological terms than the African heritage in Dominican culture. A study of this kind is extremely complex from a methodological point of view since so many shadows hover over it, making it difficult to pinpoint, and the facts at our disposal are few and fragmentary. For this reason, one might believe that the spirits of veteran and famous maroon leaders—Ocampo and Lemba and Vaquero and Juan Criollo—are wandering through the savannah, forests and paths inciting their brothers in the race to conceal their ethos in the old *manieles*[1] of Baoruco, to the exasperation of the ethnographer and ethnohistorian and as revenge for the exploitation of black people by white slaveowners.

The cultural contribution of African ethnic groups to Dominican society presents a knotty and multifaceted problem for the researcher because of the taut social weft that has been woven since the very beginnings of African enslavement. Once the Africans had crossed to the New World they stopped being known as such in order to become, as Ianni notes, blacks or mulattoes (1977: 53). This condition, rather than that of being African, in the eyes of the slave master, defines the biological, psychological and cultural characteristics that distinguish, differentiate and devalue them in relation to whites. Moreover, the problem is further exacerbated by the fact that both whites and blacks sought, and still seek, to identify themselves in terms of a mutually exclusive set of references.

These prefatory remarks should enable a more in-depth examination into the heart of the matter. Above all, a reasonably pertinent inventory of the Black African traits found in the Dominican culture of today is totally useless if the characteristics and forms of enslavement of black people in the New World, especially in the regions where the so-called plantation economy prevailed, are not fully investigated. The plantation economy absorbed the largest numbers of the odious slave trade, also allowing the most diverse and complex mechanisms to emerge. Without this knowledge, any attempt at Afro-Americanist research is bound to result in resounding failure.

Undoubtedly, the most important of these mechanisms is deculturation. Moreno Fraginals defines deculturation as a conscious process to eradicate the culture of one human group for the purpose of economic exploitation. This group is used as a cheap, unskilled workforce to facilitate the expropriation of the natural riches of the territory where it lives or is settled (1977: 14).

In terms of the enslavement of black people in the Americas, Moreno Fraginals' definition is flawless, but deculturation is not necessarily a conscious process, nor is it determined by economic factors. Numerous communities have felt the impact of this process without the intervention of the characteristics that Moreno Fraginals highlights in his definition. Moreover, deculturation, as Fraginals further points out, is typical of all types of colonial or neocolonial exploitation. In the case of the black slaves brought forcibly to the Americas, the deculturation to which they were subjected had devastating consequences for their respective cultures.

Black Africans arrived in the Americas as slaves. With their unpaid labor, they provided the Spanish conquistador with the riches of the discovered continent. On account of slavery and servitude, black Africans did not reach the Indies with their cultures intact. Uprooted from their land, they were taken and transplanted in a new environment, integrated into a society which was not their own and where they found themselves in a state of complete social and economic subordination. Thus black Africans experienced the destruction of their tribal and political structures, their forms of family life, their value systems, and ultimately, their original cultural patterns.

Africans from different ethnic groups were enslaved. Those from the same ethnic group were separated and allocated to different units of production in order to accelerate the endoculturative process as much as possible. The colonial authorities also sponsored and encouraged inter-ethnic rivalry by means of institutions such as the *cabildos* and the *cofradías*. It was a clearly a case of preventing slaves from organizing and developing a critical political understanding of their alienation which would impel them to fight against their servitude in a rational, collective and, if you like, revolutionary manner.

However, all of this would have been to no avail if the slave-owner had not subjected black people to another process that was necessarily complementary and essential to the task of rooting out their mother culture. I'm referring to endoculturation, a mechanism by which an individual is encouraged to adopt the culture that is impose on him or her. Endoculturation demanded that the slave consider the master's culture superior to his own and, even worse, that he consider that his own conduct—that of the serf—proceeds along channels below the level of conscious thought.

For a number of reasons, complete deculturation and endoculturation, which totally destroy and sweep aside a people's culture in order to replace it with another, are almost impossible to achieve. In the case of black people, far from passively allowing themselves to be stripped of their culture, they resolutely dedicated themselves to preserving it by various means, even if these were only partially successful. The fact that they were forcibly removed from their environment and transferred to a new, though similar one, had adverse consequences for their material culture. It prevented them from using their African skills and caused a radical break in their ergological practices. In cases where they were able to preserve areas of their *ethos*, it was usually those of a spiritual nature since these presented an impenetrable barrier to all attempts at altering their personality.

One exception to this general rule was when black people, rather than taking refuge in their most intimate and deepest being, or secretly keeping their cultural patterns safe, risked actively resisting through revolt and flight. Hiding in their *manieles, cumbes, palenques* and *quilombos* or whatever one chooses to call them—the Spanish colonists contemptuously called them "dens of thieves"—the slaves attempted to reconstruct their ancestral cultures; they also clearly expressed their opposition to the system that oppressed them and their unstoppable longing for freedom which is a prerogative of all mankind regardless of color.

In some cases, the results of this were successful. In Surinam, the maroons or Bush Negroes escaped into the densest forests, eluding the Dutch to the point where the latter decided to abandon them to their fate. As a result, the social and religious systems of African cultures—especially those of the Fanti and Ashanti of the Gold Coast—managed to survive largely intact. Many of their cultural elements would also, by virtue of continuous contact, become part of the culture of the indigenous people of the region. This did not happen in other American territories such as Venezuela, Mexico, Colombia, Jamaica and Santo Domingo where the aforementioned experiment was limited to a way of life in which the syncretism and transculturation that occurred when the slaves were bound to the hard labor of the sugarmills and *haciendas* had already left an indelible mark.

On the other hand, neither the slave masters nor the authorities made great efforts to completely stamp out the cultural values of the black population. It was enough to suppress those values that presented a real obstacle to the accumulation of capital from enforced labor. For the owner of a sugarmill or any other socioeconomic unit, the slaves were simply a factor in production. Hence attitudes towards them were characterized by a pragmatic view in which the only consideration was the slaves' cost-effectiveness. The well-worn and much debated issue of the alleged good treatment of slaves in the Iberian colonies, in contrast to the cruelty of the English possessions, is superfluous, irrelevant and not useful if one does not bear in mind that this treatment was linked to the particular social development of each territory and ultimately conditioned the social relationships of production.

The American slave legislation shows that in most of the colonies, the ruling class favored and encouraged the preservation and development of isolated and harmless elements of black African culture which could, in some way, help to reinforce their subjugation (Moreno Fraginals 1977: 14) and even result in greater economic advantages. The famous dean of the Real Audiencia de Santo Domingo, Don Agustín Amparán y Orbe, was the younger son of a noble family "of good breeding but little income," as Malagón puts it (1974: lxii). The architect of the very famous and misnamed Código Negro Carolino of 1784 had no objection to "innocent pleasures"—as he called them—of dancing and music among the slaves. But this favor, apparently tinged with humanitarian and beatific sentiments, reveals its true intention when he adds that, thanks to it, slaves will not feel the hardships or weaknesses "of the hard labor of cultivation." It will also distract them from "other harmful gatherings and pastimes," for the security of the colony. What the illustrious author of the Código does not state openly, however, is that the dancing, which sometimes had an erotic quality because it is closely linked to fertility rites in African cultures, also served to arouse the libido of the blacks. As a result, nine months later, the master increased his slave workforce at no cost beyond a cow or two to liven up the *calenda*.[2]

What the dominant class was not able to foresee or suspect, and what is peculiar about the processes of deculturation and endoculturation mentioned above, is the fact that, although these were used by the ruling class to exercise control freely, they also had the opposite effect. Black people exploited the available chinks to preserve their native culture, albeit in a fragmented form. This was most common in the Spanish and Portuguese colonies and must be borne in mind when attempting to assess the differences between Iberian and Anglo-Saxon slavery.

The *cofradía* of Saints Cosme and Damián, considered to be twins in Catholic hagiography, was founded in Santo Domingo by *arará* or Dahomeyan blacks. In Dahomey, twins were regarded as otherworldly beings and hence endowed with supernatural powers. In this way, slaves of this ethnic group could safely continue worshipping the twin cult under the pretext of devotion to these saints.

The *cofradías* were primarily urban institutions. As a result, when studying African retentions in the American cultures, differences between the plantation worker and the urban slave, whether household workers or day laborers, are also important. The sugarmill and the city are the two opposing sides of the slavery system. In the former, slaves were forced to work long days; in the latter, outside of household chores or the short working day in the market and on the streets selling fruit, charcoal and water, enslaved blacks were largely at leisure.

In the sugarmill, which was a social microcosm and a small empire ruled with an iron fist by the owner, whose wealth rested on a dependent workforce organized to produce agricultural goods destined for the European market and, as a result, a greater primitive accumulation of commercial capital (Wolf and Mintz 1975), the social relations between master and slave tended to be extremely personalized.

The dominant class justified its power and exploitation by means of a benevolent despotism that regarded the subordinate group as inferior and uncivilized. The distance between the owner of the sugarmill and his laborers involved a whole series of precise sumptuary and formal norms, even when the benevolence implicit in the despotism nonetheless permitted a certain "intimacy" between each party (Van der Berghe 1971: 57–61). The stereotype of the arrogant and sadistical master who took pleasure in tormenting the black, which has been extensively promoted by hardline Africanologists, does not correspond to the reality. The slaveowner harbored economic interests, not perverse ones, and his relationship with the slave was merely an economic resultant (Moreno Fraginals 1977: 15).

In spite of the paternalism and the fact that many slaves lived in the same area—the sugarmill—the plantation system did not result in the development of a strong and cohesive local community. Instead weak, unstructured and fragmented social bonds developed—and the political life of the slave declined to the point of extinction. And since the sugarmill was a radical ecological innovation (Harris 1973: 79), all the rich African heritage of farming and craft techniques of ceramics, metalworking and weaving barely managed to survive the process of this innovation. Moral values, customs, beliefs and religious practices were more likely to survive in the sugarmill. The Catholic religious practice of the sugarmills, with its devotion to the saints promoted by Counter-Reformation Spain in response to the spread of Lutheran doctrines, favored the creation of organic cults that became firmly integrated into a *corpus* that still retains all the features of true religions today. Vodú, Candomblé, and Santería offered strong competition to formal Catholicism.

Although they can be evaluated in their own right, all these retentions reveal the priority of the sugarmill, in terms of the subject under discussion; essentially, cultural traits were reworked and complexes of African origin were adapted to the new living conditions of the blacks. In the heat of the economic and social autarky of the sugarmill, this reworking resulted from a complicated arrangement of slavery relationships and structures generated. Consequently, the cultural remnants of purely African origin must be placed alongside the neo-African elements that became interwoven into the culture of the continent. As has been mentioned, these developed throughout the cycle of the plantation system.

In the cities, anonymity favored the preservation and transmission of beliefs and practices of African origin. In the city, slaves and free blacks—the latter sometimes more numerous than the slaves—enjoyed greater freedom than in the sugarmills.

Opportunities for meeting, engaging in conversation on different topics, getting together and attending meetings and parties, did not, as on the plantation, depend on the few rest periodsand holy days of obligation; they arose at any opportunity. Street life which was filled with different kinds of vendors was almost exclusively a black domain. In daily wanderings, friendships, associations and tribal reunions were established. The free blacks' houses were meeting places where those gathered dedicated themselves to their rituals and ceremonies in a carefree fashion—and were shielded from indiscreet gaze. African-derived traits and complexes became established and perpetuated themselves, though not in a pure form of course, since the dominant presence of the Spanish culture slowly but inexorably modified them.

The enslavement of black people in the Americas went through various stages. Although the slavery system must be considered as a homogenous and undifferentiated phenomenon, studies carried out in all the countries of our continent reveal diversities and particularities that can be observed over time. These are based, not as Freyre (1952), Tannenbaum (1968), Elkins (1969) and others suggest, on ideological and institutional forms, but rather on the different stages of development of the slavery systems and their respective modes of production. If this is accepted, the systematization of data, information and studies about the cultural contribution of the enslaved African and their descendants to the American societies can be approached in the light of three different working interpretations or hypotheses.

The first interpretation establishes that the African culture which arrived with the slaves exists as such—that is, as African and therefore distinct from European or Asiatic cultures—in numerous and varied aspects of American culture. Preserved by the present-day descendants of Africans, these aspects are cultural survivals passed from generation to generation.

The second interpretation maintains that African culture could not survive as such, and was recreated by slavery so as to produce a culture of its own and *sui generis*: so-called black culture. It is this culture and no other which survives today in many different areas of American life. The pure African traits and complexes disappeared as a result of the social relationships of production that emerged out of the slavery experience and were readapted to the new social and political reality.

The third and final interpretation states that both African culture, strictly speaking, and the black culture that emerged out of the slavery experience are deeply embedded in the capitalist culture that predominates in American societies. Elements of the African and the black cultures can be easily identified, but their significance can only be explained in terms of the relationships and structures of the capitalist mode of production.

According to Ianni, the three interpretations are not mutually exclusive yet his view locates black and African cultures within capitalism and as subordinated to it (1977: 57–7). For example, if we follow this line of inquiry into the religious syncretism that produced cults such as *vodú* and others, it will be necessary to clarify, as Cartaxo Rolim suggests (1978: 42–3), the issue of the presence of some Catholic symbols such as the cross—and not others symbols—in those cults. How can we explain the existence of images of the saints in *vodú* temples and not other symbols directly linked to the mass? Were the symbols chosen by the African slaves, consciously or unconsciously, and adopted by them according to a Catholic conception of the world or rather from a uniquely African perspective? Are these symbols

Catholic reinterpretation carried out by Africans, or did they reinterpret them in terms of their own cosmogony? These questions evidently lead us to question those who advocate understanding religious syncretism in terms of the religion of the slaveowner, that is Catholicism, and who favor the Marxist axiom that the dominant ideology is that of the dominant class.

By seeking to deny any influence of black Africans on the national culture, traditional historiography in Santo Domingo invented an ideological scheme that presents an idyllic image of slavery. Those in favor of this thesis—one promoted by racist Trujillism as it penetrated deep into the fabric of society—are, for the most part, armchair and airconditioning researchers. They have never spent a sleepless night amid the merry uproar of a rural fiesta or the rhythmic beating of the drums which are a very essential feature of the ritual typical of a vigil to honor a saint. They propose an ideology based on two myths which essentially justify the profitable arrogance of the privileged classes achieved through the forced or indirect subjugation of other human groups.

The first myth maintains that master-slave relations in the colony of Santo Domingo were based on humanitarian sentiments. The tendency towards social equality prevailed, as did the absence of prejudice and discrimination that was typical of the Spaniards, who were open to racial mixing with black women. This enormous fallacy fails to withstand even the most general analysis of the documentary sources. The slave legislation of Santo Domingo, caustically formulated, has three basic dimensions:

a) one aimed at protecting the master's authority over the slave and the reverence, respect and compliance owed by the people of color to whites;

b) one which attempted to instill in black people, enslaved or free, the belief that they belonged to an inferior and barbarous race, incapable of managing on its own; and

c) one which punished by means of a wide range of penalties—ranging from the lash to killing by quartering and mutilation of the limbs—acts displaying a lack of deference, but especially acts of rebellion, poisoning and marronage.

The mutilation of sexual organs was prohibited—and the reasons behind this exception seem obvious.

In fact, this legislation simply reflects the Spanish ideology that prevailed until the nineteenth century. It emphasizes ideas such as purity of blood and the formation of a society or regime with a rigidly stratified caste structure.

The obsession with purity of blood, which has religious connotations, dates back to the Reconquest. A judicial inquiry into the family of Isabel de Bargas, the mother of Hernando Pizarro, conducted in Toledo on April 28, 1544, reveals that the family "was held and found and commonly reputed to be an old noble Christian one of clean blood without any relationship to Jews or converts or Moors or even villeins" (Caro Baroja 1978: 494).

Two and a half centuries later, a file relating to the license applied for by don Nicolás de Montenegro, the cavalry's second lieutenant stationed on the southern frontier of Santo Domingo, to marry the Creole Ursula de Figueroa, a document reproduced in "Milicias de Santo Domingo" by the historian Rodríguez Demorizi, essentially repeats, with formal variations, information about the fiancée and her closest relatives' purity of blood. All of them—according to a statement made by the witnesses—were "white persons held and reputed as such" and "free from a bad reputation as Jews, Moors etc..."

Ursula de Figueroa had proven her pure lineage. However in

1775, three years later, another document sent to the king by Montenegro, now a lieutenant, reveals the same application for María de la Luz Logroño. What romantic reasons led Ursula and Nicolás to break their engagement? The new fiancée lacked the dowry required by Spanish military law for all future spouses of the king's officers, but Montenegro did not shrink from this problem and offered his own hacienda, which included fifteen slaves, as a guarantee that María de la Luz would lead the life worthy of the wife of a hidalgo. His Majesty authorized Montenegro to marry her on August 16, 1775 (Rodríguez Demorizi 1978: 294–327). One wonders if the marriage ever took place.

The case greatly aroused my curiosity since the file ends without telling us anything about this matter, but sometimes fate intervenes on behalf of the researcher or I am tempted to believe that providence came to my assistance to alleviate my curiosity. While reading some Puerto Rican documents on the migration of white families from Santo Domingo to the neighboring island on account of the invasion by Toussaint L'Ouverture, I came upon Doña María de la Luz Logroño, widow of Lieutenant Colonel Nicolás de Montenegro—as one can see, this officer had an exemplary career —and a resident of the city of San Juan. Doña María, to whom her then fervent lover had offered the hacienda that he owned as a token of his devotion, was living off the work of two day laborer slaves that she had been able to keep with her, as—a woman after all—she had taken the precaution of sending them on ahead to Puerto Rico in June 1799 (Szaszdi 1967: 1445).

Blood, purity, race... A holy trinity pursued and venerated by the Spaniards throughout their history! All of them? The people who codified such requirements, typically old Christians without any mark that might stain their ancestry, are serious and worthy men. Although people accepted it or resigned themselves to it, there were *hidalgos* who, certain of their social position, made fun of it. In the *Libro de Chistes* by Luis de Pinedo, this brief anecdote is recounted:

> A nobleman of this kingdom was reported to the Inquisition for eating meat when it was not allowed. When he appeared before the inquisitors, the first thing he did was to recount for them his genealogy, which was clean. Then he added: "As, gentlemen, you have seen that I am neither Jewish, nor a convert, nor a Moor, I would like you to know that nor am I remarkable. And removing his cloak, he stood there completely naked, walking around the room just as his mother had brought him into the world. He was really a man of very puny appearance and disposition. Turning around, he took the cloak and left the place without any shame, leaving those present laughing heartily. (Caro Baroja 1978: 495)

Many serious and worthy men lived in Santo Domingo in the colonial era. One of them was the citizen Don Gaspar de Arredondo y Pichardo. In the report that he wrote on his departure from the island on April 28, 1805, following the siege by Dessalines, he thanked heaven for giving him rich, virtuous parents of noble birth, who naturally had not neglected his education. A man like that, of such ancient lineage, must have suffered terribly from the insult he received when, as he himself tells it, at a dance given in the Dominican capital to celebrate the entry of Toussaint's deputy General Moyse, the master of ceremonies did him the honor of getting to dance with a former slave of his household, a young woman and one of the leading young ladies at the fiesta, simply because, as he says, she "was pretty" (cited in Rodríguez Demorizi 1955: 132). When such an eminent and offended citizen, whose story reveals thinly veiled racial prejudice, has no alternative but to admit that his slave was pretty, one can only imagine the kind of woman she must have been.

Absence of racial prejudice? Social equality? King Alfonso X the Wise said in one of his famous Partidas[3] that one has to pity the captives because they are "deprived of their freedom, which is the dearest thing men can have in this world." The king's advice apparently did not apply to him, since despite his noble sentiments he had no objection to issuing extensive legislation on slavery. Instead of asking others to lament, he could have granted the slaves freedom.

Racial prejudice pervaded the Spanish-American legislation. The first shameful epithets against blacks were directed at *ladino* slaves.[4] The Hieronymite Fathers state that they proved to be "very knavish" and that the kings were "the worst and have the worst habits," "a bad race of people who are very insolent and of a bad disposition" (Utrera 1976: I, 386). The good black, the good-natured black, the peaceful and submissive one was the *bozal*,[5] the one who lives in the heart of Africa and was not contaminated by the evils of civilization. The *bozal* was the "good savage," simply because the *ladinos*, the only kind of black people who went to Santo Domingo in the early years of its colonization, were the ones who led the rebellion against the white master and oppressor. When the *bozales* also rose up and escaped to the forests, their hitherto virtuous image was radically altered. In a document dated September 28, 1532, the Empress called them "haughty," "disobedient," "troublemakers," "incorrigible" and "having a bad way of life" (Encinas 1946: IV, 383).

The prejudice against black people, which clearly has its origin in economic motives, persisted in Santo Domingo throughout the entire slavery period. One of the leaders of the colony, Don Andrés de Heredia, when presenting his report on the drawing up of the Código Negro, resolutely opposed the manumission of slaves—something that clashed with the much-trumpeted tendency to social equality—because, according to him the black was an individual of "perverse inclinations" and the society would suffer morally as a result of such indulgence (Malagón 1974: 111). In addition, Don Agustín de Amparán did not hesitate to prohibit black and mulatto children from attending public schools because, if they were opened indiscriminately to the most outstanding youth, the mixing between them could give rise to "sinister impressions of equality and familiarity" (Malagón 1974: 171).

Of course, ideology is one thing and reality is another very different thing. The former discriminated but this discrimination did not prevent whites, prompted by inevitable passions, from entering into sexual unions with indigenous and black women. Mörner states that, in a certain sense, the Spanish conquest of America was a conquest of women (1969: 33). The black woman was the property of the white master, and as a result, she was an easy object for the master's sexual gratification. In the face of this, any desire of a pigmentocratic or aesthetic nature, seen from an ethnocentric point of view, disappears. What happened is that the erotic urge did not lead the slaveowner to seek out the black woman because she was black but because she was a woman; yet one should not assume that his excitement always freed him from racial prejudice, since often the sexual preference was the mulatto woman rather the darker-skinned female.

Such unions were mostly concubinage. Although marriage between white men and black women was known in Spain before the discovery of America, the most common relationship between the two was concubinage, both in Spain and in the New World. In Paraguay, known as the "paradise of Mahomet," every Spaniard had an average of 20 to 30 women (Recopilación VI, I, 6). Whoever gave that territory its nickname certainly did not visit Santo Domingo, since harems like the ones in Paraguay also abounded on the Dominican island. Francisco de Ceballos, the *regidor* of Puerto Plata, the mayor of his fortress and one of the most notorious smugglers of the north side of Hispaniola, had as his main consort a certain Fulana Manga, a good-looking black woman, and as stand-ins, various other slaves belonging to him, with whom he brought into this world a considerable number of mulatto children. His report mentions the activities of this area by Captain Juan de Garibai y Aguirre. The governor Pedro Menéndez de Avilés ordered him to live for a time in those parts to deal with the recovered items. Ceballos was married to one of the daughters of Judge Grajeda, an extremely powerful figure in the second half of the sixteenth century. He was also the father-in-law of one of Christopher Columbus' children. The writer of the report adds that Ceballos caused his wife to go mad on account of the whipping he gave her every day (Utrera 1950: 1), but I believe that her madness was the result of not knowing what to do in that harem of her husband.

The second time-honored myth hallowed by traditional historiography maintains that the black slave always considered his master to be superior, often preferring to remain a slave under the Spaniards than to be free along with the Haitians who, led by Toussaint and Dessalines, attempted to make the island "one and undivided."

This assertion is, undoubtedly, partly true. But in order to illustrate this fully, it is necessary to place it within the appropriate context of slavery relations and ideology. The deculturative process would require that the slave accept his inferiority — that is, that he was less gifted than his master because he was born with the permanent and indelible stigma of a biological degradation that was genetically transmissible on account of its presence in his chromosomes. He could not free himself from this because it was part of his human nature, as fatal and irreversible as death itself was fatal and irreversible.

This ideology, when combined with the political, social and legal structure of the colonies—a structure whose purpose was to uphold a slavery system based on exploitative labor, maintain public safety from crime, and retain power in the hands of a ruling class that was made up of peninsular and Creole whites—created a servile personality in many slaves, as David Brion Davis has demonstrated (1968: 216). This expressed itself, among other ways, in a longing for the master to be understood as something unconditional.

On the other hand, upon close examination it can be concluded that the *ethos* of every slavery society, and even more so the Spanish one, was dominated by an aristocratic ideal that instilled in all free men, even those belonging to the lower social class, not only the habit of giving orders, but also the desire to acquire riches without working. Thus the black was encouraged to adapt his behavior to the actions and expectations of the white man (Davis 1968: 217).

However, the attitude of servility was not the only one that predominated in the black slave. Marronage, which lasted for centuries in Santo Domingo, showed that a very strong tendency to rebel existed alongside this servile personality. Black uprisings were so frequent that they greatly disrupted life in Santo Domingo and resulted in a tempering of the treatment meted out to those under the yoke of slavery. Documents from the sixteenth century—the peak period for marronage—stated that the blacks rebelled so frequently that their masters, fearing that they would lose them, dared not punish them.

The claim that Dominican slaves preferred to live with their master than to take the freedom offered first by Toussaint and then by Boyer is contradicted by events themselves. During the period known as the Reconquest, conspiracies such as the mismamed "Italian revolt," were led by blacks and mulattos who sought to place the colony under the protection of Haiti. The 1796 slave rebellion of Boca Nigua was inspired by that of the blacks in the French colony of Saint-Domingue and aimed to exterminate all the whites. The dual and often contradictory psychological processes that made slaves oscillate between servility and rebellion can be clearly seen in the behavior of the ringleader of the thwarted uprising of Boca Nigua. After inciting other slaves to take up arms against the whites, Francisco Sopo betrayed the plot on the following day (Andreu Ocariz 1970). If the Dominican slaves were living so happily and contented in their chains, how could one possibly explain the attempt of the blacks of Monte Grande to rebel on the night of February 27, 1844, following the rumor that the *trinitarios* were planning to reinstate the slavery which had been abolished by Boyer in 1822?

If I have spent more time than is desirable exposing these two myths fabricated by traditional historiography, it is because their harmful consequences continue to live in the collective unconsciousness of ordinary Dominicans today. By accepting these myths, the analysis and description of the African heritage in Dominican culture would suffer from gross errors of theoretical and methodological interpretation. Slavery in Santo Domingo had, as is natural, its particularities, but in general, it operated exactly as in other American countries.

I also believe it is essential to alert everyone to the premises and conclusions of some interested parties who, fired by enthusiasm, venture to make statements lacking in scientific rigor and who speculate happily on the subject, getting—as one says in colloquial speech—"everything in a mess." It is clearly absurd that, in a "historical overview of the development of the introduction of black people into Santo Domingo and their evolution," the crowning of Miss Penny Commisiong as Miss Universe be included as part of this evolution.

If we are convinced that important, though sometimes negative patterns of African and neo-African behavior are present in the Dominican culture of today, then the task of discovering and studying them should be approached very seriously. We need to go beyond listing outmoded correspondences between tribes or ethnic groups and beyond the traits, complexes and material remains of African origin in Dominican *ethos*. For instance, it is unreasonable to state that the appearance of a musical instrument apparently of pygmy origin in Santo Domingo offers conclusive evidence of the existence of pygmy slaves on the island. This is simply to ignore a whole series of processes, such as diffusion or loan, which must be taken into account if one wishes to provide an accurate analysis of the subject. How could pygmy slaves reach Santo Domingo or other parts of the Americas when the slave traders very deliberately ensured that the blacks offered for sale matched the buyers'

demands for physical strength, age, height and other requirements? The so-called *"piezas de Indias"* [6] had to be one meter
eighty centimeters tall.

The expressions of African origin that are easily identifiable
in a culture such as that of Dominican Republic are often cited
as the only measures of the degree of Africanity or as palpable
evidence of it when, in fact, what is obviously African may ultimately reveal less about the retention of common patterns of
values, beliefs and other black behaviors than the more "altered
and difficult to identify cultural aspects" (Mintz 1977: 389-90).

Perhaps the greatest African influence in our culture can be
seen in music and dance. The African cultures are especially
musical. Rhythm is characteristic of black people and pervades
their whole life. Although Africa has a great variety of musical
instruments, the drum is undoubtedly the one which expresses
rhythm more precisely. The drum is an extension of hand clapping, and clapping is the most common musical accompani-
ment among black Africans. Alongside the drum, the human
voice is also extremely important. "Call-and-response" singing
is the most common technique of vocal groups and the musical
phrasing is generally short and repetitive.

In Africa, music and dance are essentially functional. The
concept of music as a purely aesthetic experience is alien on the
continent. Even when black people derive pleasure from music,
this is a result of the music, not its purpose. Africans worship
their deities to the sound of music—and also use it to spur on
their labors, promote their women's fertility, and so forth.
Furthermore, one basic characteristic of the African rhythm is
the use of two or three metrics, instead of using one. Using two
or more different ones in a single passage, for example, one
drummer would play in waltz time and another in marching

time. This rhythm is also produced by "contrasting beats repeated in irregular patterns" (Storm Roberts 1978: 12–19).

In an in-depth study of Dominican music and dance, Storm Roberts detected deep-rooted African survivals, although the European elements mean they can be classified as neo-African. The music of the *congos* of Villa Mella, for example, clearly conforms to the rhythmical and metrical features of African music and has a choral style that is most probably of Congo-Angolan origin. Nevertheless, the dance is specifically Spanish without identifiable Africanisms.

In the Antilles and other Afro-American territories, the best-known dance of the African slaves, as described by Pére Labat, was the *calenda*. Dances of African origin, all of which may have been derived from the *calenda*, according to Fradique Lizardo (1975), include the *sarandunga*, the *congos*, and the *jaiba*. But one particular characteristic of Dominican music and dance are the *palos* (long-drums) used to perform the *salve*. According to the well-known ethnomusicologist Martha Davis, this is the most typical of our traditional musical forms. It has two styles: one that is clearly Spanish and ametrical and antiphonal; the other is a polyrhythmical, a strong hybrid mix of the Spanish and the African (see Lizardo, introduction). Among the instruments of African origin are the *balsié*, the *gallumba*, the *marimba* or *marímbula*, and the *palos*, which comprise three drums.

The magico-religious beliefs that survive in the rural and popular sectors of Dominican society reflect the Christian-African syncretism dating from the colonial era. Dominican *vodú* is undoubtedly of Haitian origin, but its distinctive features have been very much adulterated. Many native divinities or *loas* have been incorporated into the Creole *vodú* pantheon, although the

110

main correspondences between the *loas* and Catholic saints are similar to the Haitian ones (Deive 1975).

Vodú is not the only Afro-Dominican religious expression. Although other religious expressions also have syncretic elements, they are the result of an extended process of selection, synthesis and reinterpretation of African elements. This process reveals a determined and eager reaffirmation of the original African values within a search for a suitable means of perpetuating the vernacular religious forms.

A religion is essentially characterized by the contact between the sacred and profane worlds. In religions like Christianity, this contact is especially arduous because man is obliged to elevate himself to the level of God. In Christianity, dialogue with the Supreme Deity calls for a specific corporal technique. The body should remain motionless and contracted as small as possible. The mystical ecstasy of the Catholic saints implies elevating the soul towards God and detaching the body from it since the body is corrupt matter and therefore mortal.

The Christian dialogue is the exact opposite of that found in the African and Afro-American religions, where corporal techniques reveal a dramatic expression, dionisiacal exuberance, and a physical joy that turns the body into the abode of the sacred (Heusch 1973: 255). In these cults, man does not elevates himself towards the deity or deities; they descend and possess him. The deities often become embodied in the faithful and stamp their personality on them.

Thus possession is central to Dominican popular religious expressions, as in the so-called *velaciones* or *velas de santos* (vigils), during which the whole atmosphere—music, singing, dancing, drink, etc.— induces the mystical trance, turning the ritual into a fiesta. One could also say that the fiesta ends in the mystical trance, the high point of the ritual on which everything converges.

Possession cannot be interpreted in medical terms, or more specifically, psychiatric ones, but sociological ones. Let this clarification satisfy those who, armed with their Eurocentric and Freudian theoretical baggage, see the individuals who are "mounted" as unfortunate hysterics requiring urgent therapeutic attention.

The ritual around death closely relates to popular religiosity. The funeral ceremonies that still exist in the rural areas as well as in cities, though to a lesser extent, *were derive* from the importance of the ancestor cult for Africans. The concept of a dual soul, the burial rites, expulsion and incorporation, and the taboos and magical beliefs that accompany them closely resemble those found among many ethnic groups in West Africa, a region from which the largest number of slaves were taken to the Indies. Clearly, all of these prescriptions display a high degree of Christian-pagan syncretism and transculturation. The period of exclusion from the moment of death up until the act of incorporation lasts for nine days—a period during which the deceased is still present among the living and visits and pesters them before joining the world beyond the grave forever. This has a magico-archaic significance in which the number nine features prominently. Its significance seems to allude to some sort of vital prime number. By way of illustration, one need only recall the Greek myth of the flood and the nine days Duecalion remained in his ark. In many of the vigils, the spirit of the deceased possesses one or more of those present.

One of the funerary rites is the *baquiní,* which has a combined religious-festive nature and is performed when a very young child dies. During the *baquiní,* songs are intoned; there is dancing, gambling, and storytelling and riddles are improvised. Bastide explains the origin of the *baquiní* or wake for a dead child, noting that, owing to the high rate of infant mortality caused by social contact in the Americas, the European clergy invented the belief that dead children would become angels and thus their departure from this world should be a joyful occasion rather than a sorrowful one. Despite his rather authoritative tone, the well-known French sociologist and ethnologist is mistaken in his assessment of the ideology behind the *baquiní*, since the ritual is also found in Europe, and especially in Spain, where it has the same significance and function, also exhibiting the same type of celebratory behavior. The same could be said of American countries such as Argentina and Chile where the incidence of African cultural patterns is almost nonexistent.

Even if it is, as I believe, a case of parallelism, it seems obvious that the use of the word *baquiní* in Jamaica, Puerto Rico and Santo Domingo reveals that this ritual was more common among the population of African origin than the white. In terms of the word itself, Martha Beckwith locates its origin in the English *back in it* – in Jamaica *back in it* – referring to a desire expressed by the black people during the nine nights of the ceremony, that the deceased should go back into their grave (1929: 74–8). However, one should consider the more likely possibility of the reduplicated verbal form *kini kini*, " I greet/greeting," that is typical of the languages of several peoples in eastern Dahomey and southwestern Nigeria, from which is derived the ritual word *bakinikini* "greeting the *orishas* (Yoruba deities) with respect." Another possibility points to the Bantu word *bakini* "dancers" (Cassidy and Le Page 1967: 16). Another word that has a certain phonetic and semantic similarity to *baquiní* is *banco*, used in the Código Carolino of Amparán to denote the dances held by the blacks to praise the dead, along with other rituals and in their own languages (Malagón 1974: 164).

While religious syncretism occurs in three different spheres—ecological, ritual and that of collective performance (Bastide 1960: 380)—magic obeys a specific structural law: accumulation. In Santo Domingo, the beliefs, formulas and rituals for practicing magic originate both in Africa and Europe and are legacies of the colonial era. The whites imported many of their magical practices which the enslaved Africans considered to be superior because their own practices could not free them from their chains. This does not mean that the black disowned his magic; he used it against his master and added the master's magic for greater efficacy. Incantatory formulas, Catholic prayers for curing diseases or neutralizing sorcery, were adopted by the slaves, but the whites were always in awe of the magical powers of the slave, who was able to prepare deadly philters and poisons to get rid of his oppressor. For example, in the French colony of Saint-Domingue, the authorities were continually perturbed by the ongoing deaths from poisoning caused by the slaves and were unable to discover what type of substances they used for their potions and philters (Cabón 1933: 251–2).

The ambivalence of both blacks and whites towards their respective forms of magic and the existence of magical and superstitious behavior and beliefs that are common to both, such as the evil eye, as well as the fact that syncretism in magic does not only consist of incorporating elements borrowed as a result of simple contact between the two cultures, but, very often, an entity produced displays an intensification of either one of the two types of behavior. All of this prevents me from stating, with my current understanding, which of the two types of magic in Santo Domingo—the African or the European—is more syncretic. However, Dominicans frequently turn to African deities —*luas* and *orishas*—to seek solutions to personal problems or cause some harm to their enemies.

The aspect of family organization has been practically unexplored in the study of the African heritage in Santo Domingo. This undoubtedly calls for urgent and extensive fieldwork, employing a perspective that would make it possible to examine and unpick the actual historical and contemporary significance, as well as structure and economic content of the family organization in Santo Domingo.

A brief glance at family structures and Dominican kinship systems reveals the coexistence of the stable nuclear family, monogamous and legally sanctioned, and a devalued model characterized by successive or simultaneous polygynous unions with a network of consanguineous relationships that are based around matrifocality. These unmarried, promiscuous and unstable unions produced large numbers of illegitimate children, making the extended family within the domestic realm particularly important. Nevertheless, matrifocality ensured that women—the mother or the grandmother, who is almost always the one who takes care of the children—dominate in the home. This had a significant impact on aspects of social behavior. Polygyny and matrifocality were notable patterns of Dominican rural family organization, but serial polyandry was also be found alongside these practices. However, in these cases the man played a fairly marginal role in running the household.

Several theories have attempted to explain these two forms assumed by the Afro-American family, especially the latter. Perhaps the most widespread theory suggests the retention of an African pattern that originates from slavery times and can still be found in societies that do not recognize both forms of polygamy. This theory tends to emphasize the destructive effects of the plantation on the African family and the sexual imbalance among the slaves that gave rise to a tense climate of sexual repression and obsession. In many cases, the tense climate was sublimated by storytelling, dances and such, yet at times it gave rise to pathological deviance that led to crimes such as those committed by the famous "Black Glutton," for example, who is mentioned by Casimiro de Moya and studied by Bernaldo de Quirós. Another consequence was the absence of permanent unions and the concubinage of white masters and their black slaves. Moreno Fraginals attributes the plantation slaves' lack of economic, personal and family responsibility to the fact that all their activity was regulated by the means of production typical of the sugar mill. He says: "In societies originating organically, especially in the feudal and precapitalist periods, there is a concrete relationship between production and family institutionalization" (1977: 23). This is another Marxist proposition, one that maintains that family and kinship structures can ultimately be explained in terms of the means of production that typify a society. Although this may be applied to those communities where the social relationships of slavery still prevail, the proposition needs to be reconsidered since it is clearly not universally applicable. In a study of two tribal societies in Madagascar, the well-known ethnologist Maurice Blosch has conclusively demonstrated that although the superstructure in the case of the Merina ethnic group conditions the kinship system, for the Zafimaniry that system forms part of the infrastructure (1977: 241–68).

For detailed studies, the field of mutual aid institutions, with likely features of African origin, may be of fruitful interest. One of those institutions that was very common in Santo Domingo is the system of revolving loans known as *san*. A term also used in Venezuela, *San* consists of setting up a common account or fund, made up of the weekly, fortnightly or monthly contributions of several people who are generally known to each other or related by marriage. The person who sets up the *san* is in charge of collecting the contributions—which are the same as the number of members—and has the privilege of being the first to receive the total sum of money collected.

The *san* has its exact counterpart and specific origin in the system of rotating credit called *esusu* by the Yorubas. Nigerian *esusu* and *san* have almost identical features. For one thing, it is a system that operates without written accounts and relies on the mutual trust of its participants. And secondly, both *san* and *esusu* are organized by and made up of women who, as a general rule, have a low level of income. In addition to encouraging saving, this system primarily aims to provide the person who initiates it with an immediate cash sum from all the contributions collected so as to be able to meet an urgent and unavoidable need. In their study of the markets and merchants of El Cibao, Norvell and Billingsley have shown that, out of the various resources used by the vendors for obtaining funds to finance their operations, twenty percent used *san* (1971: 395). *San* is known as *susu* in Trinidad and in Guyana as *boxy money* (Herskovits 1947: 77, 292). The same system also exists in Jamaica (Katzin 1959) and Curaçao (Marks 1976).

Another very common mutual aid institution in Afro-America, and thus in Santo Domingo, is the *convite* or *junta*, a group of peasant farmers who meet occasionally or periodically to perform various agricultural tasks such as sowing, harvesting, felling trees, etc. This system of loaned labor is almost always voluntary, but the owner of a farm who asks for the help of relatives or friends is obliged to repay the loan by participating in another *junta*. This reciprocity is known in Dominican rural popular speech as *tornapión*.

The *convite* or *junta* is not exclusive to Afro-America. Although similar agricultural cooperatives exist on other continents, it seems beyond all doubt that the commensal features and style of working reflect those of other mutual aid associations found in various regions of West Africa. The typical model most commonly used to relate the *convite* to Africa is the *dokpwe* of the Fon of Dahomey, described in some detail by Herskovits (1938: I, 63). The Haitian *convite* appears to be most similar to *dokpwe*.

The most common African features, which also appear in the *gayap* of Trinidad, the *coup de main* of Martinique (Benoist 1972: 142), the Venezuelan *cayapa*, the Ecuatorian *minga* (Whitten 1965: 69–72) and the *cuadros* of the *palenque* of San Basilio near Cartagena (Escalante 1954: 595–602), reveal a style of working characterized by the beat of drums and call-and-response singing by the farmers. This serves to coordinate and spur on the work while food and drink are consumed in order to regain strength. At the end of the day there is usually a fiesta or communal feast, paid for by the person who has called the *convite*.

Another example of this kind of mutual aid is the so-called Galician *malla* or threshing of rye and other cereals. The request for help made to neighbors by the owner of the sown field is called *roga* (request). Each group of pounders vies with the other by beating the sheaves of grain more vigorously. In order to increase the noise, some areas of the threshing floor are hollowed with old pots and pans. The *malla* also offers tests of strength between males and females and encouragement in the form of resonant and sustained *aturuxos*, or guttural cries of jubilation. The obligation to return the loaned labor is called *tornaxeira*. Widows and invalids are exempt from reciprocating. Note the similarity between the terms *tornaxeira* and *tornapión*.

The importance given by Dominican peasant farmers of African origin to funeral rites is evidenced by the mutual aid societies that aim to guarantee a good burial for their members. The requirement that the funeral ceremony, which has already been described in this essay, be performed without omitting any ritual that could impede the deceased's incorporation into the next life, calls for substantial expenditure that an individual or family is often unable to meet. Hence the existence of associations like the Hermandad del Congo, from Villa Mella, which are dedicated to this purpose.

In anthropology, culinary habits have been studied in terms of ecology, techniques for the preparation and preservation of certain products, the behavioral patterns of family life, the taboos of a religious, or in the case of illiterate communities, totemic nature and the transculturation processes resulting from the contact between two or more cultures.

In the case of Santo Domingo, the culinary transculturation reveals a triple origin: Spanish European, indigenous and African. Other studies show that the Dominicans diet still has food products and habits of indigenous origin which the African slaves were instrumental in passing on. Of course, the Spanish cuisine appears to be easily identifiable, yet the same cannot be said of the African cuisine.

Identifying vegetable products, condiments and oils of African origin presents fewer problems. One of the plants brought by the enslaved Africans is the edible fruit called *guineo*—an abbreviation of *plátano guineo*—which are different varieties of the Musa banana family. The use of the word *plátano* (plantain) which appeared in the chronicles of Mártir de Anglería, Fernández de Oviedo and Father Acosta continued throughout the sixteenth century. The latter mentions the small, delicate, white *plátano dominicano*, which he says is called thus in Hispaniola (1940: 283). The *plátano dominicano*, also called the *Congo plátano*, was introduced to the island in 1516 by Brother Tomás de Berlanga of the order of Dominican monks, as Father Cobo explains (1891: II, 447–8). Other plants of African origin are the watermelon, the *guandul*—which is related to the Kikongo word *wandu* 'type of pea'—and *ñame* (yam) whose name derives from the same onomatopaeic forms present in various languages of the Niger-Congo family that repeat with slight variations the idea of 'eating' or 'food', such as *ñamñam* in Wolof, *ñango* in Fula, *ñama* or *iñame* in Bantu languages (Alvarez Nazario 1974: 242). Fernández de Oviedo describes African palm oil and its production process. Among the fauna, one can also mention the guinea fowl.

When speaking of cuisine of black origin, it is important to draw a distinction between that derived from a purely African cultural legacy, and that which developed out of the plantation system. In the colonial era, the role of cook and the art of preparing dishes were reserved for black women in domestic service. Recipes and those special touches which make a meal tasty have been irretrievably lost because they were part of an oral tradition; perhaps the cooks, mistresses of imponderable culinary secrets, refused to reveal them to their mistresses. The dominance of black women in colonial cookery may be a very plausible explanation for the custom, very common in Santo Domingo and which seems to be reserved for women, of preparing certain foods and selling them by going through the streets or from portable stalls.

The food habits of the slaves in the sugarmills continue to prevail in Dominican cuisine. *Casabe, tasajo* (jerked beef) and *plátano* formed the basis of the diet of the enslaved black. The *tostón*, a fritter made from pressed green plantain, a phonetic variant of *tontos bananas*, typical of the dialect of the French Antilles, may be related to the negroid word from Surinam *tom-tom* or the Jamaican *tum tum*, both etymologically related to the Tshi root *tum tum*, which imitates the sound of the mortar in the preparation of the dish called *fufu* (Alvarez Nazario 1974: 277). The slaves added a large amount of carbohydrates from sugar cane to this diet, including the *guarapo* extracted from the cane juice, the brown sugar scrapings that stuck to the sugar pans, molasses, sugar stolen in the sugarmill storerooms, as well as chewing the cane while cutting it; all of these culinary practices have survived and made Dominicans such lovers of sweet things. Another product derived from plantation life is the breadfruit, which was introduced from Tahiti to Jamaica and then to others in the Caribbean following the great famines of the eighteenth century (Villapol 1977: 328).

Other African cultural legacies include particular cooking methods such as boiling, roasting over an open fire or steam cooking. In Santo Domingo, the latter is done with banana leaves that are used to wrap, for example, the so-called "pasteles en hoja" prepared with plantain, meat and other ingredients. In Santo Domingo, the well-known sauce called the *sofrito* or *escabeche*, which is generally made from onions, pepper, garlic and tomato, is also used as a condiment. *Sofrito* is very similar to the *ata* sauce of Yoruba cuisine. Using annatto to color the *sofrito* yellow may originate from the attempt to reproduce the color of African palm oil.

Dominican cuisine which is usually prepared by soaking dried grains and then grinding them uncooked and frying them with garlic, hot peppers, etc. to make fritters or buns is common in different African countries. In Azua, corn is softened in bleach, washed, pounded in the mortar and then made into a kind of pancake or bun known as *chacá*. Among the Yoruba, these fritters or fried cakes are called *akara*. Grains are pounded or ground with a pestle in a mortar, an essential piece of equipment in Dominican homes. In the rural areas, the mortar is of considerable size and, as in different parts of Africa, it is used outside the house. In the Dominican Republic and elsewhere, women usually handle the mortar.

The *mofongo* is a Creole dish made with fried and pounded green plantain to which pieces of pork crackling is added. The root of the word may originate in the Cape Verde dialect, where the word *cufongo* means "ball of corn." If Moreau de Saint-Méry were alive today he would not have to lament, as he did in the eighteenth century, that the women of Santo Domingo do not know how to make a stew called *calalú*, which, he says, can provide a wonderful excuse for fiestas or pleasures "that a happy secrecy covers with its shadow to make them even more agreeable" (1976: 87). Although a Creole of the time did not need that stew in order to enjoy such pleasures, *calalú*—known elsewhere in the Caribbean as *Quingombó* or *gombó*—is a dish that was introduced into Dominican cuisine by the *cocolos*, the black workers from the British Lesser Antilles. It is made with *yautía* leaves,[7] okra, meat and fish. The Dominicans also owe another very tasty dish to the cocolos: *fungi*, made with cornflour, salt, okra, and stewed fish. In Puerto Rico it is called by the variant name of *funche*, but both forms derive from the Bantu root *nfundi* or *nfungi* "bread made from cornflour" (Alvarez Nazario 1974: 273).

In addition, there is an urgent need for an in-depth study of

Afro-Negroid influences on the Spanish of Santo Domingo. Today, these influences are hardly appreciated by our linguists. The true African influence on the Spanish of Santo Domingo is not found in the vocabulary—in which it is indeed limited—but in the phonetic, morphological and syntactic structure of our dialect. The scanty evidence of African morphemes in the Dominican vocabulary can be explained by the fact that slaves of the same ethnic group were usually scattered throughout the various sugarmills and other units of production on the island. Since the slave was unable to communicate with other individuals of the same ethnicity in his or her vernacular tongue, the black person was obliged to learn the language of his masters. This eventually became the lingua franca of all the slaves, in addition to which Spanish was the only possible means of communicating with the white masters.

In our culture, the Spanish language underwent changes that occurred for various reasons. Above all, the African linguistic fund typical of the regions of the slave trade, and in particular the Guinea-Sudanese and Bantu, has phonetic and morphosyntactical features which, when they came into contact with Portuguese, were greatly altered. These changes were in turn relexified when the enslaved blacks went to Spain. First, the Afro-Spanish of the *ladino* slaves or those who were bought in the Lisbon markets reached Santo Domingo. This Hispano-Negroid substratum was then restructured with the arrival of the *bozal* slaves, who were brought to the Dominican Republic directly from Africa without passing through Spain. This symbiosis resulted in a typical form, both phonetic and morphosyntactical, of Dominican speech which was preserved and remains practically unchanged.

A quick glance at the Dominican linguistic system is enough

to detect, among other characteristics, variations in the use of vowels—replacing one sound with another, the absence of diphthongs, apenthesis, etc. For example, *melecina* for *medicina*, *siñor* for *señor*.... The use of consonants also presents features such as an inability to distinguish between the sounds of the letters 'b' and 'v' and substituting 'r' for 'l' in the initial or intervocal position when grouped together: *comel* (*comer*), *marvado* (*malvado*), *mejol* (*mejor*), *puelco* (*puerco*). The lack of inflection to denote number or gender in the agreement between noun and adjective is also noticeable, as in *lo hombres* for *los hombres*, *longanizas frita* (s). The 's' at the end of a syllable – such as *papele* (s) – is suppressed, exemplifying a phonetic trait that, in its turn, gives rise cases of aphaeresis, such as *etá* for *está*, *uté* for *usted*, *guta* for *gusta*. The nasal occlusion of the initial *ñ* features in words of African origin such as *ñame*, *ñaco*, *ñeñe*. The suppression of sounds, especially in the weak pretonic or posttonic syllables, is also a singular feature of the Spanish of Santo Domingo. A typical case of aphaeresis is that of *ño* for *señor* and *siñá* for *señora*.

In terms of vocabulary, I will only mention some more commonly-used words such as *bemba*, 'thick lip', of Bantu origin *ibebo* or lips, in the Bubi of Fernando Po, *ebebo*, with the same meaning in the Bakosi of former Spanish Guinea; *monga* 'flu', perhaps an abbreviation of the Kikongo dialect *ekemongo*, 'a disease that makes breathing difficult'; *cogioca* 'eagerness to obtain gains by illegal or doubtful means, embezzlement or secret deal' and which, according to Ortiz, derives from the verb '*coger*' (to get) and the Congo frequentative suffix *ojioka*, which expresses the idea of 'persistent repetition' (1924: 124); *ñangotearse*, 'to squat down', *niongota* in Kikongo conveys an idea similar to 'crawl'; *abombarse*, 'water and other liquids start to decompose', from the Kikongo verb *bomba* 'to rot, decay'; *fucú* 'bad luck', 'unlucky', a variant of *fufú*, 'sorcery, witchcraft', and which in the Ewe language of Dahomey and Carabalí[8] from southern Nigeria, means 'dust'; *taita* 'father' and its variant *tata*, the latter a word that appears with the same meaning in many languages of the Guinea-Sudanese and Bantu groups; *bachata* 'fun, revelry', 'spree', 'noisy fun'; *titingó* 'disturbance', 'uproar', which can be related to the Mandinga word *tungtungo* 'repetition', to refer to the noisy sound of the drum; *fuácata*, used in the phrase *'estar en la fuácata'*, 'to be broke or poor' or denoting the idea of 'to hit' or 'beat'. Curiously, the meaning of this word, which stems from the Kikongo verb *fwakata* 'to stuff one's face', reveals in its principal Antillean usage a contrary semantic development which is negative or ironic in relation to the original sense; *manigua* 'forest', 'jungle', whch many people believe is an indigenous word, is composed of the prefix *ma* and the Bantu root *gua*, 'prickle', 'thorn' or 'spike' (Alvarez Nazario 1974).

The word *mambí* has been the subject of varied linguistic investigations. Mambi is well-known and widely-used in Cuba because in the last century it denoted all of those who rose up against Spanish colonial power in Cuba. However, its origin is in Santo Domingo where it was initially applied to the runaway blacks who disappeared into the mountains. But before it passed to Cuba with the aforementioned meaning, the word reappeared in the Dominican Republic during the Restoration War (1863–65). *Mambí* was the Creole who fought against the troops that were loyal to Spain. A well-known verse referring to Antonio Guzman, who after remaining loyal to the *peninsulares* closed ranks on the side of the Dominican guerrillas, goes:

Antonio Guzmán,
no me gusta a mí,
primero cacharro
y después mambí.

Antonio Guzmán
I don't like him
First a cacharro
And then a mambí.

Cacharro was the nickname that the Dominicans gave to the Spanish soldiers because of the excessive kitchen baggage that they carried in their backpacks (Rodríguez Demorizi 1973: 86).

Rodríguez Demorizi notes that the word *mambí* may perhaps come from the Dominican officer Juan Mambí, who was assumed to be one of the main ringleaders of the revolutionary plot of the people of color—blacks and mulattos—organized for the night of 15 to 16 August, 1812. But the actual meaning of the word remains unresolved although it actually stems from the African root *mbi, ambi*, which in several languages of the Congo expresses the idea of 'bad', 'cruel', injurious', 'abominable' (Ortiz 1951: 77–8). This assumption is endorsed by the fact that the Congo slaves called their maroon comrades *mambís*, "in this way transferring their hatred of their masters towards them and the offensive words they called them" (Ortiz 1946). Evidently, the word *mambí* retained its original African meaning when used to refer to the Dominican and Cuban *guerrilleros* in their struggle against Spanish colonialism.

I hope that the various aspects presented thus far will be sufficient to prove that the black African inheritance in Dominican culture of today is relevant and cannot be regarded as a marginal or mimetic contribution. On the other hand, it will have been evident that I have limited myself to discussing the heritage of purely African origin and that which originates in the plantation culture, without touching on all the influences from the different migrations of people of color—*cocolos*, North American freed slaves, Haitians—whose descendants eventually integrated into the national ethnicity. One of the most interesting magico-religious complexes, which appears to be wrapped up in a whole intricate set of social relationships, is *gaga*, a product of Dominican-Haitian transculturation; June Rosenberg studied it in her most recent contribution to Afro-Dominican anthropology.

In conclusion, the study of the black values should not be viewed as a response to those who attempt to deny the importance of these values, nor as a nostalgic evocation of a past that has partly been superseded. In fact, the study should be carried out objectively and dispassionately. In my opinion, the bourgeois intellectual who adopts an anti-black stance is as reactionary and racist as the intellectual who, carried away by a retaliatory spirit, adopts an anti-white position.

Furthermore, the African heritage cannot be regarded as a mere addition of cultural patterns, which when placed alongside the Spanish and indigenous ones, make up a kind of mosaic Dominican culture. The African, the Spanish and the indigenous—the most significant trilogy of Dominican culture—have been hybridized by virtue of a long, contradictory and complex process which began when the three ethnicities converged on the island. Neither the indigenous culture, nor the Spanish, nor the African survived intact in Santo Domingo, as this was prevented by endogenous and exogenous factors. If the black and the indigenous people became partly Hispanicized, then Spaniard also ended up becoming Africanized and indigenized. The Dominican culture of today is the original and unique end result—and whether acceptable or not, this very culture conditions our behavior and our vision of the world.

References

Acosta, J. de, *Historia natural y moral de las Indias*, ed. Edmundo O'Gorman, Mexico, 1940.

Alvarez Nazario, M., *El elemento afronegroide en el español de Puerto Rico*, San Juan: Instituto de Cultura Puertorriqueña, 1974.

Andreu Ocariz, J., "La rebelión de los esclavos de Boca Nigua," *Anuario de Estudios Americanos*, XXI, Seville, 1970.

Bastide, Roger, *Les religions africaines au Brésil*, Paris: Presses Universitaires de France, 1960.

_____, *Las Américas negras*, Madrid: Alianza Editorial, 1967.

Beckwith, Martha, *Black Roadways: A Study of Jamaican Folk Lore*, Chapel Hill, NC: University of North Carolina Press, 1939.

Benoist, J., ed., *L'archipel inachevé*, Montreal: University of Montreal, 1972.

Bloch, Maurice, "La propiedad y el final de la alianza," *Análisis marxistas y antropología social*, Madrid: Anagrama, 1977.

Cabon, P. A., *Notes sur l'histoire religieuse d'Haiti*, Port-au-Prince, 1933.

Caro Baroja, J., *Las formas complejas de la vida religiosa. Religion, sociedad y character en la España de los siglos XVI y XVII*, Madrid: Akal Editor, 1978.

Cartaxo Rolim, F., "Religões africanas no Brasil e Catolicismo, um questionamento," *Africa. Revista do Centro de Estudos Africanos da Universidade de São Paulo*, 1, 1978.

Cassidy, F. G. and R. B. Le Page, *Dictionary of Jamaican English*, Cambridge, 1967.

Cobo, Bernabé, *Historia del Nuevo Mundo*, ed. Marcos Jiménez de la Espada, Seville, 1890–93, 4 vols.

Deive, Carlos E., *Vodú y Magia en Santo Domingo*, Santo Domingo: Museo del Hombre Dominicano, 1975.

Elkins, Stanley M., "Slavery in Capitalist and Non-Capitalist societies," in

Laura Forner and Eugene Genovese, *Slavery in the New World*, Englewood Cliffs, NJ: Prentice Hall Inc., 1969.

Encinas, Diego de, *Cedulario Indiano*, Madrid: Ed. de Cultura Hispánica, 1946, 4 vols.

Escalante, Aquiles, "Notas sobre el palenque de San Basilio, una comunidad negra en Colombia," *Divulgaciones etnológicas*, III: 5, Barranquilla: Universidad del Atlántico, 1954.

Freyre, Gilberto, *Casa Grande e Senzala*, Rio de Janeiro: Jose Olimpio Editor, 1952.

Harris, Marvin, *Raza y trabajo en América*, Buenos Aires: Siglo Veinte, 1973.

Herskovits, M. J., *Dahomey*, New York: J. J. Agustin, 1938, 2 vols.

_____, *The Trinidad Village*, New York: Knopf, 1947.

Huesch, Luc de, *Estructura y praxis. Ensayos de antropología teórica*, Mexico: Siglo XXI, 1973.

Ianni, Octavio, "Organización social y alienación," in *Africa en América Latina*, ed. M. Moreno Fraginals, Mexico: Siglo XXI/UNESCO, 1977.

Katzin, M., "The Jamaica Country Higgler," *Social and Economic Studies*, 8, Kingston: University of Jamaica (Mona), 1959.

Lizardo, F., *Danzas y bailes folklóricos dominicanos*, Santo Domingo: Fundación García-Arévalo-Museo del Hombre Dominicana, 1975.

Malagón, A., *Código Negro Carolino (1784)*, Santo Domingo: Ed. Taller, 1974.

Marks, A., "Male and Female and the Afro-Curaçaoan Household," Royal Institute of Anthropology, no. 77, Leiden, 1976.

Mintz, Sidney, "Africa en América Latina," in *Africa en América Latina*, ed. M. Moreno Fraginals, Mexico: Siglo XXI/UNESCO, 1977.

Moreau de Saint-Méry, M. L., *Descripción de la parte española de Santo Domingo,* Santo Domingo: Editora de Santo Domingo, Sociedad Dominicana de Bibliófilos, 1976.

Moreno Fraginals, M., "Aportes culturales y deculturación," in *Africa en América Latina*, ed. M. Moreno Fraginals, Mexico: Siglo XXI/UNESCO, 1977.

Mörner, Magnus, *La mezcla de razas en la historia de América Latina*, Buenos Aires: Ed. Paidos, 1969.

Nolasco, Flérida de, *Vibraciones en el tiempo*, Santo Domingo: Editora del Caribe, 1974.

Norvell, D. and R. V. Billingsley, "Traditional Markets and Marketers in the Cibao Valley of the Dominican Republic," in *Peoples and Cultures of the Caribbean*, ed. Michael M. Horowitz, Garden City, NY: The American Museum of Natural History, 1971.

Ortiz, Fernando, *Glosario de afronegrismos*, Havana, 1924.

_____, "Algunos afronegrismos en la toponomia Africana," *Afroamérica* (Mexico), 2, 1946.

_____, *Los bailes y el teatro de los negros en el folklore de Cuba*, Havana, 1951.

Rodríguez Demorizi, E., *Invasiones haitianas de 1801, 1805 y 1822*, Santo Domingo: Editora del Caribe, 1955.

_____, *Poesía popular dominicana*, Santiago: Universidad Católica Madre y Maestra, 1973.

_____, *Milicias de Santo Domingo*, Santo Domingo: Ed. del Caribe, 1978.

Storm Roberts, J., *La música negra afro-americana*, Buenos Aires: Ed. Víctor Lerú, 1978.

Szaszdi, Adam, "Apuntes sobre la esclavitud en San Juan de Puerto Rico, 1800–1811," *Anuario de Estudios Americanos* (Seville), XXIV, 1967.

Tannenbaum, F., *El negro en las Américas: Esclavo y cuidadano*, Buenos Aires: Ed. Paidos, 1968.

Utrera, Fray Cipriano de, *Historia Militar de Santo Domingo*, Santo Domingo: Tipografía Franciscana, 1950, 3 vols.

Van den Berghe, Pierre L., *Problemas raciales*, Mexico: Fondo de Cultura Económica, Coleccíon Breviarios, 1971.

Villapol, Nitza, "Hábitos alimeticios africanos en América Latina," in *Africa en América Latina*, ed. M. Moreno Fraginals, Mexico: Siglo XXI/UNESCO, 1977.

Wolf, E. and S. Mintz, "Haciendas y plantaciones en Mesoamérica y las Antillas," in *Haciendas, latifundios y plantaciones en América Latina*, Mexico: Siglo XXI, 1975.

CHAPTER FIVE

The *Hato* and the *Conuco*:
The Emergence
of Creole Culture

RUBÉN SILIÉ

The *hato* is known as a piece of property that comprises the
land corresponding to shares granted, called *derechos de tierra*
(land rights), on which an owner was entitled to raise as many
animals as he chose and to take possession of the wild or stray
animals (Ots Capdequi, 95).

The following royal provision establishes the framework for
setting up the *hato*s: "that the pastures, woodland and waters
and areas may be commonly held and in Santo Domingo it is
understood that, within a boundary of ten leagues surrounding
the city...that the pastures, woodlands and boundaries be commonly held." This was a general tenet obtained in Spain as well
as in Santo Domingo. It continues: "In terms of Santo Domingo this is understood to be areas of ten leagues which we
allow and deem fitting, that a *hato* with cattle have an area of a
league in circumference, so that within it no other may make a

131

corral for cattle, nor a house, it is decreed that the pasture of all this may likewise be common; and where there may have been *hatos*, sites may be provided for sugarmills and other farms and each site may put up a stone house and it may have no fewer than two thousand head of livestock, and if it had over six thousand, three sites, and observe where there may be title or our favour that decrees another thing" (Ots Capdequi, 22).

The *hatos* were large expanses of land without fixed fences or boundaries to impede the movement of the animals. This was possible because the cattle-raising economy did not clash with the other economies—that of the plantation or major export crops. During this period, there was an "unlimited supply of lands" and their value was not very important: "...a cattle *hato* or an *estancia* (ranch) with cattle, horses and mules or sheep, goats and pigs, is represented by a piece of land and a number of head of livestock; but what has economic value is not the land but the livestock" (Ots Capdegui).

The *Hatero* and His Environment

"Those extremely sober men, known by the name of "hateros" live on dairy products alone. They eat meat which they like very much and are able to buy at extremely low prices, but nothing can make them abandon their frugal and avaricious principles. It is undoubtedly in the Spanish *hatero* that we find the most perfect example of the rich man sheltering from the elements, just as we have described, in dreadful hovels open to all weathers, the best of which do not require much labor. On the other hand, he has the advantage of not needing to spend much on clothing as the hot climate of Santo Domingo allows him to disregard the seasons" (Arch. Nat. Section Outre Mer. D.E.F. Carton 5 folio 918: "Prècis de voyage faut du Cap à

Santo Domingo pendant le mois de Brumaire, en 7, par Mr. Vincent. 1789").

Various French travelers of the eighteenth century, who visited the eastern part of the island for different reasons, wonderfully described the lives of the hateros. Overall, the opinion was that the hateros were very rough men, dedicated to an inactive life and reconciled to the designs of nature.

Although the *hateros* of the eighteenth century were unlike those who lived in the previous century ("the Century of poverty"), the quality of life was still at a low in material terms. It could not be compared to the splendor of the French landowners, who lived in great luxury. One could also compare the public buildings and works of infrastructure such as irrigation channels. The same can be said of eating habits; whereas in Santo Domingo the diet was very basic, the French consumed products that were extremely exotic for the colony.

The wealth of the *hatero* was calculated by the number of corralled animals they owned, as these animals were the only ones that were quantifiable and could be sold at a given moment. Thus the acquisition of animals (like that of slaves) was necessary for moving up the social ladder. Also, as will be illustrated later, taxes were collected from the *hatero* on the basis of the number of animals. Every year, the authorities required landowners to present an account of their possessions, indicating the number of full-grown as well as the young animals. From this total animals for the exchequer and the ecclesiastical tithe were deducted as well as those animals which could be sold to the French, those that the owner could consume, and finally, those to be used to replenish the herd. These were known as *multiplicos*.

The *corrales* of the eighteenth century bear no relationship to the stock farms of today. They consisted of several leagues over which the herds roamed freely, disappearing into the woods without the constant vigilance of cowboys. Under such conditions, although one may speak of *multiplicos* or livestock breeding, the breeding itself depended more on the animals and the weather rather than on the landowners. The owner only supervised the movements of the herd in order to gain the benefit of the offsprings provided by nature.

Work on the *Hatos*

The owners themselves did not always carry out work on the hatos. In most cases, "a mulatto or black generally held the position of *mayoral* (overseer). There were two or three other assistants who rode on horseback from daybreak, going round all the places where the herd was in order to treat the new-born calves and the animals wounded in fights or accidentally. On these farms they were also concerned about attacks by wild animals" (Del Monte y Tejada, Antonio, "Historia de Santo Domingo," citada por Oscar Gil Dias en "Apuntes para la Historia," 167).

There were only *mayorales* in the *hatos* of large-scale *hateros*; however, the majority of the hateros were so poor that they simply could not put *mayorales* in charge of their properties. Hence many owners also took on this role.

Since most of the animals were scattered in the forests, periodic round-ups were organized to catch them. These round-ups were usually carried out in the spring with the assistance of other neighboring farmers. Once the animals were rounded up, they were enclosed in corrals for different purposes: consumption, sale or breeding.

Such rudimentary methods revealed the low level of productivity of the *hato*, since it depended on the annual rise or fall in the number of animals. This, in turn, was subject to the vagaries of nature and the animals' ability to withstand the climate and remain alive until the roundup time.

Thus cattle-raising in the eighteenth century cannot be envisaged as a venture that had been set up from the start by the colonists to operate as they chose, but rather it involved the use of resources offered by nature without human intervention. As Gilberti rightly points out, referring to the Argentine cattle ranch, it was: "similar to someone cutting down a forest or plucking fruit from a wild tree." As a result, it had great advantage over any other activity that required technical skill and a greater investment of time. Thus the most important thing for a *hatero* was to own a piece of land where he could "make a place for a corraled herd" and on which the *casa de campo* (as the houses found on the farms were called) was generally located. In this way, the occupation of the land was effectively restricted to the area around the house along with the corrals of the "*corralera* or tame" animals.

As described by Sánchez Valverde, the main work of the *hateros* involved the following:

> Working with the *corralera* animals was no easier than with the *montarreses* or wild ones. The shepherds of Hispaniola who are responsible for breeding animals have to rise very early each day and go out barefoot, stepping in the dew or mud, to look for the horse that they must ride on their expeditions. As the horse has to fend for itself it tends to be very far away or hidden among the bushes and woods so that it is very dif-

ficult to find. The shepherd leads it to the house and
once he has saddled the horse he breakfasts on a
baked plantain if he has it and a cup of ginger or coffee. This is all he eats until the time he returns. Having
breakfasted thus, he mounts the horse and goes,
enduring the heat of the sun and the discomfort of the
rain, through mountains, woods and savannah, sometimes galloping, sometimes running, to identify the
animals scattered over many leagues, rounding them
up where possible and leading back to the corrals
those which he sees are worm-eaten or have some
other disease needing treatment." (Sánchez Valverde,
185)

The work of the hunters was also as hard as that of the others:

The hunter generally goes out barefooted and on
foot with a spear and his dogs. If he goes on horseback
he has to leave it at the entrance of the wood or forest
because they are impenetrable except on foot. Even so,
he has to perform a thousand contortions in order to
go in and be able to follow the hunt. He frees one, two
or more dogs. Exercise and necessity rather than natural inclination enable them to track the beasts. When
they bark the hunter runs with his spear, catching himself on the trees, leaving behind tatters from his shirt
or pants and often his flesh. He considers himself fortunate if he finds a good bull or large *becerro* (type of
wild boar), which rushes at him at top speed and with
which he fights until it is dead. After skinning it he
cuts it into strips, leaving the head and a large portion
of it, only taking that part of the meat that he can

carry on his shoulders as far as his house or he leaves some and returns with the necessary help to carry it… His feet develop a crust or patch a finger thick from continually walking barefoot. The thorns which are many and vary in size or type tend not to go right in. When they return from their exercise and cut the soles of the feet with a knife they are like surgeons working on a foreign body or a wooden leg. Throughout the day spent hunting he sustains himself by quenching his thirst with sweet or bitter oranges, depending on what he finds, and defying the natural heat with some fresh wild fruit that is found in the country. (Sánchez Valverde, idem)

According to J. B. Lemonier-Delafosse, there were also excellent horsemen:

One should know those horsemen, true horse-men, as they were called by Indians, the first Spaniards on horseback who set foot on their land!… They are so good on horseback, so powerful, that one could imagine they form a single body with the horse. Armed with a sharp spear, no Baskir can compare to them; they could fight the most skilful Cossacks. The hunt is where one may admire their speed and dexterity!… Scarcely is the animal wounded with the weapon thrown from a galloping horse than does the horseman jump down onto his prey! Ordinarily they hunt wild pig and they use another method for the oxen.

Nor is it like the lasso of the Pampas: here the horseman waits for the moment when the ox, running, falls down on its front legs. He then grabs it by the tail which remains up in the air. At that moment he raises it forcefully, twisting its bottom vertebrae; the animal loses its balance and falls nose down on the ground. The man promptly passes the tail he is holding in his hand in front of the animal's back leg. This maneuver forces the animal to remain still while he uses a small sword to wound it behind the horns at the point where the head meets the spinal column. (151–2)

The rigors of the work of a *hatero* meant that these kinds of jobs were reserved for men with strength and dexterity, which was not common among all men of the time, as well as a thorough knowledge of the terrain. The latter was very important as hunting the cattle required knowledge of the places they frequented, as well as the short cuts and paths where the cattle might be found.

With these requirements, work on the *hatos* could not be based on slave labor, since, apart from the independent lifestyle of the *vaqueros* (which offered the possibility of escape), the risks encountered on a daily basis by the herdsmen in their hunt for the animals would be hard for the slave to endure. In addition, the limitations of the slave trade and the *hateros'* lack of capital to participate in it meant that they were unable to buy large numbers of slaves. As a result, it was not uncommon for a *hatero* to have free blacks working on his farms and enslaved blacks as domestic servants.

The Hatero's House

According to Moreau de Saint-Méry: " The place where he shelters, he and his family, is a hut, made out of badly joined-together stakes and boards, covered with straw with a living room of between 12 and 18 foot square, in which there is a table, two or three stools and a hammock. There is a second room for sleeping, smaller than the first and one or more beds like those I have previously described. When it rains, the drips formed by the holes let the water fall inside and very soon the floor, which is not paved with brick and is only distinguishable from the field in that footprints have destroyed the grass, is covered in mud." Similarly, Lemonier-Delafosse, who visited the easternmost part of the colony, observed that the countrymen lived in actual huts built from raised stakes roofed over with branches.

The capital city was also somewhat different, as indicated by Sánchez Valverde, who points out that, by the end of the eighteenth century, there were some stone buildings and the majority of the houses were made of wood covered with royal palm (*yagua*) and were, as he said, "sufficiently comfortable and spacious."

So the housing had not developed much from the time of the Tainos or the styles typical of the Africans that were reproduced in the French part under the name of "*ajoupas*." They were of such poor quality that, according to G. Débien, it was not worth listing them as property in sales documents.

Unfortunately, these styles of housing are still found in the Dominican Republic today, with the furniture in these houses being very much along the same lines. Some authors note that in the countryside beds were made from forked poles and straw, or the people would raise small forked poles and stretch cow hides between them. In the best of cases, hammocks were used. In the capital, the poor families could not improve much on the comfort of the countryside, since more or less the same thing is repeated in some inventories or distraint proceedings found in different sources. In the case of the distraints that appear, for

139

example, in the documents of the Incháustegui collection, recently published under the title of *La vida escandalosa en Santo Domingo en los siglos XVII y XVIII*, it was discovered that these distraints were never carried out because of the lack of value of the goods or else ridiculous items were seized. For example, one of those documents states: "We did not find any possessions that could be impounded as they were made up of useless junk of no value and in the hut where the said Isabel Lorenza lives only a bed of benches was found and on it an old kapok mattress, a chamber pot and a cauldron."

In other inventories, large earthenware jars, small trunks, mortars, earthenware jugs and cauldrons were included. Essentially, the furniture was quite crude, just like the housing— and one would not find it very different from that used in many parts of the country today.

Blacks in Hatero Society

The described *hatero* setting was not complete without the presence of black people who made *hatero* society their own world, attempting to elude the forms of exploitation to which they were subjected by Spanish or Creole whites.

The black population was classified into slaves, free blacks and mulattoes, with each of these categories occupying different positions within the occupational structure, such as day laborers, domestic servants, hunters, and trades such as tailoring, stonemasonry, carpentry, etc. However, the black hustlers fell outside this occupational structure. These men, as witnesses of the time explained, were not notably different from their masters or white Creoles in general, since the conditions of life in the colony were so appalling that rigid demarcations could not be established. Unusual forms of social engagement showed that other factors determined the highly flexible relations between masters and slaves. In the case of the *hatos* and the *conuco,* one refers to *certain* determining factors, such as the agreement by both sectors to have the chance of getting ahead within colonial society. Most importantly, however, on account of the nature of these relations, the colony became a focus of attraction for slaves from Saint-Domingue who continually crossed over to Santo Domingo.

In addition, it is important to examine the different views regarding the reasons behind the continuous flight of slaves from the French part. Most of the documents and books by modern authors suggest that the main reason for the crossing was simply the Spaniards' milder treatment of their black population. For example, Don Américo Lugo would have one believe in an attitude peculiar to the Spaniards which makes people forget the classist nature of the Spanish slave-owning regime. It in fact hides the behavior meted out to the slaves by the requirements of the system in place in Santo Domingo, where the shortage of labor and the lack of access to the slave trade forced the slaveowners to hold on to the slaves or free blacks by whatever means and to extend their lives for as long as possible. It was the opposite of a plantation economy which needed to obtain the greatest amount of work from the slave even if the slave died in the process.

In short, it amounts to a question of different systems of slavery with the Spanish method of domination as the only alternative because of the impossibility of participating in the slave trade and the lack of capital to develop a plantation economy. As a result, a comparison between the French and the Spanish systems should be conducted on the basis of the typical characteristics of each and not in terms of moral values.

Therefore, the issue cannot be considered in any other way than that the Spanish society on the island did not have contractual labor relations, and the Spaniards had a slavery system that was also based on force and violence and where the whip was the best tool of conviction and persuasion. The codes or rules for control and authority over the slaves, drawn up in the Spanish colonies, in which the coercive nature of the society is obvious, are also proof of this.

If we limit ourselves to the question of better or worse treatment, or to who may have been kinder, we will find ourselves up a blind alley. For example, the French said that they were kinder to their slaves than the English and the English would say that they were better than the Portuguese, etc., so that it will always be a vicious circle. It is necessary to consider the issue in terms of the social character of a particular society, as only the social categories are valid for analyzing society since history is generally driven by class struggle and not by good or evil.

Furthermore, one form of slavery or another is the difference in behavior of slave masters of the same nationality in different times or colonies, as in the case of the Spaniards in Santo Domingo and the same Spaniards on the island of Cuba. In the latter, if a plantation system remained tied to the slave trade, its form of control had a much less rigid basis than that of the Spanish in Santo Domingo.

In the case of Santo Domingo, it is impossible to consider the flight of slaves to the Spanish part in terms of the search for better living conditions. However, they did not become completely socialized in Santo Domingo. One must bear in mind the expulsion factors in Saint-Domingue. It is also necessary to link the escapes to the support received by the runaways on Spanish territory, where all kinds of reasons were given for not returning the slaves who arrived there. There was talk of guaranteeing the right of asylum as well as retaliating for border infringements (and not only in Santo Domingo).

In this particular case, some letters from the Conde Solano (Governor of the Spanish part) are revealing. He says that he authorized the detention of blacks captured on his territory in retaliation for the problems created by the French who were attempting to seize land that had traditionally belonged to the Spaniards. But in the same document the French try to explain the real reasons for the support given to the runaway slaves by the Spaniards, saying that since the Spaniards generally did not have the financial resources to buy slaves, they took advantage of the situation to appropriate the French runaways, regardless of the number that escaped into Spanish territory.

In any case, none of these cases involve improvisation or a pragmatic attitude on the part of the colonists, rather all was set forth in various royal letters patent (*cédulas reales*). In order to clarify these views, we provide two reasons—that is, to avoid a return to the paternalistic view of nineteenth-century historians of the Dominican Republic and to reveal the true nature of relations in the country's slavery society.

In the first place, characterizing a particular society in terms of the way the opposing classes relate to one another is impossible, since society retains its form or structure independent of this relationship. The relations of production, we believe, always determine this structure. Hence any explanation of the mildness or the kindness of slave masters cannot escape this structural reality, which is why the form of the relationship does not alter the true nature of Dominican slavery. This can only be considered when explaining certain attitudes—and not when characterizing a type of society.

Regarding good treatment, the labor relations established in the colony as well as its laws in fact demonstrate the Spaniard's intentions. Don Agustín Emparán y Orbe explained the interpretation of the laws, even if, as he himself says, the Código Negro was drawn up to improve the lot of the slaves: "They will also guide our laws to the extent that it contributes to their important goal, the useful and diligent occupation of free and enslaved blacks in the cultivation of the products needed by the metropole. Their appropriate division into classes and races; the office and trades that are applicable and their perfect subordination and respect to the magistrates, to their masters and generally to every white person."

Therefore it is necessary to ask whether the laws relating to the blacks were in fact beneficial to them—or if it was a simply a question of readjustments to improve the colonial economy. There is no doubt about this, especially if one analyzes the said Código, because even with it the slaves did not become completely socialized.

One confusing factor about the conditions of the slaves in the island's two colonies is that the differences in treatment between Santo Domingo and Saint-Domingue were more obvious because the Spanish *hateros* or *estancieros* were much poorer than the French planters. Hence, social status in Saint-Domingue and in Santo Domingo differed greatly. However, one cannot overlook the huge differences in material living conditions of the Spanish slaves and their masters.

In the case of Brazil, Fernando H. Cardoso also illustrates the difficult of deducing a particular and unchanging social form of domination from a narrow gap of material living conditions between slave and master. That to say that in spite of the poverty of the slave master, he continued "exercising his social powers like someone who has sufficient means to attain the objectification of his will and of his interests through the action of the slave."

In the Dominican Republic, poverty of the slaveowners undoubtedly played a role in the "mellowing" of relations because the Dominican landowners generally had fewer slaves. The master himself oversaw the directing of agricultural tasks (leaving little room for the absenteeism that was so rife in other parts of the continent), doing everything possible to hold on to his few workers since his profits partly depended on the slaves' physical condition.

In all of these cases, the lack of participation in the slave trade, which among other things, in resulted in the high price of the slaves, contributed to improving the treatment of the slaves.

Those forms of race relations clearly revealed the Spanish Creole's need to preserve his own *hatero* system, and despite the many dispositions and recommendations by the Crown or its representatives that blacks be treated otherwise, the particular conditions of the colony prevented the Spanish Creole from following them.

The free and enslaved blacks remained attached to the *hato* and the *conuco* in conditions that represented a specific alternative and in which, although it partially socialize them, they also found an environment that did not force them to seek other opportunities for survival in the face of exploitation, as was the case of marronage in the plantation economies.

The Creole society began to take shape mainly in the eighteenth century, with its main elements being the *hato*, the *hatero*, the *conuco*, free and enslaved blacks, and mulattoes.

The following paragraphs illustrate how these elements combined to define both the Creole and Creole culture.

In a general sense, the *hato* as an economic unit in the Dominican Republic became the answer or solution to the "abandonment" by the "Mother Country." As a geographical-political unit, it was organized using the remaining elements of the initial attempt to establish a plantation economy on Hispaniola—that is, unlimited amounts of land, limited labor, little technological development and a large number of cattle.

These factors were taken into serious consideration by the inhabitants of the colony because they were the means by which they could achieve their personal goals, in terms of acquiring prestige, wealth and power.

The concurrence of the aforementioned factors, among others, lay behind the establishment of a cattle-raising economy in this part of the island. The *hato* and the tenant farmers had control of the lands (at least de facto, especially if we remember that in land matters as in many others, the laws of the Crown were not worth the paper they were written on). Most importantly, they developed certain methods of subjecting the enslaved and free labor force, which was different from what normally occurred in the plantation economies where supplies depended mainly on the exterior by means of the "trade." In terms of the animals, as already mentioned little was required and the scarcity of technology did not affect the consolidation of this economy; hence conditions were ideal.

These clarifications reveal how the world of the cattle-raising *hato* progressively established itself using a formula that was of both Creole and the Spanish Crown. Having nothing more to offer its subjects in this territory, the Spaniards were obliged to try and reconcile their own interests with those of the rest. And thus royal dictates were issued in order not to lose control of the colony; however, one cannot say that economic motives were the main incentive because expenses were actually created since the bureaucratic and administrative costs were covered by a *situado*[1] from outside.

While colonial control was maintained by administrative and military means, the control and running of the abovementioned systems by internal groups in the colony continued—and this would later serve as the basis for their political independence.

Within this context, one can see the way in which the *hato* and the *conuco* are connected, the latter being conceived in terms of the characteristics described by Bernardo Vega in his essay on the indigenous heritage in the Dominican culture of today.

El *Conuco*: An Essential Unit within Hatero Society

Bernardo Vega's essay examines the Taino origins of the *conuco* and its spread throughout the Dominican Republic. However, this unit of production still exists today; the eighteenth century was no exception, and on the contrary, the conuco was very important in that century.

The *conuco* formed part of the activities of both white Creoles as well as Creole blacks and mulattoes. Of the former, Moreau de Saint-Méry said: "They rise at dawn to go and visit their little plots which provide their subsistence... (102). On the blacks' incorporation into the *conucos,* he notes: "In Santo Domingo they call *conuco*s the farms of agricultural produce of the country, which are regularly made in a certain number of yards of land by the free blacks etc, or the day laborer slaves. The owners who cannot cultivate the area belonging to them grant it to them for the sum of five pesos a year. Once this period of a year has passed or at the most, two, the tenant abandons it and goes on to clear and sow another piece for the same grant" (Sánchez Valverde, 170).

*Conuco*s were typically maintained using totally primitive resources; initially it was "slash and burn" agriculture which, as per the previous quote was repeated from place to place, thus reinforcing its widespread practice. Furthermore, the work tools used in the eighteenth century were little different from those used in the previous ones; there were the *coa*, the hoe and the machete.

Thus agricultural activity took place mainly within these small units, as an appropriate solution that was capable of guaranteeing the food supply. When speaking of self-sufficiency, this should be conceived in absolute terms, since although the *conuco* could guarantee the basics, there was always room for exchange in the limited internal market, especially in the main urban centers. For example, the blacks often arrived in the capital to sell their products, using the money to buy other foodstuffs which they could not produce or clothes and imported items.

The *conuco*, unlike the *hato*, was often fenced in to prevent the onslaught of cattle and pigs which tended to attack the sown fields. Because attacks became very common, the inhabitants constantly complained to the authorities, asking them to impose certain measures to protect their plants.

Although the individual economies maintained by the enslaved blacks, free blacks or free mulattoes ensured the required self-sufficiency demanded by the cattle-raising economy, these forms of production were an integral part of the hatero economy and essential to its operation.

From the plots of land granted to the workers, the *hateros* and the colony as a whole were guaranteed the main food products, lending continuity to the *hato*'s very variable relationship with the external market. Besides, and above all, it was a form of payment and thus of binding the labor to the *hato*, which was the main unit.

It may be for this reason, among others, that the free and enslaved population of color did not feel obliged to seek another alternative (such as marronage in other colonies). Instead, a tacit agreement based on the principle that although the population of color would be subjected to certain pressures from the Spaniards, the type of work involved was a more satisfactory option than that offered by the plantation economy with its harsher forms of exploitation. For the Spaniards too this was the ideal arrangement, given the impossibility of obtaining and keeping the required labor by other means.

In addition, while the *hato-conuco* combination guaranteed the colony's internal subsistence, import activity was also included and finished products from the metropole were placed on the market, largely preventing the development and accumulation of more varied crafts as a step in the direction of manufactured goods. The craft items were not much of an improvement on the traditional Taino and African crafts.. Among these objects were clay vessels, washing troughs, canoes, hammocks, and the *macuto*, all of which did not become crucial to the economy of the period. Hence, the current poor state of crafts in the Dominican Republic despite the stimulus it might have received from the development of the tobacco economy.

If one were to present a panorama of Dominican architecture, only a few important examples from the seventeenth and eighteenth centuries would be available. Although the seventeenth century has been characterized as one of "poverty" in relation to the eighteenth century, the economic boom of the latter did not result in a significant advance or progress in terms of the forces of production. In fact, as mentioned earlier, the growth of the *hatero* economy occurred through increase, that is expansion of the cattle rearing lands, attracting more labor, etc.—without the incorporation of new elements of production.

In contrast to the plantation, no new forms were incorporated into the hatero economy, much less new technical elements. The impossibility for *hateros* to accumulate capital contributed to this, as can be deduced from the economic situation of the period which experienced a constant outward flow of capital to the metropoles (especially France and England). Although one can state that in the eighteenth century many people emerged from the poverty of the seventeenth century, it is impossible to claim that they experienced an era of grandeur as was the case of the neighboring colony of French Saint-Domingue. An example is provided by travelers from the French part, such as Moreau de Saint-Méry, who visited the east and remarked on this subject: "The Spanish Creole, up until then indifferent to the treasures of all kinds that surround him, spends his life without desiring a better fate. A capital that is obviously in decline, settlements scattered here and there, some colonial establishments which to call them factories would be to exaggerate, huge *haciendas* called *hatos* where animals are raised carelessly; here we have everything found in a colony where nature offers its riches to men who are completely deaf to its voice" (82).

Thus the *hato-conuco* combination was not exactly destined to fundamentally improve the miserable living conditions of that period. This, added to the absence of an economy with greater technological and cultural demands, hindered greater development. In the nineteenth century, Dominicans mainly worked on the *conuco* in order to get provisions for their basic needs and survival.

The Creole and the Creole Culture

In order to explore how Dominican national culture evolved, it is important to establish the difference between the Creole person and Creole-ness. The definition of a Creole person does not pose too great of a problem since anyone born on the continent was considered Creole, though over time this term was replaced by specific nationalities. Thus we find that Juan José Arron's chronology of the Creole began in the sixteenth century with José de Acosta, then it moved to the seventeenth century with the Inca Garcilaso de la Vega, for whom the concept shifted to the following: "It is a name invented by the blacks.... To them it means a black person born in the Indies; they invented it to differentiate those who come from here, who are born in Guinea, from those born over there, because they consider themselves to be more honourable and of higher status on account of being born in the homeland, unlike their children since they were born outside and the parents are offended if they are called Creoles. The Spaniards have similarly introduced this name into their language to denote those born over there. Thus they call the Spaniards and the Guineans who are born over there Creoles" (88).

For various reasons, the term Creole was reserved for anyone born on the American continent. In the nineteenth century, it became modified to mean "the national, native, that which is typical and distinctive of each of our countries" (92). Thus in Santo Domingo and elsewhere in the Caribbean, the term was mainly used to refer to black people. The need to indicate the origin of the slaves made this even more important, as it determined their value and differentiated them from other slaves. Thus, for example, in the slave markets, details would be given as follows: "A black Creole woman, our slave, called Francisca, around twenty eight years old"; or one could also state: "A slave of his property called José Manuel Miranda, a Creole from Guinea," or simply: "A little black girl of around 10 years of age, my slave who is a native of Guinea."

Especially for slaves or free blacks, the term was in current use. In addition, the children of Spaniards, whites or mulattoes born on the island were also considered Creoles, since Sánchez Valverde, a contemporary, used the term to refer to the latter. In the following paragraph comparing the longevity of the Creole to that of his French neighbor, SánchezValverde notes: "In short, nothing can be more fanciful than to characterize the French as being energetic about their work in Santo Domingo, when in terms of the kind of life which you have just described, it is a fact that their national delicacy makes them less suited to that climate, even more so than the European Spaniards; I am not referring to the Creoles (…) But as the Creoles move away from their European origins they become healthier, stronger and live longer" (163). (The last paragraph is a quote from Charlevoix.) Moreau de Saint-Méry used the term in the same way in an earlier paragraph, when he refers to "the Spanish Creole."

Thus in order to classify blacks it was necessary to add their place of origin to their name on account of the need to specify their status. This was not so pressing in the case of whites.

However, the references mentioned offer an idea of the term's common usage. It is another matter when one considers the issue of "Creole culture," which is made up of contributions from different social sectors of colonial life. However, claiming that each sector contributed equally would be naïve and deny the classist nature of *hatero* society.

Due to the relationship between the cattle-raising *hato* and the *conuco* and also between men of color and whites, it was not unusual that the whites should be culturally dominant since they controlled the colony and were able to remain the main axis around which all the other cultural elements revolved. As a result, from the beginning of the colony, black people were always the one who were "converted," not the Spaniards, so that gradually the blacks who arrived later began a process of "creolization." Although they arrived with their own cultural forms, these forms never managed to predominate.

Broadly speaking, people of color also generated their own vision of creolization, given that the preserved series of beliefs and practices among them may not spread to the dominant groups. These practices remain the principal markers of authenticity which were not marginal in the lives of those groups. As part of everyday life, these markers allow for true cultural identification.

Accordingly, the Creole culture can be considered to have two main dimensions, one of which is predominant. Further, the predominant dimension is more important in the process of consolidating the national project, as it differentiates between the foreign and the native. Consequently, a second meaning, referred to by Juan José Arron, is formed; that is: Creole is the same as "the national, the native, that which is typical and distinctive of each one of our countries." With this meaning, Creole-ness assumed the official; therefore the practices preserved by the dominant groups stopped being such and suddenly and without any explanation the black person born in "The Indies" stopped being Creole and his or her culture even less so. Both became regarded as African or in the best case, as something approximating this. And it is clear that everything identified with the former was then fully Creole.

Over the centuries, especially in the eighteenth, the sense of belonging to the territory of Santo Domingo began to be consolidated. This is clearly due to the nature of the *hato* as an economy that was run mainly by Creoles. Although this consolidation was achieved with the participation of blacks, there was no official recognition of their contribution to the configuration of a new cultural universe. For example, although whites might call the blacks lazy, they could not do without their labor. Some aspects of black material culture such as farming techniques, styles of building their dwellings, food habits, were especially important as well, yet they were overlooked because the *hatero* economy could not expand by renewing its material resources.

Since the white society was typically devout and Christian, the greatest rejection of African culture was mainly in the spiritual order: beliefs, traditions, rituals, music, dance etc. But for the same reasons the most important elements that shaped the personality of people of color were those that were most often used to stigmatize them.

Nevertheless, they attempted to preserve a large part of their own system of beliefs, as well as other material aspects of their (African) culture such as farming practices, culinary habits, crafts, religious traditions and rituals. The greatest emphasis was laid on ritual to the extent that it remains very present even today. Realizing that in order to have as few problems as possible in the colony, the people of color were willing to also accept western culture. Thus they organized many aspect of their lives so as not to come into direct conflict with this culture. Eventually, they were caught in a dilemma that compelled them to operate in two cultural dimensions: their authentic one and one that was imposed on them.

Consequently, the African descendants were caught in the

trap that would eventually make them feel ashamed of their true origins; although in fact they continued carrying out their own practices. We are convinced of the universal nature of the predominantly African Creole culture, in the sense that answers to all existential aspirations and achievements, whether material or spiritual, were discovered within it. In the worst case, this led to reinterpreting the dictates of Spanish culture and discovering a kind of expression and support which differed from that of European origin.

Regarding the term the "indio category," as the "Creole" blacks were for the most part free or had the possibility of buying their freedom, runaway slaves from the French part, who constantly crossed over into the Spanish colony hoping to pass as "Creoles," began calling themselves "indios" as a way of having recourse to the most indigenous element of the island: its original inhabitants. That was a very decisive factor for preventing greater influence by the African cultural aspects, because, as eighteenth-century black population in the Dominican Republic came mainly from the French part, the blacks were already conditioned not to renounce their own traditions, but certainly to subordinate them to the Spanish ones. It was a compromise to maintain their freedom. Previously I demonstrated how even the term "indio," used as a color category was later revived by the white Creoles and became a way for blacks to forget their immediate origins; this revival involved cutting out an intermediate stage and returning to the original inhabitants of the Island, whom the dominant class had made into the ancestors of all groups in Spanish Santo Domingo.

In summary, the metropolitan Spaniards, true representatives of the Crown, were unable to recreate their own culture for material and spiritual reasons. Hence, to a certain extent, they were also sponsors of the white Creole culture, which only contradicted the Spaniards on matters relating to legal-political control and the economic monopoly imposed on them by Spain. For these reasons, the Spanish Creoles did not experience major existential problems other than, in a general sense, that they symbolized the version of the internal dominant class. The black Creoles, on the other hand, appeared to be the most repressed culture and the one forced to lose its own authenticity. Thus within the Dominican Republic in the eighteenth century, two strong cultural tendencies were in operation, each having its own system of representations.

The eighteenth century was the century of recovery a greater economic growth for Latin America. It was also a period of expansion for Spain, and as the American colonies became consolidated, the Spaniards intensified the mechanisms of control relating to these colonies. As a result, tensions between the white Creoles and the peninsular representatives increased; at this stage, Creoles controlled the economy with the *peninsulares*[2] who were left in control of legal and political matters. As Pierre Cahunu points out, "To tell the truth, the existence of the peninsulares in the administration is nothing more than the inevitable compensation for their lack of importance in the economic structure. The owners of the mines, land, businesses and, paradoxically, of the very interior of the monopoly are Creoles" (23).

Throughout the nineteenth century, there existed a reinforcement of the main characteristics of the eighteenth century and a lack of maturity in the consciousness of the Spanish Creoles in deciding to gain independence from Spain. The main reason for this was the capacity of the *hatero* economy to sustain itself despite the presence of the metropole. This contrasted with those countries where plantation economies became established and for which the need to break the colonial ties was more pressing.

In the Dominican case, the hatero sector definitely dominated the struggle for independence. In terms of the particular characteristics of the movement, the idea of the nationalism began as a vindication for this sector and one in which the inclusion of other Creoles was sought during the long independence process until the "Restoration."

The dominance of the Spanish Creole sector has resulted in the struggle to recover cultural aspects corresponding to the African influence within Dominican social formation. Although both cultures existed alongside each other, the majority of the Dominican population did not accept the importance of the blacks. Hence the problem of creolization cannot be resolved like any other acculturation phenomenon resulting from equal symbiotic relations between the component parts of a national culture. Instead, Dominican national culture must be established without a true cultural identity since homogenization had only been achieved at the official level, marginalizing a large sector of the population which was never *fully* represented within it.

Thus a lack of identity should not be understood as a lack of culture, but simply as such: the definition of the Creole culture involves an identification with the national project of the dominant classes which has been unable to cancel out the cultural practices of certain sectors yet has presented these practices as separate from Dominican culture. Even Dominican whites share a great many of the cultural traits that are of African origin and have been highlighted by various anthropological works. That is to say, for them, these are also a part of culture that is considered, as Sidney Mintz states, " a body of beliefs and values socially acquired and formed, which serve a group organized within a society as a guide for its behavior" (Mintz, Sidney, "África en América Latina: Una Reflexión Desprevenida" en "África en América latina" de Manual Moreno Fraginals. Siglo XXI Ed., UNESCO, 1977).

As a result, what actually takes place is that an identification occurs which is then rejected on ideological grounds without real practical alternatives that nullify the ancestral influences. As a result, the Dominican negates himself or herself at every attempt to deny the African contribution.

On the other hand, skin color also becomes an extremely important element in colonial society, this element took precedence over all the other factors of stratification within the social structure and thus a relationship between ethnicity and occupation or social position was established.

Therefore, when one speaks of a lack of identity we are not referring only to people of color, since whites are also Dominicans and participate in this culture. Any claim that attributes the lack of an identity to the people of color only would contradict this statement by René Depestre, with which I am in total agreement: "Historical creativity has not been the exclusive privilege of a social group considered in isolation. America, unilaterally called Latin or Anglo-Saxon, arbitrarily called white or black is, in truth, the combined social creation of multiple ethnicities, whether indigenous or from different African and European countries. It is the ethno-historical result of a painful process of mestizaje and symbiosis which has transformed or even transmuted, with the precision of a nutritive phenomenon, the original social types, the multiple African, indigenous, and European essences and contributions, to produce ethnicities and cultures that are completely new in the world history of civilizations."[3]

In addition, the predominance of the white Creoles in the case of the Dominican Republic and the entire Hispanic Caribbean stands out clearly; however, the "American-ness" or Creolization of the predominant culture achieved its status on account of the fact that, when it merged with the other cultural dimensions, it became subordinated to it. This is shown by the way that the natives or Creoles constantly attempted to hide and very often even abandon those cultural elements that did not derive from the predominant version. But as Nina Friedemann rightly points out in the case of Colombia: "that is the path that the non-whites had to follow in order to gain access to formal, specialized education and in order to be able to aspire to positions at the level of socio-economic decision-making.[4]

In conclusion, today's Creole-ness can be understood as everything produced by the national Dominican society—and is undoubtedly an expression of the two main dimensions that have shaped Dominican idiosyncrasy over time: the white Creoles and the Black Creoles, without leaving out the contribution of the indigenous peoples, filtered through the influence of those other elements. In addition, the seventeenth and eighteenth centuries with the cattle-raising economy, an alternative that fitted the interests of those classes, constituted the time and space in which the main foundations of Creole society were consolidated in the Dominican Republic.

Thus, the authentic national and Creole culture can become a true instrument for our national development if the majority of Dominicans identify with the main components of their culture. And most importantly, if the Dominicans are able to preserve the most valuable elements of their historical-cultural heritage, the country's national sovereignty will be guaranteed.

CHAPTER SIX

Immigration in the Late Nineteenth and Early Twentieth Centuries and Its Contribution to Dominican Culture

JOSÉ DEL CASTILLO PICHARDO

In the social sciences, culture refers to the way of life of any society, not just "the areas which society itself considers more important or desirable."[1] Thus this essay begins with the definition that "culture is the configuration of learned behavior and the results of the behavior, whose elements are shared and transmitted by the members of a society."[2] These results include what has been designated *material culture*, or "the objects that members of society have customarily manufactured and used," as well as *immaterial culture*, that is, ideas, value systems, customs and such.[3]

I begin with these dilemmas, all of which necessitate an inventory of the contributions of the different groups of immigrants who arrived in the Dominican Republic at the end of the nine-teenth and beginning of the twentieth centuries. They brought with them new languages, religions, ideologies, institutions, customs and ways of life; they also brought about radical transformations in the prevailing ways of life by introducing new productive technologies, modern forms of transportation and communications, and by driving the capitalist relations of production according to the business models of the period.

The Nineteenth Century and Its Transformations

The final decades of the nineteent and the beginning of twentieth centuries are key moments in the transformation of the planet in every respect. In those years, propelled by vigorous capitalism, the world economy became centralized, incorporating into its sphere those regions that had remained outside of it. This resulted from the export of surplus capital from the more developed countries who went in search of new sources of primary materials and new markets for metropolitan manufactures.

These were the years of territorial expansion and the emergence of a new colonizing movement among the major powers. Between 1876 and 1914, the United States, Germany, Japan and France extended their dominions by fourteen million square kilometers, an area one and a half times the size of Europe. This brought 100 million people under colonial control. If we include old England, it alone had thirty-three million square kilometers of colonial territory and 393 million inhabitants.[4]

World trade experienced extraordinary growth due to the mass production that was made possible by major innovations in industrial technology and stimulated by rapid transformations in transportation and communication methods. It rose from the 7.8 billion dollars attained in 1883 to 20.9 billion dollars in 1913.[5]

At the same time, the industrial nations experienced the rise of different forms of business mergers as a logical result of the process described above. The struggle to control the markets led to the formation of trusts and cartels and thus the development of the much-discussed and undoubtedly influential multinational corporations such as Standard Oil of New Jersey (today Exxon), US Steel, the General Electric Company, American Sugar Refining and others. In 1902 US Steel and its affiliates alone employed 168,000 people.

One of the pillars of these transformations was metallurgy, driven by the steel mills that produced a more consistent product than iron. It was used for manufacturing machines, tools, means of transport (boats, railways) and transportation tracks (rails and bridges). England and the United States led the "railway revolution." At the beginning of the twentieth century, the internal combustion engine and oil production combined to give rise to new industrial activities such as the automobile and oil industries. At the end of the nineteenth and the beginning of the twentieth century, electricity enabled what some authors have called the "second industrial revolution." Used for lighting the cities and, especially in the early stages, it also powered trams and urban underground trains. The automobile and the airplane would later complement the development of transportation based on the railway and steam ships at the beginning of the twentieth century.

Although the railway had already been an everyday reality in Western Europe and the eastern United States before 1870, it became widespread after this date. The railway was significant for the Dominican economy, within which internal communications were based around the *recuas* or mule trains, and since the capacity of one average cargo wagon was equivalent to 100 mules. However, the railway's importance lay not only in lowering the cost of transporting passengers and goods (by reducing the time and providing greater security). The expansion of the railway also tended to give value to the agricultural or virgin lands through which it passed, as in the case of El Cibao. In addition, it made the profitable farming of large tracts of cane-growing land by the sugar industry possible, giving rise to the sugarcane *latifundio* and the large sugar central, as Ramiro Sánchez illustrates in his *Azúcar y Población en las Antillas*.[6]

Throughout the nineteenth century, the steam ship struggled for supremacy of the seas in open competition with the clipper, the fastest sailing ship of the time. The steamboats that went up the Mississippi from New Orleans—immortalized by Mark Twain in *Huckleberry Finn* and *Life on the Mississippi* and by the magic of Walt Disney who incorporated them into Disney world—offered proof of steam's superiority for river transportation.

If the railway and the steam boats expedited the movement of passengers and goods, the development of telegraphic and telephone communications facilitated long distance connections and the instantaneous transmission of news. With rapid economic transactions possible, the tea and sugar markets of London and the coffee and sugar markets of New York grew, transforming the planet into what a communication sociologist has termed "the global village," referring to the rapid circulation of information from one point of the globe to another.

The Universal Postal Union, set up in 1874, also made international correspondence cheaper and more reliable. The electric telegraph was adopted widely from the middle of the nineteenth century, with the first submarine cable from Calais to Dover laid in 1851, linking England to the continent of Europe. In 1867 the 4,000 kilometer transatlantic cable linking the old continent to America was completed. In 1874 the Pernambuco cable connected Brazilian coffee to the world markets. The telephone, invented by Bell in 1876, spread in the late 1870s and the early 1880s.

Other communications media such as the radio, the phonograph and the cinema completed the tableau of communication innovations bequeathed by the nineteenth century. The phonograph, invented by Edison and the Frenchman Charles Cros in 1877, performed the miracle of recording the human voice and sound, transmitting and preserving it. Its use would make classical music, the waltz and other musical expressions a truly universal heritage. In 1895 the cinema held its first session in the Gran Café on the Boulevard des Capucines in Paris, thanks to the ingenuity of the Lyonnais industrialist Louis Lumiòre. It went into commercial distribution at the beginning of the twentieth century. Radio, which was developed in 1896, would become widespread at the beginning of this century. All these advances revolutionized not only the world of communications but the population's recreational habits.[7]

The nineteenth century became the setting for important changes to work regime and for population movements. Slavery and the slave trade were abolished, and new forms of transitional servitude emerged as well as the imposition of free labor. In addition, the mechanization of industry snatched women and children from the home, involving them in the vortex of the factory. Dickens in *Oliver Twist* skillfully recorded these societal transformations. In short, it was the century that marked the emergence of a labor market of worldwide dimensions.

The cities that emerged from the new settlement patterns that accompanied industrial development multiplied around the globe. In 1850, forty-four cities in Europe and seven in the Americas had over 100,000 inhabitants. By 1914 this figure had risen to 180 and 69, respectively.[8]

International migrations with their cargo of transculturation and the frenetic search for new horizons expressed the mood of the times, creating a new kaleidoscope of ethnicities especially in the emerging nations. In 1875 Old Europe sent off 250,000 emigrants a year. By 1890 this was 750,000 and in 1913, over two million. On the other hand, the United States received twenty-eight million foreigners between 1860 and 1920. In only one year, 1913, Brazil and Argentina attracted 194,000 and 364,000 immigrants respectively. Most of these immigrants were incorporated into the industrial or agricultural labor force, or were pioneers who opened up new routes into the vast unexploited regions of the American territories.

Along with the Irish, Russians, Polish peasants, Jews persecuted by pogroms, southern Italians, Spaniards and other Europeans, other immigrants arrived in these lands. They were needed by the plantation economies which, as the century advanced, had experienced the reduced possibility of buying slaves or hiring freed slaves.. Contracted under a new form of temporary servitude and known as coolies, Chinese and Indians arrived in hundreds of thousands in British Guiana, Trinidad, Jamaica, Cuba, Peru and other countries.

The Arabs, with their traditional commercial acumen, completed this contingent of new inhabitants of the Americas, especially in the final years of the nineteenth and beginning of the twentieth century.

There was a movement of population within the American

continent itself. Chileans, Bolivians and Mexicans set off for California fired by "gold fever," an experience lived and recounted by Vicente Pérez Rosales in *Recuerdos del Pasado*, and recreated by Neruda in *Fulgor y Muerte de Joaquín Murieta*, his one attempt at playwriting. The northern Chilean nitrate fields, the reason for the War of the Pacific between Chile, Peru and Bolivia, were populated by Bolivian and Peruvian workers. This inspired Luis Advis' *Cantata de Santa María de Iquique* and was portrayed in Latin American film by Miguel Littin in his *Actas de Marusia*. Argentinian Patagonia attracted Chileans and foreigners of all kinds to farm the plains. This was also the theme of another very important film, *La Patagonia Trágica*. Work on the Panama Canal brought in Antillean workers at a time when the Central American banana plantations and work on the railways was also attracting workers. Carlos Luis Fallas portrayed this in his *Mamita Yunai*.

The extraordinary development of the material forces of production, science and technology was matched by a new mentality and related value system. The positivism devised by Auguste Comte (1798–1857) heralded a new reign, that of science, which would transform morality and politics into activities whose norms were determined by the positive spirit with a fundamental nature that lay in the discovery of the natural and unchanging laws of progress. These were as irrefutable as the law of universal gravity, driving the advance of society, which evolved towards higher levels of organization and greater control by man over nature. For Comte, the new era could be characterized by the predominance of positivist ideas on the intellectual plane and of industry in material life, as it was based around a social unit made up of all humanity under a universal order sealed by a sentiment of benevolence. He believed this new order would "put an end to the state of crisis" ushered in by the French Revolution.[9]

New elements were added to Comtean positivism, especially by Herbert Spencer (1820–1903) who was influenced by the organicist evolutionism of Charles Darwin. He insisted on a strong liberalism which would limited the role of the State in directing the social process. Spencerian theories became widespread, consolidating their popularity through the attitudes of the entrepreneurs and an important sector of the middle classes of the western world, especially its intellectuals.[10]

Within the sphere of politics, liberalism came to symbolize the era, with its platform of human and political rights, modern constitutional organization, economic freedom and competition in business, as well as the ending of restrictions and privileges and the limiting of state intervention.[11] Both liberalism and positivism were the ideological elements of a world infused with boundless optimism and spurred on by the religion of progress.[12] Its practical translation could be summarized by the motto, Work, Order and Progress, proclaimed by the bourgeoisie whose historical realization inevitably occurred in the closing decades of the nineteenth century as a result of the consolidation of centralist regimes. For this reason, although it may appear incongruous, by assimilating the historical processes through a unilinear and Manichean evolutionist approach, Ulises Heureaux, Porfirio Díaz and other dictators demonstrated the practical application of the liberal propositions. They appropriated them according to the prevailing economic and social reality and the inherited patterns of traditional political culture.[13]

Did the Dominican Republic take part in this movement of capitalist expansion and modernity that enveloped the planet? Or did our society remain on the margins of this process, as

Pedro Henriquez Ureña suggests, implying that if one was born in 1884 then he or she in effect been born in the eighteenth century? Or, if we disagree with the interpretation of our great humanist, did our society, like other Latin American societies, become incorporated into the movement of the era, assimilating its general trends through the filter of its own particularities?[14]

Dominican Society at the End of the Century

The nineteenth century with its atmosphere of change on all fronts made its entrance on the Dominican stage, not in the twentieth century as Pedro Henríquez Ureña would have it, but from the 1870s. Riding spiritedly on the back of the steam engine attached to the iron mill for extracting cane juice, it appeared in the vacuum of the sugar caramelizing pans and in the centrifuges that separated the crystals from the molasses, then advanced swiftly along the railroads, breaking the monotonous silence of the countryside with the whistle of the smoking locomotive of progress. The telegraph and telephone lines trickled along and steam navigation spread in the nineteenth century during which ideas of positivism and liberalism were articulated, with their gospel of work, order and progress.

And on the crest of this nineteenth century wave, as its flesh, muscle and guiding head, immigrants positioned themselves as businessmen, intellectuals and professionals, small shopkeepers, farmers, laborers and artisans, completing the picture of emerging capitalism in the Dominican Republic.

By the 1870s, Dominican society relied on an economy based on the export of valuable woods and dyewoods processed in the sawmills of the southern strip and in certain coastal areas in the north of the country such as Monte Cristi; on tobacco production which became concentrated in El Cibao on family farms with a network of traders whose main collection centers were

Santiago and Puerto Plata, the exit port for Europe (Germany via Hamburg); on the operations of sugar and cane syrup mills which were mainly family-run and spread over the traditional sugar cane areas (especially the hills of Ocoa, the plains of Azua, Baní and San Cristóbal) whose production was destined for domestic consumption and whose surpluses increased our export lines; on the traditional cattle-raising *hatos* located in the extensive plains of the east; and on the production of the *conucos* which aimed to supply the population's food requirements.

According to Hazard and other foreigners, the uneven development of internal communication routes could be added to this picture. Traveling around the country on muleback, wading across rivers, negotiating rough mountain terrain, they experienced innumerable vicissitudes as part of an undertaking that involved a certain element of risk. Thus a society that was very much divided along regional lines emerged and was exacerbated by production specializations and corresponding social structures, all of which provided a natural base for regional and local autocratic government, political instability and the uneven national integration into a project that would lead to greater consensus among the population.

At the beginning of the 1870s, the Dominican population was estimated to be between 150,000 and 207,000 by the commissioners of the North American government who inspected the country in order to sound out the viability of Báez's[15] annexation project. However, in 1869 Abad estimated it at 252,000 and Javier Angulo Guridi had calculated 300,000 in 1866,[16] a projection that appears to be exaggerated. Despite the discrepancies in these figures, what is certain is that the Dominican Republic had the lowest population density in the Antilles, a telling sign of an eventful history of epidemics, the devastation of towns, genocide, mass emigration and other demographic catastrophes which decimated the population, without the counterbalance of immigration and natural increase that may have overturn this trend.[17]

Despite the attempts at populating the country promoted by Boyer in the 1920s with the immigration of freed North American blacks who settled in Puerto Plata and Samaná,[18] and the immigration of Haitians during the period of occupation, one year after the Dominican State was set up, the *El Dominicano* newspaper devoted a long article to the demographic problem suggesting the solution in the title: "Immigration." The fate of the independence project itself was clearly expressed in the concerns of *El Dominicano*. The writer of the article directly linked the demographic problem to the state of the country's agriculture, indicating the intended destination of potential immigrants. According to the author, "not only the population of the Spanish part which has always been tiny in relation to its land area, but various factors have combined to prevent the results that might nonetheless have been expected from agriculture with a small number of workers." The reasons he considered fundamental are extremely thought provoking and reflect opinions that have been held for many years and repeated by different authors, and which are still in the catalog of assumptions of the dominant ideology.

According to *El Dominicano,* our agriculture was in a deplorable state because of the following reasons:

> In the first place there is no doubt that the scorching climate of the zone in which we live is enervating and predisposes one to idleness; from eleven in the morning until two in the afternoon one feels a press-

ing need to rest in the shade; and such is the allure of this idleness that it extends itself imperceptibly until one ends up resting all day and acquiring a horror of work.

In the second place, one must relate the productivity of the land to the idleness of our laborers since a month of work is sufficient to ensure their subsistence for a year; there are banana plantations that were planted more than a century ago and will probably last another thousand years without requiring more than the minimum of effort.

In the third place, the climate contributes to idleness in another sense. It is a fact that men meet their needs through their efforts; and what are those needs in our country? Food? We have already explained how easily this is acquired. Clothing? As there is strictly speaking no winter in our country, one does not need more clothes than those required to cover oneself; that is, some pants and a canvas shirt which do not cost more than three or four pesos are sufficient to clothe our country men for six months, both in winter and summer. And do you think it would be so easy to induce men to work for ten or twelve hours, when without doing so, they can eat, clothe themselves and be sheltered?[19]

The Panacea of Immigration

The efforts to attract settlers from abroad were evident in the legislative measures and official and private immigration plans of the Dominican Republic. Distinguished intellectuals and public figures wrote about the migratory problem. From Bonó,

Espaillat, Billini, Hostos, Luperón and other nineteenth-century figures, to José Ramón López, Tulio Cesteros, Francisco J Peynado, Peña Batlle and Balaguer, it has continued to be a central issue in Dominican social thought.

In terms of official initiatives, Dominican leaders from the early years of the First Republic prioritized the immigration problem. In 1847 an immigration law had already been passed on account of "the great scarcity of inhabitants." In 1852 Báez sponsored similar legislation. Later, in 1867, Cabral's government issued a law on agricultural ventures, colonization and immigration. In 1876 the government of Espaillat granted immigrants unrestricted rights to land belonging to the State. In 1879 the Executive Power decreed the concession of certain exemptions to "all immigrants who come to the country under contract to a rural farm owner or by companies set up for the purpose." In the same year, Congress passed an immigration law in which the government undertook to cover the one-off travel costs of immigrants incurred by the contractor. This law was no longer in force under the provisional government of Horacio Vásquez in 1902 as it was considered that the exemptions granted had led to abuses that were damaging to the treasury.

Three years later in 1905, the government of Morales Languasco issued a resolution regulating immigration, which was then repealed by Congress six months later. Finally, in 1912 a new immigration law was issued that contained restrictive clauses referring to the "natives of the European colonies in America" (meaning *cocolos*), "those from Asia, Africa and Oceania, as well as laborers of races other than the Caucasian." This legislation was later extended by the North American government of occupation and by Trujillo's regime.[20]

The immigration plans ran alongside legislative measures. In

1851 the National Congress had already authorized President Báez to accept a loan of two million, part of which would be allocated to "facilitate the entry of foreign agricultural workers." In 1860 the State signed a contract with the businessman Manuel Pereira to bring in families from the Canary Islands, establishing *Juntas de Inmigración* in the provincial capitals and in Samaná and Puerto Plata.

In 1884, under the regency of Billini, a project for families from the Canaries was promoted by means of a contract with the immigration agent Andrés Sosvilla y González.[21] Both projects achieved poor results, with only a few handfuls of immigrants arriving in the country. Previously, in 1882, Gregorio Luperón had made efforts in Paris to steer "the tribes persecuted in Russia and Germany" towards the Dominican Republic. It was a project for Jewish immigration which was approved by the Alliance Israelite Universelle and financed by the Barons de Rothschild. Nonetheless it ended in failure.[22]

Another project that suffered a similar fate was that of Leonte Vásquez, who was granted a license by the state in 1891 to establish a colony of immigrants in San José de Ocoa. Faring better than Vásquez, a firm named Montandon, Descombes and Co. established a small colony of Europeans in Sabana de la Mar in 1888, with the aim of promoting cocoa farming. The farm La Evolución was established for this purpose.

In spite of the fact that the State set aside funds for promoting immigration on several occasions, such as in 1884, when thirty percent of the export income was set aside for that purpose—a measure that was in place for barely a month—and in 1891 when the same thing was done with five percent of the municipal income, with the exception of the *patente*[23] payment, and in 1901 when the same measure was approved with thirty percent of the income generated by customs in La Romana, the efforts to attract population under its encouragement were generally unsuccessful.

Nevertheless, the country's immigratory crisis continued. In 1883 it reached a point during which Indian coolies were imported through the Sociedad de Emigración India of Guadeloupe, and later Yucatecan and American Indians were hired as laborers.

The primary aim behind most of the immigration projects was the settlement of uncultivated land that was in abundant supply. Thus immigration and colonization became inseparable as the essential ingredients of a two-pronged policy: selective population in racial terms—preferably of Caucasian extraction— and promoting agriculture by means of a technically qualified labor force capable of modernizing the traditional methods employed by Dominican farmers. In terms of the latter, it was claimed that every agricultural colony would be a breeding ground that would spread the most advanced methods of agricultural science and technology among the rural population located on their periphery.

Objectives specifying the ideal characteristics of this type of immigrant were linked to the summarized aims. Thus in addition to the contributions to be gained from race and technical qualifications, there were other important characteristics: the habit of saving, the spirit of enterprise, social discipline, especially as evidenced by the regular and rational performance of everyday tasks. As may be observed, it was a farm worker motivated by the ethics and habits associated with capitalism in its competitive phase.

Another factor behind the immigration projects was the aim of attracting capital into the country. It was assumed that each immigrant possessed a sum of capital that, while modest, would make up a considerable total given the large number of people mobilized.

Although these ideas were common to the authors of the period, they acquired coherent expression in the thought of Eugenio María de Hostos, whose civic apostolate had an enormous influence on the country's intellectual elite. For Hostos, immigration was "the problem of problems and the measure of measures, because it is the only thing that can resolve everything." According to him, it was about attracting "'organized families' prime economic agents and industrial instruments by reason of the principle of organization that they bring with them." These families would be settled in colonies whose hallmark would be radically different from sugar tenant farming, which implied gathering "around a capitalist who owned a piece of land and a machine-operated sugarmill a few individuals who have two or three thousand *pesos fuertes* and who by paying for the physical labor of some laborers may produce cane for the sugarmill, which they sell at the set price, earning a few thousand pesos in a few years and at the end of which they lose all rights to the land to which they have given economic value." Unlike this model, Hostos believed that "one colonizes in order to cultivate both the land and the man," synthesizing in this way the civilizing intention of his proposal.[24]

Despite the efforts deployed, the Dominican Republic was not an important destination for large international migratory movements from the old continent. Other poles of attraction acted as a magnet for the streams of European settlers. Under these circumstances, the immigration patterns that prevailed in our country were different, prompted mainly by the sugar plantations and other export farming activities as well as the political expulsion factors operating in Cuba and Puerto Rico.

The Groups of Immigrants

Let us now analyze the groups of immigrants who arrived in the country in the final decades of the nineteenth and the beginning of the twentieth centuries. A list of foreigners ordered by the Ministro del Interior y Policía in 1882 has enabled the calculation of the main groups of immigrants based in the country at that time. However, until now researchers have only been able to locate files relating to the Province of Santo Domingo (which in this record include San Cristóbal, Palenque, Baní and San José de Ocoa), [25] Azua, El Seibo, and the maritime districts of San Pedro de Macoría and Puerto Plata. Files for the provinces of Santiago and La Vega, the districts of Samaná, Monte Cristi and Barahona, covering the foreign presence in the whole country, are missing. But as the popular saying goes, when there is no bread use *casabe*.

Puerto Plata headed the centers surveyed, with 1,038 foreigners out of a total of 1,953, or 53%, followed by Santo Domingo with 773, representing 40%. Next came El Seibo with 82, San Pedro with 65 and Azua with 27.

The most important groups by nationality were the Spanish with 847, or 43%; the English with 379, or 20%; the Dutch with 215 (11%), the Danish with 117, North Americans with 109, Italians with 82, the French with 78, the Venezuelans with 34 and the Germans with 33. Nevertheless, these figures require closer examination as they conceal a much more complex situation. Unfortunately, it is only in Puerto Plata that the authorities bothered to specify the place of origin of each individual registered under a particular nationality.

A more in-depth analysis of the data indicates that out of the 408 Spanish citizens registered in Puerto Plata, only 58 were from the Peninsula and two from the Canaries, with 301 being Cuban and 46 Puerto Rican. In the case of Santo Domingo, although they did not have the foresight of the Puerto Plata authorities, a run through the list of names reveals high proportion of Cubans and Puerto Ricans registered as Spaniards, such as Juan Amechazurra, Juan Fernández de Castro and Juan Serrallés, among others. This corresponds to the fact that Puerto Plata, Santo Domingo and Santiago were the main reception centers for Cuban and Puerto Rican immigrants who came to the country during the Ten Years' War in Cuba (1868–78).

The second important national group, the English, also presents a more diverse reality. Out of the total of 379 in Puerto Plata alone, 332 came from the British West Indies, especially the Turks islands, not counting the *cocolos* based in the other centers of the country. In the case of the Danes, the same thing occurs. Out of a total of 117 settled in Puerto Plata, 92 came from St. Thomas, St. Croix and St. John.

The Dutch, in turn, came from Curaçao and were made up of two different groups: the Sephardic Jews, who were involved in commercial and financial activities, and the people of color who specialized in craft trades and probably worked within the sugar industry. Among the first group are surnames such as Marchena, Coen, Leyba, Henríquez, among others, whose presence in the country goes back a long way. In the second group surnames such as Sillié, Mangual, Prince and Leyte appear.

Among the North Americans, especially those who settled in Puerto Plata, was a group of blacks belonging to or descended from the contingent of North American freed slaves settled by Boyer in the 1820s. The other North Americans were Cubans linked to sugar industry activities such as Joaquín M. Delgado and the Lamars, among others.

Having identified the distribution of the different national

178

groups and clarified the issue of their places of origin, let us examine the characteristics of these migrations and their contribution to Dominican culture, classifying the immigrant groups according to their main areas of activity.

Business Immigration

In the 1870s, the modern sugar industry emerged in the Dominican Republic as a result of the combination of favorable international circumstances: the Cuban war, which affected the main exporter of sugar cane; the Franco-German War of 1870 —both countries were the main producers of beet sugar; the US Civil War and its effect on the Louisiana plantations; as well as the consolidation of suitable internal conditions: the ending of the second Dominican war of independence.

This renewed spirit of enterprise was greeted with enthusiastic praise for the work, progress and the peace needed to make the anticipated period of well-being a lasting one. Reflecting this new climate on its pages, the most influential newspaper in Santo Domingo defined these days as the "true dawning of the future," while an anonymous member of the Sociedad Amigos del País emphatically stated that there were "many Dominicans who might wish to hear no other bugles than the whistles of the locomotives nor any other cannons than those shooting balls of twenty *quintales*[26] [of sugar] to New York."[27]

Consequently, the province of Santo Domingo saw its land transformed from virgin forest or pasture to fields sown symmetrically with sugar cane around the sugar mills. The same phenomenon occurred in Azua, Baní, Ocoa, Puerto Plata, Samaná and San Pedro de Macorís, which, over the years, would be converted into the most important sugar-producing center of the country.

The first railway lines in the country came with the sug-armills—and with them locomotive and the railway carriages as well as iron bridges. Some of the first telephone networks were installed in the industrial establishments around the city of Santo Domingo.

The establishment of the sugarmills entailed incorporating a huge range of previously unseen industrial equipment and accessories into Dominican society which linked the country to the technology produced by the nineteenth century in more advanced countries. Thus modern business practices typical of capitalism and guided by the principles of rationality and the maximization of profit were introduced into the Dominican environment. Social relationships, especially the work regime, were transformed and important new social groups were creat-ed. Patterns of population concentration changed, turning extremely underpopulated areas such as Macorís, later La Romana, into important, cosmopolitan cities in turn shook the colonial, walled capital out of its centuries-long lethargy.

Dominicans of the time were not unaware of the contribution of the sugarmills. When Carlos F. Loynaz, a Cuban, set up the first steam-powered sugarmill in San Marcos, Puerto Plata, the press in that town wrote admiringly: Today we have witnessed the decisive proof in his sugarmill "La Isabel." In less than half an hour the recently cut cane, crumbled by the crusher, sent its juice into the evaporators where it boiled, filling the air with the delicious fumes of *guarapo*[28]; an hour later it passed through the centrifuge and its bright powder sweetened our breakfast cof-fee."[29]

Brimming with enthusiasm, the press in the capital celebrat-ed the arrival of the steam engine that was installed in the *La Encarnación* sugarmill, which was founded by the Dominican Francisco Saviñón, suggesting that a new era of work was opening up which would disable the revolutionary guerrillas. It reads thus: "In what we can term the industrial procession which conveyed the boiler, placed on two carts pulled by three magnificent pair of oxen, it was natural that its monumental bulk would attract attention and that the titanic efforts employed in its placement be considered. But there was something else that attracted the attention more fully and aptly: it was the individuals who were in charge of it, who directed the work and who almost worked like laborers and oxen drivers. These individuals were Mr. Félix M Lluveres and his sons, Pedro, Felito and Francisco. They all represented a satisfying regeneration, a pleasing hope, as until yesterday these were men purposefully devoted to the sterile task of our miserable party politics. From heroes of factions they have become heroes of work, heroes of industry; from destructive elements they have transformed themselves into elements of production, peace and progress."[30]

Another change that went hand in hand with the sugar industry was the movement of rural *conuco* farmers towards the sugarmills in search of the seasonal wage, which at that time was attractive. This involved a significant sector of the rural population surrounding the sugarmills, as well as internal migratory movements, especially from Azua towards Santo Domingo and Macorís and also from El Seybo to the latter's center. The voices of Hostos and Bonó were raised in warning at the related abandonment of the *conucos* and the resulting shortage of food for domestic consumption entailed by this movement, and also against the dispossession and proletarianization of the peasantry, this latter aspect being exaggerated by these authors.

The landholding system experienced important modifications as a gradual process of the breaking down of communal property, an essential step in the reign of capitalist relationships in agriculture, which called for unequivocal title deeds backed by the appropriate measures. After several decades, this process would assume its final form with the implementation of the Torrens system during the North American occupation.

The process of capitalist expansion, which was concentrated on the sugar industry, was entirely driven by Cuban, North American, English, French, German, Puerto Rican, Italian and Dominican entrepreneurs. Their vital contribution lay in establishing what is still the main industry in the Dominican Republic, most of which was built by them, opening the way for significant changes on all fronts.

Most of the businessmen who established sugarmills in the country were Cubans or came from Cuba, where they had been connected with the sugar industry. Thus we have Joaquín M. Delgado, a Cuban who founded the *La Esperanza* sugarmill in 1875 in the municipality of San Carlos. In the same area in 1876 one of his compatriots, Evaristo de Lamar, founded the *La Caridad* sugarmill in the vicinity of what is today the Simón Bolívar *barrio*, while a sugar mechanic from Matanzas, Juan Amechazurra, established the *ingenio Angelina* on some 10,000 *tareas*[31] of virgin forest, in a place calle El Higo on the outskirts of a hamlet described by Amechazurra himself as "four bohíos of yagua" with "a church of indefinable appearance" and which "in the capital itself little more was known about it other than that it produced good coconuts and bananas,"[32] referring to Macorís. According to Juan J Sánchez, the Cuban businessman had to "train the Dominican laborers he needed, so as to enable them to carry out the work in the fields as well as possible, redoubling his efforts in acquainting them with the tasks of the sugarmill."[33]

Based in the Dominican Republic since 1846, the Bostonian

merchant William Read founded the *Las Damas* sugarmill in Sabana Grande de Palenque in 1877, on what are known today as the pasturelands of the Vicini family which were incorporated into the *Caei*. Two years later, Santiago Mellor, also a North American, founded the *Porvenir* sugarmill which was equipped with triple action machinery and was the most technologically advanced until then.

This trend continued in 1880 with the incorporation of the *La Fe* into the sugar universe of the province of Santo Domingo, in what is today the suburban development La Fe. The firm of J.E. Hatton & Cía, composed of the Briton Joseph Eleuterio Hatton and the North Americans Alexander Bass and Carlos and Juan Clark, founded it. All of them came from Cuba and were connected with the sugar business. In 1881 Señora Dolores Valera de Lamar, a Cuban, set up the *Dolores* sugarmill in Sabana Grande de Santo Domingo. This establishment was apparently incorporated in the same year into the *Stella*, under the direction of the North American Geo Stokes.

Within the same period, several sugarmills were established in the vicinity of Pajarito. The Cambiaso brothers, Italian traders who had been established in the country for a long time, entered into partnership with Augusto Cisneros and founded the *San Luis* sugarmill, today called *Ozama*; at the same time, Ricardo Hatton, the English son of Joseph Eleuterio, and Mariano Hernández, a Cuban *hacendado*, founded *Jainamosa*, on what years later would become the farm of Don Agusto Chotin and whose canefields would be transferred to the Ozama of today. In its turn, the French company, Societé des Sucreries de Saint Domingue, founded the *La Francia* sugarmill, in the same spot where Molinos Dominicanos are today.

Alexander Bass and the German businessman Frederick Von

Krosigh, also from Cuba, founded *La Duquesa* on the lands of El Higüero, in Sabana Grande de Santo Domingo and in San Carlos, where today lies the colony with the same name as the *Rio Haina* sugarmill and an establishment of the IAD (Instituto Agrario Dominicano).[34]

The firm, Padró, Solaun & Cía, formed by Cubans, founded the *Consuelo* sugarmill in Macorís in 1882. Over time, this mill would become the most modern in the region under the ownership and administration of the dynamic North American businessman William L. Bass, son of Alexander. At the beginning of the 1890s, Bass's enterprise was hailed in the *Eco de la Opinión*, which observed that "men of the mettle and capital of William Bass are what the Dominican people need in order to rise. Businesses of this kind may appear at every turn and we will be saved by the REASON of work or by the FORCE of the capital invested."[35] Bass promoted the *colonato* (sugar planter) system, giving seventy-five pounds of sugar for each tonne of cane handed in by the planter. He increased the productivity of *Consuelo*, gaining the leading position previously held by *Santa Fe*, and he extended the railway lines and the number of locomotives and railway cars. The *batey* (outbuildings) of the sugarmill had seventy houses for the laborers, one for office workers and the home of the Administrator. It had telephone communications, its own pier on the River Maguá, and a little steamer and barges. It employed 800 day laborers at the time of the harvest and had "a busier and better stocked market than the city itself," according to Sánchez.[36]

Consuelo had its own newspaper, *The Hawk*, dedicated to providing "a daily report of the progress of that *hacienda*; always spicing up its columns, sometimes with interesting anecdotes, sometimes humorous items about the managers and employees of the sugarmill or reprinting selections from literature or about the inventions of the period."[37] In fact, Bass was an inspired poet, and I was able to read his books of poetry in the Library of Congress in Washington, appreciating his incisive caricatures of the United States Sugar Trust against which he conducted a frenzied lobbying campaign in Congress. For his part, Bass was an expert in sugar technology and he patented several of his inventions in the country. These included the "Guarapo Rectifier" as well as modifications to the cane carts. He wrote several works on the subject. He also ran the Pioneer Iron Works a company that manufactured industrial equipment for the sugarmills which he inherited from his father.

In 1882 the Cuban businessman Juan Fernández de Castro founded the *Cristóbal Colón* sugarmill, hailed by the press as one of "the great industrial enterprises" and characterized by "the partnership of large-scale capital, cultivation and production, improved mechanical equipment, and a fixed and portable railway to serve the farm."[38] Fernández de Castro would also set up the *Quisqueya* sugarmill at the beginning of the 1890s.

Santa Fé was founded in 1882 by the firm, Vásquez, Rousset & Cía, of which the Frenchman Augusto Rousset was a member. This sugarmill would later pass into the hands of the Cuban Salvador Ross, whose relationship with the San Pedro de Macorís community was evidenced by the construction of the Salvador park opposite the Catholic church, the donation of the clock for the church tower and the draining of the "ancient and pestilent swamps, which caused so many malarial fevers in this city,"[39] and by the purchase of a fire engine and numerous works which led the Town Council to present him with a medal of Gratitude in a solemn ceremony that also honored Juan Amechazurra.[40]

During the same period, the Puerto Rican Juan Serrallés established the *Puerto Rico* sugarmill at the place called Las

Cabuyas on land leading to the new bridge at Macorís. At the same time, the firm of Lithgow Brothers founded the *San Marcos* sugarmill in Puerto Plata, using sugar technology unknown in the country, which had been patented by Fryer, an Englishman. This consisted of the manufacture of something called *concreto*, a compacted mass containing sixty percent sugar and forty percent molasses. Its foundation was greeted with enthusiasm by the people of Puerto Plata, who were amazed at its "iron buildings," its "majestic chimney," its railroad which ran from the sugarmill to the port and especially the two locomotives which arrived in 1883 and were christened *Puerto Plata* and *San Marcos*. When these became operational on August 18 of that year, according to the Puerto Plata press: "a railway train operated for the first time in the country."[41] This illustrates that it was from 1884 onwards that the sugarmills in the province of Santo Domingo began to install rail transportation. The French engineer H. Thomasset, who was at the time the sole representative of the "Decauville iron roads," played a prominent role, laying the first lines at the *La Fe* and *Esperanza* sugarmills.[42] Following the same trend, *Cristóbal Colón* put its railway system into operation in November 1883. This event was written up in the press as follows: "In San Pedro de Macorís the locomotive whistled during the trial run of the railway installed on the 'Colón' farm of Don Juan de Castro farm (the star of them all)."[43]

Also in Puerto Plata, Miguel Andrés Peralta and Eduardo Hachtman set up the *La Industria* sugarmill in 1879, later called *Las Mercedes*, using a hybrid technological model that incorporated elements from the industrial era into a system that was still manually operated.

Italia, known today as *Caei*, was the only sugarmill directly

THE CONTRIBUTION OF IMMIGRATION

founded by Juan Bautista Vicini, who would acquire the largest number of sugar establishments in the nineteenth century. His operations began in 1882 in the place called Caoba Corcovada and were affected by the storm of San Germán in the following year that caused one of the worst floods of the River Nizao. Vicini established a mixed system, consisting of a supply of sugar from planters and from the sugarmill itself (which is called today "*caña de administración*"). The industrial equipment was manufactured in France by Fives-Lille, with its "engineers, mechanics and laborers" responsible for the installation. A considerable part of that equipment is still in working order. From the beginning it was equipped with a railway, which came into operation in March 1883 and went as far as Palenque, the port of embarkation for its sugar. Attached to the sugarmill was a Savalle still, used for making rum and other types of alcohol.

Immigrants as well as Dominicans founded other sugarmills. At the same time, foreign businessmen continued to be linked to the sugar industry in its various stages of development. The social structure that emerged on the sugar plantations still has characteristics that are unchanged, especially in terms of the work regime and the polarized ways of life; these features are evident in the living conditions of the *batey* with its overcrowding, unhealthiness, undernourishment, and low levels of education as compared with the conditions of the upper-level employees and executives which are the exact opposite in terms of security and income. These themes have been skillfully portrayed in Dominican literature by authors such as Marrero Aristy in his *Over*, Pedro Mir in his book of poems, *Hay un país en el mundo* and Bosch in some of his stories (*Luis Pie, La Nochebuena de Encarnación Mendoza*).

The spirit of enterprise did not stop at the sugarmills, as the

Dominican Republic saw the emergence of other large-scale agricultural ventures, including the cultivation of bananas in Puerto Plata and cocoa in Samaná.

In the industrial and manufacturing sphere, the main cities experienced a veritable boom in the production of chocolate, cigars and cigarettes, rum, alcohol and beer, soaps, candles, matches, pastry, tiles and bricks and other goods that have remained part of Dominican traditional production and to which immigrant businessmen significantly contributed their enterprise.

Some mining projects were proposed, and in San Cristóbal they were heralded in newspaper articles such as "La Futura California Dominicana (The Future Dominican California)" but all remained at the developmental phase.

In 1884 the French submarine telegraph company, better known as Cable Francés, began installing the country's telegraph network, "under the direction of a Frenchman." According to Hoetink, by the next year there were schools of "practical telegraphy" in Puerto Plata and Santo Domingo. In the years that followed, the telegraph network extended throughout the country, linking the main cities Sánchez-La Vega, 1887; Monte Cristi, 1890; San Pedro de Macorís, 1895; Azua, 1898.

The importance of the telegraph was not only experienced in the world of business for carrying out rapid transactions, it also acquired particular political significance as a means of control. This was the reason why Heureaux made up a Telegraphic Code for official communications which became a wonderful catalog of political Machiavellianism.

With regard to the telephone, by 1886 it was already in operation in Santo Domingo. In that year work was carried out to connect the sugarmills surrounding the capital. The *Eco de la*

Opinión considered the advantages of this innovation, stating that:

> Communication with the sugar mills on the out-skirts of the Capital is valuable for their owners or agents, because they are kept abreast of what is happening and can be alerted in time about accidents on the farm; for the traders, because in the space of a moment they can make a profitable deal, etc; for the individuals employed in these establishments because they can communicate and enjoy moments of agreeable relaxation with their family and friends during the sad and monotonous periods that weigh down in the solitude of the countryside; and finally for the authorities, who, by means of these lines, will be better able to monitor public security.[44]

By 1888 there were already some forty-six telephones installed in Santo Domingo, according to a directory published in the newspaper.[45]

Most of the railway projects were the initiatives of foreign entrepreneurs or of Heureaux' government in association with foreign entrepreneurs, almost all of whom were British or North American. Although the first concessions were sold off at the end of the 1860s, construction only started between 1879 and 1880.

In 1887 the Sánchez-La Vega railway became operational, opening up a new route for exports from El Cibao which had been practically monopolized by Puerto Plata. Federico García Godoy described the construction works, revealing that "at this moment under the direction of skilled engineers almost two hundred men are involved in laying track and building bridges,

and over one thousand three hundred in the building of em-
bankments and setting the gauge." For García Godoy, the railway would bring value to the Aledaña land. It would attract
hardworking immigrants and turn La Vega into a key center of
El Cibao.[46] But Sánchez would also become important. In the
same year, Hoetink points out that "this muddy town was divided into an enclosed section with the houses of the Company";
(meaning the Compañía Escocesa, in charge of the railway)
"and the rest, where (…) some 2,000 pioneers were seeking their
fortune; a quarter of them Dominican, another quarter
Europeans, and half immigrants from the Virgin Islands, the
Turks and Curaçao."[47] In 1895 San Francisco de Macorís was
connected to this network and in 1909, Salcedo.

In 1897 the Ferrocarril Central Dominicano joined Puerto
Plata and Santiago, accelerating the links that traditionally unit-
ed these two cities, and in 1909 it was extended with the Moca-
La Vega branch line.

Immigration of Traders: Germans, Italians, Spaniards, Jews and Arabs

A large part of the commercial activities, especially the export
and import trade, was in the hands of immigrants who settled
in the country. They introduced more aggressive business practices, connections to overseas firms and, in some cases, acted as
a catalyst for improving the quality of our exports.

The Germans had established themselves as a force in the
tobacco business, especially in Puerto Plata, from where they
shipped the El Cibao leaf to Hamburg. A chronicler of the period reveals that in 1884 he had "met on a road more than twenty-five travelers of this nationality, all of them doing excellent
business."[48] In San Pedro de Macorís, some German traders

financed the *colonos* and bought sugar for export, at the same time as they ran businesses selling imported merchandise. This was the case of Elhers Friedheim, who established sugarcane plantations with tenant farmers. In Monte Cristi the German traders established a tradition that would end during the First World War as a result of measures taken against them by the government of occupation.

The Italians set up in trade in the capital Puerto Plata, San Pedro, and Azua, among other places, becoming very influential in Dominican society. Juan Bautista Vicini and the Cambiasos are typical of the more outstanding cases. Vicini eventually had a hand in all kinds of business, being one of the biggest exporters of the country's products, an importer of merchandise, a leading moneylender—the State was one of his main debtors —and the owner of coasting vessels, an agent for wharfs and port warehouses. He owned houses, manufactured rum and alcohol and ended up with more than ten sugarmills under his control by the end of the century. His political influence may be seen in his close relations with Heureaux during his long period in power.

In general, the Italians integrated fully into Dominican society, commonly marrying Dominican women and taking part in religious activities, social clubs, etc.

Spaniards from the Peninsula occupied an important position in the wholesale export trade, a tradition that has remained today. In Santiago the North American commissioners who visited the country in 1871 listed them among the "most prosperous traders."[49] In Puerto Plata, the house of the Catalan trader Cosme Batlle would become one of the most prominent in the import and export trade and as a moneylender to the State, gaining notoriety on account of its close links to President

Heureaux. In San Pedro de Macorís, José Armenteros, who arrived in the city in 1897, founded the firm of José Armenteros & Compañía, one of the most prosperous trading companies in the town. Later he moved into industrial activities, such as the manufacture of soap and stearin candles, along with his compatriot César Iglesias, retaining and expanding both companies. Another example is Juan Parra Alba, who stood out on account of the huge variety of his business initiatives, appearing in 1907 in the Deschamps *Directorio* as a distiller in San Pedro de Macorís, while owning a match factory, a chocolate factory, an icemaking plant and a modern bakery in Santo Domingo.[50]

Although the Spanish traders married Dominican women, they founded their own institutions, especially social clubs such as the Centro Español in San Pedro de Macorís and the Casa España in Santo Domingo. On the other hand, they were prominent in the senior management of the Chambers of Commerce, Agriculture and Industry. (Carlos Dobal has knowledgeably covered other contributions made by the Spaniards in his essay in this volume.)

Although their immigration began from the 1840s onwards, the Sephardic Jews who came from Curaçao and, less frequently, from St. Thomas, were linked with trading and financial activities from the first quarter of the nineteenth century. During this period, there is evidence of the close ties between the Dominican economy and the ports of Carlota Amalia and Wilhelmstadt and links between Dominican politicians and the traders who were based there. These immigrants or their counterparts in the aforementioned cities financed the many costs of the war against Haiti and even of the domestic "revolutions" in 1896 Jesurun y Báez was one example. Thus the Jewish traders became key players in Dominican financial politics. In 1866

Cabral authorized Jacobo Pereira to arrange a loan in Europe of 400,000 pounds sterling in a transaction that failed on account of the refusal by Congress. Two years later, Báez delegated Jesurun to arrange a loan. This resulted in the well-known Hartmont loan of 1869. Later in 1888 in Amsterdam, Eugenio Generoso de Marchena signed for a loan of 770,000 pounds from the Dutch bankers Westendorp.[51]

Outside of financial activities, Sephardic Jews were major figures among the import and export trading houses of Santo Domingo and in other urban areas on a much smaller scale. At the end of the nineteenth century, the houses of Samuel Curiel & Co., E López Penha, Eugenio de Marchena, and J de Lemos appeared among the most important in the capital's directory.[52]

The Sephardic Jews did not remain a closed group characterized by endogamy and attachment to their religious habits and traditional educational practices as the key mechanisms of group cohesion, as their limited numbers conspired against this type of behavior. Hoetink points out, citing Ucko, that their spiritual needs were satisfied by their membership of freemasonry, an institution that was in vogue at that time, as well as conventional acceptance of Catholic rites, especially matrimony. On the other hand, from one generation to the next, a change in orientation of their activities was occurring. While trade and finance predominated among the first generation, by the second generation, new activities were introduced such as education, journalism and politics. This culminated in a third generation with the clear predominance of the liberal professions and politics. In this sense, the Henríquez family serves as a typical example of this process of intergenerational change in orientation, having provided Dominican society with a large and distinguished group of educators, men of letters, journalists and politicians who have exercised undeniable intellectual leadership over various generations.

The Arabs, especially Syrians, Lebanese and Palestinians, began to arrive in the country in the 1890s and at the beginning of the twentieth century. They settled in almost all the important cities, devoting themselves to retail and itinerant trade. In Santiago they set up hardware stalls in the Market, offering credit that had to be paid off on Saturdays. This stands out as one of the keys to their success.[53] The 1907 Deschamps *Directorio* carries an advertisement for Nacif and Julián P Haché, while various Arab surnames, such as Diep, Elías, Jelú, Hahnet, Jacobo, Jorge, Shadalá, Suet, Safet, Tallay, Zaen and Isaías, appear listed as traders. Thirteen years later, the *Libro Azul de Santo Domingo* includes a detailed description of Baduí M. Dumit & Co., established in 1900 in Santiago, which, as it points out, was "one of the largest" in that city, adding that Señor Dumit also owned six "fine houses in the city." In the opinion of the book's compilers, one of the factors behind the Syrian immigrants' success was "the attractive prices at which they sell, always lower than the rest."[54] The progress of the Arabs in Santiago was evident in the contributions they made to the adornment of the city, for example, "the electrical illumination of the cathedral" and the "chapel in the town cemetery."[55]

Another important destination for Arab immigrants was San Pedro de Macorís and the surrounding sugarmills where they traded aggressively, seeking out clients in the canefields and *bateys* of the sugarmills. Initially the established traders in San Pedro de Macorís resented this, alleging that their peddling was unfair competition. On the open land at the entrance to the Consuelo sugarmill, where Sánchez notes that a market of considerable size was set up, especially on Sundays, the Arabs cornered the market with their fabrics and various bargains. The extraordinary trading ability of the Arabs led some sugar companies to grant them the concession to run their *bodegas* (grocery stores), in what seems to be a form of compromise in the battle to control the retail trade.

In San Pedro de Macorís, one finds a higher ratio of Arab traders in 1907, with names such as Abud, Chain, Curé, Camastro, Duluc, Elías, Hazim, Abraham, Jorge, Nicolás, Manzur, Salomón and Merip appearing. In this city, the progress of the Arab community is evidenced by their influence on the textile trade, their inroads into clothes manufacturing (Antún) and even the sugar industry as important *colonos* (Acta). Their leadership at the community level was demonstrated by the positions of *senadores, munícipes* (municipal council members), and *rectores* (university presidents), occupied by members of the second generation and to a lesser extent those of the first.

In Santo Domingo, during the same period, surnames such as Azar, Elías, Alma, Abud, Hasbún, Heded, Mansur, Miguel, Melhen, Terk, Zaiter were registered as traders. Almost all are located on Separación street (today El Conde). However, Mella Avenue was the site of Arab dominion, especially in the area of textiles and bazaars. The rapid growth of the Arab businesses is exemplified by the case of Nemen Terk, who in 1920 took up a whole page of the exclusive *Libro Azul*, stating that he was one of the most important merchants involved in importing goods as well as exporting the country's products. He employed twelve clerks, two agents, two traveling salesmen and sixty workers. He owned urban farms and a schooner for traveling the Caribbean.[56] Yet the mobility of the Arab community based in the capital would be best illustrated by the foundation of the Club Sirio Libanés, which some traditional families of the city joined.

The upward mobility of the Arabs in Dominican society has been extraordinary. They became the principal traders in many of the country's cities and played an outstanding role in industrial activities, mainly the textile industry. The second generation has undergone a considerable change in occupational orientation, from business—though without abandoning it—to the professions, politics and the military. The participation of the second generation in academia has been extremely significant. In the Universidad del Estado alone, out of the seven rectors who emerged following the "reformist movement," four have been descendants of Arab immigrants: the doctors Kasse Acta, Cury, Tolentino Dipp and Rosario Resek. In the same period, four vice-rectors have also been descendants of Arabs: Abinader, Lalane José, Tolentino Dipp and Schecker. To large extent, the Universidad Central del Este is the creation of its rector José Hazin, who has energetically promoted it.

In almost all the university careers, the list of the descendants of Arabs speaks for itself, and is especially noticeable in almost all the medical specialisms. To only mention a few, the names of Antonio Zaglul in psychiatry and of Emil Kasse Acta in pediatrics are significant.

In the world of politics, second-generation Arabs have played an outstanding role. The ranks of the public service are filled with the descendants of immigrants who have held ministerial and embassy posts and been senate and committee members. The list also includes secretaries of state, and even one vice-president of the Republic. Arabs have held leadership positions in the wide range of parties in the country today. In the military, individuals such as General Wessin y Wessin and General Estrella Shadalá have risen to the highest ranks.

The Arab contribution to Dominican cooking has also been

significant, to the extent that many Arab dishes are an important part of our cuisine, such as *quipe* (*kibbeh*), stuffed cabbage, and stuffed eggplant, among others.

Middle-Class Cuban and Puerto Rican Immigration

During the course of the first war of independence in Cuba (1868–78) and the anti-colonial struggle in Puerto Rico, an important migratory wave of Cubans and Puerto Ricans arrived in the country. Their influence on Dominican society was significant in various spheres. We have already analyzed their entrepreneurial element. Now we will look at the middle class groups that formed part of this immigration.

The political motives behind this immigration are reflected in the activism that characterized its members, who made Puerto Plata their main base. In Puerto Plata, Eugenio María de Hostos, Federico García Copley and other famous immigrants formed patriotic associations, edited newspapers and performed a huge number of civic duties. They were associated with the liberal Dominican elements which, like Luperón, saw the independence of Cuba and Puerto Rico as tied to the preservation and development of Dominican sovereignty. Thus a Cuban like García Copley appeared as the founder of the Liga de la Paz, a body that received support from Hostos and which, under the leadership of Luperón, led the struggle against the government of Ignacio María González.[57]

Although the Dominican press welcomed the contributions of the Cuban patriots and enthusiastically supported their struggle, the Cubans and Puerto Ricans also founded various newspapers.

In 1875 Hostos contributed to the newspaper *Las Dos Antillas*. González closed it down, but it re-appeared under the name of *Las tres Antillas*, then later becoming *Los Antillanos*, which was edited by Hostos. Federico García Godoy founded *El Esfuerzo* in La Vega in 1880, and in 1889 *El Pueblo*, while in 1885 Juan Amechazurra edited *El Oriente* in San Pedro de Macorís. On the occasion of the second Cuban war of independence, *El Cubano* was published in Santo Domingo, *Albricias* in Monte Cristi, and *Cuba y Quisqueya* and *Prensa Libre* in Santo Domingo.[58]

In the field of education, the work of these immigrants was outstanding. In 1873 Ursula Godoy, along with her husband García Copley and their son Federico, founded the Academia de Niñas Santa Rosa for primary education in Puerto Plata. Her husband taught grammar and rhetoric at the Escuela Superior Municipal and the Escuela Superior de Niñas Santa Teresa in Santiago. Their son was the deputy head of the Colegio Municipal de Puerto Plata. In Santiago, where a large section of the Cuban colony settled; Rafael Díaz Márquez, a doctor, founded and ran the Colegio Salvador, while Dr. Juan Justo Osorio organized the first gymnasium in that city.[59] In Baní, Enrique Loynaz and his wife Juana Castillo taught, according to Incháustegui, producing "good characters."[60]

Hostos' work in the field of education was undeniably important, as it introduced into the country the basis for an education guided by positivist principles, providing a more dynamic role in the educational process for the State. The insistence on laical education, the founding of the Escuela Normal, the inauguration of the chairs of public law and political economy at the Instituto Profesional, the publication of his books *Lecciones de Derecho Constitucional*, *Moral Social* and *Tratado de Sociología*, from which many young people of the Dominican intellectual elite absorbed his ideas, are a few of the Master's many and rich contributions to Dominican culture.[61]

An important group of Cuban doctors settled in Santiago de los Caballeros. One of them, Dr. Francisco Argilagos, was among the first to practice eye surgery in the region. Another, Dr. Castellano y Arteaga, became the head of the provincial health department, while a third, Dr. Eusebio Pons y Agreda, published *Nociones de Cosmografía*, a pamphlet on Dominican medicinal plants (*Noticias sobre algunas plantas medicinales de esta República, sus propiedades y empleo en medicina seguida de una guía médica para las familias*) and a tract on smallpox. He patented a *Jarabe Depurativo de Guázuma y Guayacán* (blood tonic syrup) which he sold in his pharmacy. Pons y Agreda also became the president of the town council and ran the San Rafael hospital. A fourth, Dr. Pedro Pablo Dobal, practiced surgery extensively and was Lilís' personal physician as well as a founding member of the Centro de Recreo and vice-president of the town council.

This immigration also included public works contractors and even a composer, a pianist, a conjuror, and a quick-change artist.[62]

The two phases of Cuban immigration are linked to the two wars of independence in Cuba. When Cuba gained its independence, the majority of the immigrants returned to their country, but another section remained integrated into the heart of the Dominican community through family ties. This included the García Godoys, the Loynaz and the Zayas.

Proletarian (Lower-Class) Immigration: *Cocolos*, Puerto Ricans and Haitians

Along with the sugar industry, the railway and other production activities, thousands of foreign workers arrived in the

Dominican Republic, especially from the mid-1880s, the beginning of a long period of low sugar prices that would continue until the years of the First World War. This depression forced the sugar businessmen to reduce wage levels, thus discouraging the Dominican peasants who took part in the harvest.

The immigrants from the small Caribbean islands, called *cocolos*, whom Hazard had seen in Puerto Plata in the 1870s working as day laborers in the port and the women as washerwomen, and who in Santo Domingo formed a small community of artisans, provided the solution to the labor shortage in the Dominican Republic. From the end of the nineteenth century and during the first thirty years of the twentieth century, they arrived in numbers of several thousand per year to work in the sugar fields and in manufacturing in San Pedro de Macorís, Santo Domingo, Puerto Plata and later in La Romana, as well as on some cocoa plantations in Samaná, banana plantations in Puerto Plata and on the gangs building the Sánchez-La Vega railway.

Accordingly, their combination of physical labor, talent and discipline contributed significantly to creating wealth in the Dominican Republic.

This immigration was not problem-free. While an entrepreneur like William Bass was boasting of his profitable contributions to the sugar industry, certain newspapers echoed the interests of the traders who felt they had been adversely affected by the saving habits of immigrants returning home with a large part of their earnings. Displaying a thinly veiled racial prejudice, the traders described the immigrants as a "sloop of calamities" characterized by their "ethnic inferiority," etc.

The numerical significance of this movement is shown by the fact that in 1919–20, out of almost 6,000 immigrants who arrived in the country in that year, sixty percent were laborers brought in by the sugar companies, not counting family members and other laborers who came for various jobs outside the industry. Out of those immigrants, forty-two percent stayed on in the country after harvest, with almost 12,000 *cocolos* recorded as being employed by the sugarmills in that year.[63] Thus, this group of immigrants became an important community, both in the sugarmills and the cities, where they formed entire *barrios* such as Miramar in San Pedro De Macorís.

The *cocolos* were better qualified than the other sugar workers. Hazard had already noted their skill at languages, stating that "most spoke English perfectly," and knew two or three languages."[64] Literacy levels must have been much higher among the *cocolos*, largely due to their religion, as reading the Bible was a basic requirement of religious practice and the churches had a leading role in the educational process. These factors influenced the *cocolos'* rapid access to sugar manufacturing jobs which called for a certain level of qualification.

The *cocolo* ethos is characterized as a community united around the family, an austere lifestyle, committed religious practice, disciplined work and saving habits and a strong sense of community, all of which resulted in what can be considered their rich and extensive contribution to Dominican culture.[65]

In terms of institutions, the presence of the *cocolos* gave rise to numerous Protestant churches which are still thriving in the Dominican Republic today. These include the Iglesia Episcopal Dominicana, the Iglesia Moraviana, the Iglesia Africana Metodista Episcopal and the Fe Apostólica. These churches, especially the Episcopal, opened a number of schools to educate *cocolos* and Dominicans, both in the cities and the sugar mills. Many *cocolo* teachers also taught elementary education and musical knowledge in small home-based schools; many taught Dominicans English as well.

The *cocolos* were actively involved in the Masonic movement, supporting the foundation of various lodges of oddfellows such as the Logia Estrella of Puerto Plata, founded in 1889, and the Loyal Lux Dominicana, established in 1896 in the same city and presided over by Luis A. Lockward. In San Pedro de Macorís, they founded La Industria in 1892, but they were ousted from leadership by Dominicans, which why they created La Experiencia in 1908.

These immigrants also founded a large number of mutual aid societies, which would support their members in the event of illness and cover the burial costs in the event of death. They also held cultural activities and parties. In his thesis on *cocolo* culture, Julio César Mota discovered twelve societies of this type established in San Pedro de Macorís and the surrounding sugarmills, while Don Emilio Rodríguez Demorizi reports on two established in Puerto Plata at the end of the twentieth century.

Apart from these societies that acted as models for the Dominican labor movement at the end of the nineteenth and early twentieth centuries, the *cocolos* ran, under the name of Black Star Line, a Dominican chapter of the pan-African society called the Universal Negro Improvement and Conservation Association (UNIA), led by the Jamaican Marcus Garvey[66] in the United States. This society, founded in 1918 and whose radical propositions anticipated Black Power, was suppressed by the occupation authorities in 1921.

In 1913, the *cocolos* organized the first union of port workers in San Pedro de Macorís, where they practically monopolized work on the docks. Their presence in the labor movement of the east was shown in the 1940s when they led the workers' pay claims alongside Dominican leaders like Mauricio Báez.

The contribution of the *cocolos* to Dominican folklore has been recorded in the dances of *el momise* and that of the *Guloyas*, both inspired by biblical themes and incorporated into the repertoire of our national folklore dance troupe, under the direction of Fradique Lizardo.

In the culinary sphere, the *yaniqueque* (Johnny Cake), a kind of bun or pancake made with flour, egg and oil and fried or baked, is undoubtedly the most widespread contribution of *cocolo* cuisine to Dominican food habits. However, at the regional level, in San Pedro and Puerto Plata, other *cocolo* dishes are highly regarded. The *domplín*, eaten at lunch and dinner, is a bun or pancake made of "flour kneaded with cream and egg" boiled in salt water and served with a fish sauce, especially cod. Apparently, there is also a variant, at least in Puerto Plata, which consists of boiling the bun in chocolate made with milk or water and served at dinner. Another dish found throughout the region is *fungi*, made with salted cornflour cooked with okra and served with fish stewed in coconut milk.

Among the other sweets that were assimilated by the Dominicans and which apparently are of *cocolo* origin is the *conconete*, made with pieces of coconut and flour. In terms of *cocolo* drinks, the most popular is guavaberry, which is drunk at Christmas and is made of fermented syrup from the berries of the *arrayán* tree (*Myrciaria floribunda* or *Eugenia Floribunda*). Today, this drink is commercially produced by Pedro Justo Carrión.

The *cocolo* community has experienced a process of evident mobility. Within the sugar industry itself, there are few who work in the canefields, where they have been replaced by the Haitians. The majority of the first generation as well as successive generations are skilled sugar-manufacturing workers. Among the technical staff in the industry are many second- and third-generation *cocolos*.

Outside the sugar industry which is characterized by a rigid social structure, the *cocolos* have progressed even more quickly, using important avenues for mobility such as education and the Protestant churches. Among the most virtuous and worthy Dominican families of *cocolo* descent are the Lockwards and the Silié , the former being linked to education and the Iglesia Evangélica. The ancestors of both families eventually moved away from the sugar industry and devoted themselves to the urban craft industry. The Lockwards arrived from the Turks Islands and established themselves in Puerto Plata while the Siliés came from Curaçao and originally settled in Santo Domingo. They later moved to San Pedro and then returned to Santo Domingo. The Lockward family has given us a distinguished group of educators, journalists, musicians, pastors, men of letters, economists and politicians, while the Silié family has traditionally produced educators, outstanding lawyers, dentists, sociologists and historians and politicians.

The descendants of *cocolos* have also been outstanding in other areas: Ricardo Carty, Ricardo Joseph, and Walter James, in the artistic sphere: Juan Lockward and Violeta Stephen, in literature: Antonio Lockward, Norberto James, and Mateo Morrison and in local and national trade union leadership, and politics, where one of them, Alfonso Lockward, was a presidential candidate.

The immigration of Puerto Ricans was promoted by the Puerto Rican businessman Juan Serrallés to work in his sugarmill Puerto Rico and by William Bass to work at Consuelo. They also came to take part in the harvest on some coffee farms in the south of the country. However, the Puerto Rican immigration did not attain the same numbers and degree of continuity as the *cocolo* migration.

The majority of the Puerto Rican immigrants came from the coffee farms of their country. Others were day laborers and artisans who were attracted by what one of them considered good pay, medical care and the "poor man's drugstore," and payment in cash instead of the tokens offered by the Dominican sugarmills. Bass only had to pay their passage and give them, upon their arrival, "a peso each so that they could eat, have a drink and smoke a cigar or cigarette before putting them up 'wherever possible" and offering them work the following day."[67]

An important new migratory wave of Puerto Ricans arrived in the country only when the work on building the Central Romana began. A large portion of the manufacturing and administrative workers as well as day laborers came from Puerto Rico. The rural guard of the Central was formed by none other than the San Juan chief of police, Captain Cabreras, who arrived in 1917 with fifty-seven of his close men, among whom were non-commissioned officers.[68]

This community of Puerto Rican immigrants has had a significant impact on local life in La Romana, setting up centers such as La Casa de Puerto Rico and founding numerous Dominican families characterized by their industriousness.

Finally, the Haitians who came to the country in thousands at the end of the 1910s, during the North American occupation, to work in the sugar harvest and the public works carried out by that government, are—as a slogan promoting tourism in our country abroad goes—the "best-kept secret" of Dominican society. Despite the fact that they carry out the sugar harvest and have been living on our *bateyes* for decades, the Dominican intellectual elite has regularly treated them with contempt. Balaguer refers to the Haitian immigrant "as a being marked by horrific physical blemishes," stating that "none of them are aware of hygiene," that they have been "a generator of laziness," and have been "a harmful influence on Dominican workers."[69] In a newspaper edited by Gregorio Urbano Gilbert, the Haitian immigrants were described as "the undesirable neighbors from the east,"[70] from "whom we cannot expect anything good."[71]

Despite these hostile reactions, the Haitians are a significant and growing presence in Dominican society. In addition to their contribution to production, they have introduced ancient and secret magico-religious practices alongside the beliefs that have become established in the popular psyche, providing the expertise of priests specialized in rites such as *vodú*. In 1904, Juan Antonio Alix had already dedicated one of his spicy *décimas* to this subject à propos of an occurrence in traditional Santiago:

> Cumpliendo con sus deberes
> La señora policía
> Ayer como a mediodía
> Sorprendió cuatro mujeres
> Que bailaban con placeres
> El judú con un haitiano
> Que también le echaron mano
> Y lo tienen en chirona,
> Porque esa buena persona
> Del Judú es buen hermano

> *In the course of her duty*
> *The policewoman*
> *Yesterday at around midday*

Surprised four women
Who were dancing with enjoyment
The judú with a Haitian
Whom they were also laying hands on
And they have him in jail
As that good person
Is well-acquainted with judú

It continues:

Entre dichas bailarinas
Había tres dominicanas,
Fragatas de cuatro andanas,
Y con buenas culebrinas.

Among the said dancers
Were three Dominican women
Four-line frigates
With good culverins.

Later pointing out:

Pájaro muy lugarú
Y gran profesor Haitiano
De ese fandango africano
Que se nos mete de lleno;
Y si no hay Gobierno bueno
Adiós pueblo quisqueyano.[72]

A fellow who is very lugarú[73]
And a great Haitian professor

207

Of that African rumpus
That is establishing itself in our midst
And if there is not a good government
Bid farewell to the quisqueyano nation.

Since those times, these practices have proliferated, involving almost all the sectors of Dominican society including educated people who practice it secretly.

CHAPTER SEVEN

Modernization and Change in the Dominican Republic

FRANK MOYA PONS

In this essay, I will be unable to cover all of the issues relating to the modernization and changes that have occurred in the Dominican Republic over the last hundred years. So much has changed in the country in less than a century, and these changes have happened so rapidly that Dominicans have hardly had the time to study them. As a result, any lecture or conversation into this field should be exploratory, presenting a broad outline of issues.

A century ago, in 1880, the Dominican Republic was almost the opposite of the country we know today. Many foreign visitors who traveled within the national territory at the end of the nineteenth century noticed that the eastern part of the island of Santo Domingo, occupied by the Dominican Republic, was essentially an underpopulated area; in 1888, the population was 435,000.

The country had only three urban centers worthy of being called cities, with each of them hardly exceeding a population of

10,000 inhabitants. The base of the economy was rather limited, with production revolving around tobacco cultivation, raising herds of livestock, and felling various valuable woods, as well as the manufacturing of rum. Land ownership involved a system of communal lands dating back to the distant years of the colonial period. This system continued practically unaltered until the end of the nineteenth century because of the small population size, the lack of an internal market and the consequent lack of demand for agricultural products.

Monetary circulation was very limited, due to the country's small export capacity and the minimal economic requirements of a small population, who, according to the travelers, was accustomed to living a frugal life. Essential items were gotten from the family *conucos* or acquired in the grocery stores of the countryside (*pulperías*), or in the few provisions stores found in the so-called urban centers.

Subsistence farming prevailed in the countryside, where agricultural production depended on primitive technology. Peasants ignored the plow, the use of fertilizers and seed selection. Fences were not used for cattle-raising, nor improved fodder. Agricultural technology was limited to the use of the *coa* and the machete, as well as the still-widespread *garabato* (long forked pole).

The bulk of this society was composed of a peasantry and a large group of laborers who had no formal education and among whom illiteracy was the norm. Thus their scientific understanding of natural laws was virtually nonexistent. Hence they understood and controlled their environment by performing traditional ancestral rites that reflected beliefs, superstitions, and magical notions about such things as the rainy season, plant cycles, the political leadership, and the success or failure of the harvests.

This was a relatively simple society, in which time passed according to the cycle of the harvests. It was also a slow-paced economy, where economic rhythm was marked by the pace of the donkey and mule trains that transported the products to the few exit ports.

Most peasants and laborers depended on a small number of import and export merchants whose agents operated at the local level in the inland cities representing the interests of the larger commercial houses located in the main ports. These import-export merchants, in turn, were agents of parent companies with central offices based abroad. Alongside with them there was also a tiny stratum of professionals and bureaucrats consisting of some lawyers and notaries, very few doctors, government officials and army officers. This was a two-tier society where the artisans, despite their numbers, were unable to form a middle class that could act as an effective intermediary between the upper classes and the rest of the population, which, as we have said, consisted of mainly laborers and peasants.

Finally, this was a society with traditional habits and a parochial and provincial outlook. Only a few of its members were able to travel abroad and come into direct contact with the outside world. Thus their knowledge of what was happening in the "modern" societies of the north Atlantic was obtained from reading the books and newspapers that reached the ports of the Republic in the ships that came for the timber, tobacco and the few products that the country exported.

Traditional customs also reflected a conspicuous religiosity which manifested itself in the mass participation on the holidays in honor of the virgins of La Altagracia and Las Mercedes and the reverential observance of the Catholic rites of Holy Week. Many of those customs derived from a mixture of

Spanish and African traditions of the sixteenth and seventeenth centuries.

Consensual unions were the norm. Extended families prevailed together with mating patterns of serial monogamy, matrifocal families, paternal authoritarianism, permanent subordination of women to men, and the natural division of labor between the sexes. In this world, the daily diet was limited to beef or pork accompanied by plantain, *yuca* and other tubers and occasionally eaten with rice and beans. Chocolate drink, which was made with water, was an ever-present ingredient because milk and eggs were scarce. As a result, the typical Dominican cuisine included an unvarying diet of a few items, and its most sophisticated dishes were the *sancocho* and the *locrio*.

Although much more could be said about the Dominican society at the end of the nineteenth century, we can summarize by stating that in 1880 the Dominican Republic did not have cities, paved roads or industries. It lacked secondary schools and universities, and its most developed institutions included a church that was devoid of priests; a caricature of an army plagued by generals and regional *caudillos* who constantly competed for leadership; a bureaucracy that was extremely inefficient and ignorant of statistics and whose administrative practices had been inherited from Spanish colonial procedures.

And finally, there was the ubiquitous cock fighting which, along with the *pulpería*, was the heart and passion of Dominican life. All the symbols of what was deemed worthy were expressed in the men's loyalty to their fighting animals, a loyalty that was superseded only by that sworn by *compadres*. *Compadrazgo* involved an entire dynamic of personal loyalties and political, family, local and regional attachments. It estab-

lished permanent bonds of friendship and familiarity that pro-
tected individuals and families from the hazards of political violence and the precarious economic situation. For most of the
nineteenth century the Dominican population was divided by
pernicious regionalisms caused by the country's poor communication between the cities and the countryside due to the lack of
roads.

In the final twenty years of the nineteenth century, the
Dominican society described above was suddenly shaken when
Cuban and North American capitalists took advantage of a
consistent policy of immigration and foreign investment incentives offered by the Dominican liberal governments, and bought
enormous tracts of the uncultivated, unpopulated and cheap
land in the Dominican Republic, which they turned almost
immediately into plantations. There they invested huge sums of
money and built steam-powered sugar mills that were capable of
processing 200 times more cane in a day than the largest of the
traditional Dominican sugar mills.

There are several studies on the impact of the introduction of
the sugar industry in the Dominican Republic at the end of the
nineteenth century. These studies show how, without warning,
technology and capital displaced the few peons, peasants, and
cattle ranchers in the pastoral regions of the country creating a
pressing need for labor which was reflected in the offering of
high wages that were previously unheard of in the country. This
attracted large numbers of immigrants, both internal and external, while a modern type of agriculture took over large areas of
the country which became dominated by modern industrial
plants whose production was supported by an equally modern
railway.

The modernization of the Dominican Republic began the same way it did in other former colonial territories, that is, with the massive introduction of capital accumulated in the most industrialized nations. These expanding economies stimulated their entrepreneurs to seek new sources of raw materials in places where land and labor where cheap. In some countries, economic modernization began with mining, as was the case of Mexico, in others with the coffee plantations, as in the case of Brazil; in other countries, as in Cuba and Santo Domingo, it began with the introduction of modern factories and plantations to produce sugar.

The development of the sugar industry in the Dominican Republic forced the rural populations living in the areas where the sugar mills were located to retreat from the plains as the flat lands were seized by the plantation owners. At the same time, these populations were forced to seek a living as workers in the same plantations that displaced them.

With the construction of the modern, mechanized sugar mills, the Dominicans witnessed the first radical transformation of their countryside. Sociologists can explain the profound implications of these transformations: dozens of rural communities and families of peons found themselves transformed overnight into an agricultural proletariat or into rural vagrants who wandered around because they lost their land, fairly or unfairly, to the sugar mills.

The territorial expansion of the sugar mill at the end of the nineteenth century not only altered the pace of the economy within its sphere of influence by imposing a new industrial routine and introducing the railway, it also immediately placed economic and legal demands on the system of land tenure. The sugar producers maintained constant pressure on the governments of the Republic until finally, in 1911, the State was compelled to issue a law for the dismantling of the communal lands system. This was the beginning of the end of the traditional Dominican system of land tenure that had been an almost sacrosanct institution for some 400 years.

At the end of the nineteenth and the beginning of the twentieth century, the sugarmill, that great agro-industrial capitalist enterprise, was the principal and most decisive factor for change in rural Dominican life in the south of the country.

Another important factor of change in the Dominican life was the introduction of the railway in the central and eastern Cibao region during the final decade of the nineteenth century. Built to open up new lands for cocoa- and coffee-growing and exporting products from the port of Sánchez, the railway also encouraged the export of tobacco and other products from the country through the port of Puerto Plata.

At the end of the nineteenth century, European countries and the United States experienced extraordinary economic affluence as a result of the wealth created by the industrial revolution. An unprecedented demand for products, whose consumption had been continually growing, was generated. The rise in worldwide demand for sugar, coffee, tobacco, and cocoa had an impact on those regions of the world where these crops could be produced. In the Dominican Republic, which had a suitable climate, all governments of the time wanted to take advantage of this juncture—even if it meant placing the country in debt—so long as the railway would facilitate the exploitation of lands that had remained practically uninhabited and totally uncultivated for 400 years.

The introduction of the railway into an economy that proceeded at the pace of the donkey and mule trains forced the

Dominicans to make huge adjustments to their lifestyle at the end of the nineteenth century. This is especially true if one observes that, along with the railway, the Dominican Republic obtained access to the telegraph by means of the French cable and opened their ports to various shipping firms whose steam-powered boats considerably shortened the distance between the Dominican Republic and the United States and Europe.

Changes in the communication structures at the end of the nineteenth century were not universal. Nevertheless, the business world was immediately transformed. Quite early in the twentieth century, new inventions and technologies were adopted by the Dominican business elite as it came into direct contact with more modern societies. Soon the typewriter and linotype arrived and written communications also speeded up with the appearance of new daily newspapers, such as the *Listín Diario* in Santo Domingo and *El Diario* in Santiago.

The pace of these changes differed in the various areas of the country. In 1910 the Dominican Republic still had only two roads that had been opened during the government of Ramón Cáceres, one of which went to the Alcarrizos and the other to Río Haina, each less than twenty kilometers long.

The spread of new elements of modern life was most evident within the sugar districts, particularly in the city of Santo Domingo and the new urban center of San Pedro de Macorís that was being built by the sugar corporations and related interests. In the north and El Cibao, the railways created enclaves of modernity in Puerto de Sánchez, in Puerto Plata, and in the cities of Santiago and La Vega, where the ruling elites had traditionally been oriented towards the exterior. Until the construction of the railroad, it was easier for an inhabitant of Santiago or Puerto Plata to travel by boat to New York than to

Santo Domingo because of the lack of roads and the difficulties of cabotage navigation.

While those changes were impacting those early "centers of modernity," the rest of the country benefited only slightly from them, as the isolation of these populations kept the rural communities and the villages of the interior largely untouched. However, the fact that the main market for Dominican sugar was the port of New York, and that at the end of the nineteenth century the United States was increasingly spreading its naval presence in the Caribbean, gradually that which was modern began to be perceived as North American as the Dominican Republic came into increasingly direct contact with the United States.

This perception became more accentuated during the First World War when the ties that the country had traditionally maintained with different European nations, including Germany, were broken by a military government that the United States imposed on the Dominican Republic in 1916. The changes produced in the country during the American military occupation between 1916 and 1924 profoundly affected key aspects of Dominican life.

One of the most decisive works of the military government during that period was the linking of Santo Domingo, the capital city, with the main productive regions of the country by building a network of highways. This was begun in 1917 and completed in 1922. The impact of the highways on Dominican life was much greater than the impact of the railways because for the first time, the national government was able to effectively centralize the Republic's administrative, economic and military life, since the highways permitted the introduction of automobiles and trucks which made the transportation system increasingly flexible and versatile. As a result, the traditional system of mule trains, which had already been greatly affected in the El Cibao area by the introduction of the railway, lost its importance.

The mule trains did not disappear overnight since the roads built by the North American military government were only the three main arteries of an entire road system that would take fifty years to complete. But from then on, the occupation of chauffeur or truck owner became a symbol of modernity that effectively competed with that of muleteer. Also, within a short space of time, the roads caused the decline of the railway business because the trucks handled freight more efficiently. A 1926 report stated that it was much cheaper to transport goods by truck than by rail at a time when gasoline cost barely a few pennies a gallon.

Thus, although a lot of agricultural cargo continued to be transported for export along the Sánchez-La Vega and Santiago-Puerto Plata lines, the statistical figures show that as the volume of cargo transported by road increased, the volume transported by rail fell. By 1950 the trains that operated in El Cibao had already become obsolete because of decreased profitability. This made new investment in their improvement or modernization impossible while each year the number of kilometers of road being built was increasing. New regions of the country were connected to the main urban centers by the three major highways.

While the railway remained for some time a declining means for transporting cargoes of agricultural products, like cane sugar, cocoa, and coffee, the roads became the preferred way for the transportation of imported manufactured goods from the industrialized countries. Thus the roads became the channel through which new cultural items from abroad penetrated the country.

Without the roads it is impossible to explain the modernization of the Dominican Republic in the twentieth century. The roads have been conduits of foreign cultures, and a precise correlation can be established between the increased kilometers of roadway construction and the increased pace of change experienced by the country over the past sixty years.

Although a lot more could be said about the impact of the roads, we should also mention some other acts of the American military government that contributed to cultural change and the transformations of the socio-economic structure of the country. The disarmament of the population, for example, was a decisive factor in transforming Dominican life since it brought an end to the revolutions; it also allowed for the establishment of a constabulary which eventually evolved into a national police and a professional army.

Regarding the disarmament of the population, it is fitting to point out something that has not been fully explored—that is, the psychological impact on the Dominican male population caused by the forced surrender of their revolvers and other guns to foreign military forces. The Dominican male lost an instrument of power and social respect as well as a symbol of virility that came from the traditional custom of acquiring a revolver at puberty, which was a kind of rite of initiation into sexual maturity. Traditionally, the acquisition of the first revolver coincided with the custom of pulling down the boy's pants and incorporating him into the world of adult malehood. A great deal can be written about the use and significance of the revolver in the Dominican Republic, and judging by the Dominicans' submissive behavior following disarmament, one can conclude that the men likely suffered a kind of castration trauma when they handed over their arms to the U.S. Marine Infantry in 1917.

Other changes in Dominican life during this period directly relate to public administration, especially in the areas of education and public health in which the military government invested efforts and money in transforming the prevailing conditions. Between 1917 and 1920, this government built several hundred primary schools, and the level of student enrollment rose to more than 100,000 in 1920 from about 20,000 in 1916. Although educational development proceeded slowly in the two decades following the end of the military occupation, it generated a growing interest in primary education in the rural areas. Until then over ninety percent of the Dominican population was completely illiterate.

The health campaigns to combat malaria, syphilis, venereal diseases and the intestinal parasites which affected most of the Dominican population also ushered in new hygiene and public health policies. Backed by international funding in the 1940s and 1950s, these policies helped bring about an impressive drop in mortality later. This led to an increase in life expectancy and more importantly, a significant rise in population growth.

Another development that had an important economic and social impact was the imposition of a new customs tariff in 1919 to facilitate the tax-free entry of American goods into the country. By virtue of this tariff, over 245 goods produced in the United States were declared free of import duties and over 700 had steeply reduced import duties. This gave rise to competition from imported products, which had an adverse effect on locally manufactured goods. In many cases, small artisans and industries found it impossible to compete with the avalanche of American goods following the implementation of 1919 customs tariff. The incipient Dominican industrial development, which could have become more significant due to the capital accumulated by the increase in prices during the military occupation, was set back by at least twenty years because competing with the American products that arrived in the country tax-free became almost impossible.

One consequence of the massive importation of American goods during the military occupation was the development of a very pronounced taste for American products on the part of Dominicans. Although in the following years, Dominicans returned to consuming European goods, from then on more than half of the Dominican imports have always come from the United States.

A marked Americanization of the language also occurred during those years due to the dissemination of trademarks in the English language on almost all the products consumed in the country. Baseball also spread widely among Dominicans. Over time, it would replace cockfighting as the national sport. Among the urban elites, American music became a sign of good taste, although there was also the reverse tendency among the masses, who dedicated themselves to dancing *merengue* more enthusiastically than before to show that they rejected foreign domination.

In conclusion, one can state that the U.S. military occupation began a process of the Americanization of Dominican customs and taste. A quick glance at the newspapers of the period reveals an increasing number of advertisements for American brands. Forty years later, when the process of industrialization began in the Dominican Republic, one of the main obstacles to the growth of local industry was the existence of very definite patterns of consumption among the Dominican population, which preferred American manufactured goods to locally produced ones.

However, one should not imagine that the changes mentioned above instantly transformed the Dominican economy and society, much less the national culture. Despite the numerous modern public works carried out during the period of military rule and the succeeding administration of President Horacio Vásquez, Dominican life still continued to flow along very parochial ways. The country's population had increased from 900,000 in 1920 to almost two million in 1945, but Santiago and Santo Domingo, the two main cities, still had no more than 300,000 inhabitants together.

The other towns were communities of fewer than 10,000 inhabitants who were attached to few commercial activities and to farming the rural holdings. These inhabitants were still served by a small number of artisans who processed local raw materials and some imported products. The local societies continued to be organized along traditional lines with their local elites belonging to the finest clubs in the larger towns—such as the Club Unión in Santo Domingo, the Casino Central in La Vega, the Centro de Recreo in Santiago, the Club de Comercio in Puerto Plata, and the Club Esperanza in San Francisco de Macorís.

The tiny middle class was made up of artisans and skilled workers who were organized into different trade and mutual aid organizations, since the country's limited industrial development had not yet generated sufficient numbers of workers within different occupational spheres to allow the formation of trade unions.

To get a picture of the economic and industrial development of the Republic during the Second World War, it is sufficient to mention the following facts: apart from the fourteen sugar mills in operation, the majority of the so-called industrial establishments were made up of small family or domestic factories that employed few workers and produced only enough to supply the local market. According to the official statistics, all the industries in the country employed only 36,632 workers, 26,407 of whom worked in the sugar mills. The other industrial establishments totaled around 1,719. Their size and scale can be measured by the observation that the capital invested in ninety-six percent of them did not even average out to 15,000 dollars. Eighty percent of the so-called industrial establishments did not have more than 5,000 dollars invested. Equally, ninety-six percent of them employed an average number of workers that never exceeded sixteen. Sixty percent of the Dominican industries of the time employed fewer than five workers, and barely twenty-five percent had between six to ten workers per firm.

As already stated, these industries were small family businesses engaged in making clothes, soap, cheese, butter, corn flour, chocolate, wallets, mattresses and pillows, ice cream, shoes, hats, starch, lard, charcoal, bread, cigars and plug tobacco, salt and drinks. The largest were several rice mills, coffee, match and cigarette factories as well as the newer vegetable fat and cement industries that were built during and immediately after the Second World War.

It was difficult, if not impossible, for trade unions and labor organizations to develop in those years. The only known attempt to set up a trade union was in the sugar industry—the only industry large enough to be able to employ large numbers of workers with a work discipline and wage structure that set them apart from the traditional artisan occupations.

In general, labor relations in the other Dominican industries, with the exception of cigarettes, cement, vegetable fats, and matches, were characterized by a highly personalized work regime which made them similar to the classic medieval European family workshops rather than firms emerging from the Industrial Revolution. Indeed, sociologists have plenty of research material regarding the level of capitalist development in the Dominican Republic forty to fifty years ago.

During the final years of the war, Dominican industrial development was stimulated by an increased demand for sugar and molasses in the United States. This had the beneficial effect of slightly improving the distribution of income between the workers in the sugar industry and the rest of the country's population. As the national income increased somewhat, so did the aggregate demand for imported manufactured goods that scarcely reached the local market owing to the import restrictions imposed by the war.

The growth in internal demand encouraged the establishment of numerous new businesses. The official figures show that between 1943 and 1945 2.3 million dollars were invested in setting up 1,154 new manufacturing firms, which then provided employment for 4,554 new workers. One should bear in mind when examining these figures that most of these firms were very small workshops, and that most of this capital was invested in the construction of a cement factory, a textile factory and an industrial abattoir. In any case, the figures show the local producers' immediate response to the shortage of manufactured goods. It can be stated that over the years many of the small family industries created during the Second World War developed into large firms that supply today the needs of the national market and produce a surplus for export.

Various processes that would lay the foundations of the current Dominican economic growth accompanied this incipient industrial development, which continued almost uninterrupted until 1958. As already mentioned, the building of roads had connected the main cities with the most populous and productive areas of the country. Gradually, migration from the countryside to the cities began. For many of the peasants and landless peons, the investment in the health facilities and sanitation infrastructure immediately made urban life more attractive than rural life. Drawn by the hope of finding work in the newly built industries, the peasants and peons soon formed a large urban labor market, whose cheap labor benefited the Dominican industry of recent years.

Health services improved notably during and after the American military occupation. The building of hospitals, the training of new doctors and the energetic anti-parasite and vaccination campaigns, as well as the introduction of antibiotics at the end of the 1940s, dramatically lowered the mortality rate and increased fertility among Dominican women. Thus the years following the Second World War marked the beginning of what is now referred to as the population explosion.

In 1944 Dominican politicians still believed that the country was underpopulated and so they encouraged people to have more children by offering incentives to large families. This suggests that the phenomenon of a population explosion was not evident until the 1950 census when the Dominican population was recorded at 3 million inhabitants. Many people congratulated the government of the time, considering it to be responsible for the country's demographic growth. This was seen as a sign of social maturity and development since it would now be possible, they believed, to provide enough workers for the Dominican economy, which had been held back by labor shortages for centuries.

The population growth obliged the government to enlarge its

bureaucracy and expand public services. At the same time, the number of men employed in the armed forces to meet the defense needs of the Trujillo regime kept growing as the dictator felt permanently threatened from outside. This means that employment in the tertiary sector increased.

As the population employed in the numerous small-scale industries and workshops kept growing each year, various middle sectors gradually began to form. These sectors experienced a significant boost between 1948 and 1958, thanks to the extraordinary growth of the Dominican economy, which experienced a favorable period of good prices for its export products.

An aggressive policy of agricultural settlement and colonization opened to production hundreds of thousands of acres of land that until then had remained unexploited. The government built numerous irrigation channels in uncultivated fields that were dedicated to growing rice and plantains. Together with the extraordinary growth of livestock and the development of new plantations of *yuca*, peanuts, and bananas the Dominican agricultural horizon dramatically expanded during the 1950s.

The population increased as agricultural production grew. The number of jobs and the level of school enrolment also rose, as did the number of university graduates. In addition, the Universidad de Santo Domingo, which had been reorganized in 1932 and had maintained a student body of around 1,000 for many years saw enrollment rise to some 3,000 students by the end of the 1950s. Around 100 professionals graduated each year, providing the country, for the first time in its history, with a new professional middle class, which would end up dominating the Dominican social, political and economic leadership of recent years.

However, all these changes failed to satisfy the basic needs of the population because economic growth was controlled by a system of family monopolies which, backed by a tyrannical political regime, used the Dominican profits to accumulate huge savings that were transferred abroad. This resulted in an uneven and totally asymmetric economic growth during which a small minority benefited from the advantages of the recent industrial development.

Meanwhile, the majority of the population had no access to the country's sources of wealth. At the end of the 1950s, it was clear that the hospitals that had been built were inadequate. There were not enough schools to serve the population and illiteracy had risen. The cost of living had gone up and wages were still frozen. More unemployed people wandered the cities, while the Trujillo family oligarchy drained the country of the capital that should have been reinvested in order to create new jobs. The countryside had remained impoverished because several million acres of land had fallen into the hands of absentee landowners who had removed the former occupants from the land and did not invest in making these lands productive. During the 1950s, it was notable how the urban classes, and especially the nouveau riche traders, professionals, and military, invested their savings in the purchase of rural properties as a means of gaining economic security and social prestige in a country where land ownership had traditionally been regarded as a symbol of power.

The emergence of a rural proletariat was another feature of this period. This proletariat grew out of the government's policy encouraging births and from the continuing loss of the peasants´ land, already mentioned. Large numbers of men and women, who were uneducated, without health care, unemployed and landless, were thrust into the newly formed *favelas* of the country's main cities. This process of marginalization was already notable in 1960, and it accelerated rapidly during the following decade, creating a ubiquitous mass of *chiriperos* (informal sector workers), hustlers and day laborers, who became a ready supply of cheap labor for the Dominican economy.

It can be said that Trujillo inherited a traditional backward and poor society in 1930, and when he died he left behind an underdeveloped society in transit towards a capitalist economy that was distorted by his own monopolist industrial development. With the control of the country's resources in the hands of a completely unscrupulous family, the nation was deprived of the opportunity to experience harmonious economic development. This left the country in a situation that was remarkably similar to, though clearly on a different scale, other Latin American societies.

Thus when Trujillo died, the country confronted the following reality: a population of four million inhabitants, sixty percent of whom still lived in the countryside and more than seventy percent of the population was illiterate; small towns and cities that were receiving massive influxes of peasant families fleeing the poverty of the countryside; an agriculture that based its productive capacity more on the opening up and the colonization of new land than the actual modernization of farming techniques; and a peasantry that hardly used machinery, fertilizer, improved seeds and pest controls (there were barely two agricultural scientists in the entire country). Since Trujillo and his associates had been the only industrialists, the local elites' economic activities were limited to commercial and farming ventures, and to practicing their professions.

A collective pessimism pervaded most of the population when Trujillo was killed in 1961—a pessimism that had been accentuated by the isolation in which the dictatorship maintained the Dominicans. At that time there were no business, professional, student, or workers' associations; Dominicans did not have real experience on democratic political participation after thirty-one years of totalitarian rule; the towns and cities of the interior suffered from their inefficient health and social services, since the urban development of the previous decades had been concentrated on the cities of Santo Domingo, San Cristóbal and Santiago, leaving the other towns of the country practically abandoned; the roads and highways were ruined due to the economic collapse the country suffered in the final stages of the regime.

The point from which the Dominicans had to start in 1961 presented such a bleak prospect that it is indeed very impressive how much the Dominican Republic has changed in the last eighteen years. With Trujillo's death, all the nation's energies were unleashed. The middle classes, which had begun to emerge, started to organize into a visible group of institutions, pressure groups, interest groups, and associations. Thus emerged a new private sector that gradually began to challenge the governmental hegemony that was the norm from Nicolás de Ovando (1502) to the Consejo de Estado (1962).

On the other hand, the political control that prevented the Dominicans from fully exercising free enterprise was lifted. Recent governments have allowed free competition against the former Trujilloist monopolies that became state property after the death of the dictator. The emergence of a new business sector has been a factor behind a new economic nationalism. Let's keep in mind that in 1941, for example, foreigners controlled eighty-seven percent of the industrial investment in the Dominican Republic. Today, thanks to the proliferation of nationalized industries, foreign control of this sector has fallen to thirty-four percent.

However, the gradual nationalization of the Dominican

industry, which began in the 1950s with the purchase the for-
eign-owned sugar mills, has not been without its consequences.
The country's recent industrial development has been financed
by foreign loans and aid. As a result, the Dominican Republic
has become indebted once more, following a period of fifteen
years during which the external debt was practically nonexistent. In a country with a limited domestic economy, the only
way to resume industrial development was by attracting foreign
capital. This is in fact what has happened as the World Bank,
the Interamerican Development Bank (IDB), the International
Development Agency (USAID) and the International Monetary Fund (IMF), increased their operations since 1962 within
the framework of the Alliance for Progress.

Thanks to the enormous flow of dollars from abroad over the
last two decades, monetary circulation has risen to unprecedented levels, and trade has expanded with the proliferation of
companies, a fact that have helped stimulate economic compet-
itiveness. It has also made possible the development of a national banking sector, which today has over fifty financial institutions in the country, including home savings and loans institutions, as well as insurance companies. The mere presence of a
large number of financial institutions is a clear sign that capitalism has finally arrived at the Dominican Republic, leaving
behind the traditional and semi-feudal economic institutions
that were the norm for centuries. In fact, no more than twenty-
five years ago (in the 1950s), peasants came to the cities to
exchange hens and pigs for clothing and shoes, which was clear
evidence of the backwardness of the monetary economy.

Population growth, and the resulting growth of the cities, plus
the aforementioned expansion of monetary circulation, enable
us to understand the industrial and commercial development of

the Dominican Republic between 1961 and 1981, since it has only been in the last ten years that one can speak of the development of an internal market capable of demanding and consuming all of the country's industrial production. Official figures from the 1950s show that the domestic market was not large enough to consume the internal production of rice, corn, plantains, bananas, *yuca*, and meat. Aggregate demand has grown so much over the past eighteen years that the country has been forced to import large quantities of basic foodstuffs. In fact, in 1981 forty percent of its import spending goes to food from abroad.

The expansion of the domestic market has meant that all types of businesses have proliferated, especially in the area of services. Thus the Dominican Republic has finally witnessed the emergence of a vigorous new middle class. Its size can be measured from such indicators as the number of telephones, the number of private and public vehicles, the number of homes owned that were built under the savings and loans system, the number of professionals graduating from our universities, the number of mid-level workers joining the thousands of firms and offices that have opened all over the country, and, if these figures could be broken down, the number of taxpayers with sizeable earnings who are registered for income tax.

The new Dominican middle class differs considerably from the middle sectors that formed before the Second World War in the bigger Latin American countries. To its credit, it has contributed to the growing democratization of the Dominican Republic through its political resistance to any new form of dictatorship. Until now, this emergent middle class has prevented the country from returning to tyranny or lapsing into communism.

The families that compose this middle class were for centuries deprived of the most minimal gratifications, and now appear extremely reluctant to forego the pleasures of consumption. This middle class genuinely feels entitled to any form of conspicuous consumption after having been bombarded with images of the "American way of life" in the cinema, press, radio and television, which constantly show how the middle class lives in other modern and developed countries, particularly the United States. This middle class has indeed emerged from the climate of entrepreneurial freedom of the past twenty years, and it will fight to its death before allowing any of its civil and economic rights to be taken away.

Another phenomenon that has accompanied the flourishing of the social, institutional and economic life of the Dominican Republic in the last two decades is the proliferation of ideological political parties. This is also a recent development. Until Trujillo's death all the parties in the country were personalistic and *caudillista* organizations, which fought for power on the simple proposition of wealth acquisition and the preservation of personal relationships based on clientelism under the protection of a *caudillo*.

Most of the Dominican political parties are immersed in a social context that preserves many traditional political forms, and they have not completely disengaged from *caudillismo*. However, they have gradually lined up behind contemporary social ideologies that are very much in vogue globally, indicating a determination by their leaders to update the terms of reference for political participation in the Dominican Republic. The growth of industry, as well as the activities of the political parties, has also contributed to the development of trade unionism by boosting hundreds of labor organizations. This was unthinkable just thirty years ago when the main industrial firms outside of the sugar industry had no more than fifteen employees.

In the face of the constant pressure created by the demand for new services such as water, electricity, telephone, sewage and schools, the governments have relied on international assistance to meet these basic needs of the population, bringing aqueducts and electricity to most towns, and extending these and other services to the rural population. As a result, the modernization of the cities is rapidly reaching the countryside because local roads are being built continuously.

The motorcycle, radio and television have reached the most remote rural communities, shrinking and often eliminating the cultural distances that previously existed between countryside and city. There are rural areas of the Dominican Republic, such as the central Cibao valley, where the boundaries between rural and urban are rapidly disappearing, and where communities that until recently had a peasant existence are being converted into suburban communities whose population now commutes to the nearby cities to sell their labor, get an education, and buy goods and services.

This modernization has not necessarily benefited everyone. In fact, the city's easier access to the countryside has placed the peasants at the mercy of the city businessman with sufficient capital, education, and technology to appropriate their lands more efficiently. The former inhabitants of these lands have been forced to relocate to the deprived urban barrios and *favelas*, or become members of the large agricultural proletariat that is growing day by day in the countryside. They provide an easy target for the new political demagogues that have emerged as a result of the country's political democratization and are exploiting a new phenomenon that was previously non-existent in the Dominican Republic: peasant movements that continually organize to illegally squatter in private lands with the support of some political organizations.

Much of the recent Dominican political instability arises out of the dissatisfaction of those large sectors of the population who have not been able to benefit from the advantages of modernization. Yet they have been sensitized by the new ideas that have reached the country in recent years and by the new political ideas regularly taught in the classrooms and disseminated in the media. As a result, the Dominican population of today is better educated politically than it was thirty years ago, but the expectations created in the masses by this education is at variance with the huge gap between them, the new middle class, and the nouveau riche elite.

From now on, the political conflicts in the Dominican Republic will not result from fighting among *caudillos* but from clashes between social groups with diverse interests. The new ideas and contemporary social ideologies will play a decisive role in Dominican political life over the next twenty years.

When speaking of new ideas one must bear in mind other cultural changes that have also taken place regarding the racial self-identification of Dominicans. Migration to the United States has brought tens of thousands of men and women into contact with a social reality that has enabled them to discover that they form part of a larger Caribbean social environment. Contact with other minorities and groups of color in the United States has allowed Dominicans to identify themselves as a group that descends from black African slaves and white Spanish immigrants, and yet not lose sight of their diversity in comparison to the Haitians.

Both migration and tourism have contributed to this discovery of ethnic roots and the formation of new attitudes to the question of race. Increasingly, Dominicans are now beginning to realize that they form a mulatto community that was hispanicized as a result of the long colonial coexistence, but which has been notably influenced by the coming and going of Haitian workers throughout this century.

In New York and other parts of the United States, the Dominicans discovered what many Puerto Ricans had found out decades before: it did not matter what they considered themselves to be, since, objectively speaking, they descended from Spanish colonists and African slaves. Half of a Dominican's origin is actually not so different from that of a Haitian. One can argue a great deal about this, but it seems that the discovery of Dominican negritude occurred on two different levels. One, as has been mentioned, was the result of the contact between Dominicans and people of color and other minorities in the United States at a time when the civil rights movement shook the United States and radically overturned art, literature as well as the media, especially in the latter half of the 1960s. A second level was of an ideological nature, and this began to manifest itself among professional groups and university intellectuals of Marxist orientation, who from 1966 on began to draw attention to what they termed "the racial and cultural alienation of the Dominican people."

Although initially unpopular, the sustained campaign of those intellectuals has gradually caught on among different urban sectors of the Dominican population who, sensitized by the experience of racial inferiority felt by many Dominican families in the United States, are slowly rejecting the previous point of view which maintained that the Dominicans were mostly white; they now believe that Dominicans are mainly people of color.

Thus the ways of perceiving race are changing as are the ways of perceiving religion, due to the process of secularization, which is the result of the growing modernization of the cities. In general, the industrialization, urbanization, improved communications, the influx of new ideas and technologies, increased international flights, tourism and migration, and the ongoing influence of the lifestyles of more modern industrialized societies through cinema, radio and television, have all also contributed to the secularization of Dominican life.

This has had a huge impact on religious practices. It seems just yesterday when the enormous Holy Week processions or the religious pilgrimages to Higüey or Santo Cerro brought together tens of thousands of men, women, and children from all over the country, revealing the significant influence of the Church on Dominican life and thought. For a time, the Catholic Church reigned supreme in the Dominican Republic and its influence was undeniable, but the economic and social changes in the country have taken away a lot of legitimacy from the Catholic Church. From a sociological point of view, this institution was better equipped to operate in a traditional society where political and social life were centralized and rigidly hierarchical, and in which the institutional pluralism and the consumerism that we are witnessing today had not become widespread. The Church has only begun to adapt to the changes recently. Instead of opposing them as it did until 1965, it has increasingly committed itself to solutions that promote social justice and respect human rights.

Evidently, all these changes in the economic and social structures have had a profound influence on the cultural and spiritual order and have also affected the sense of national identity. The problem of identity is certainly an ideological phenomenon, but it is also a social fact affected by the dynamics of human relations, which are always changing, fluid and generally difficult to pin down. One cannot engage the question of national identity without taking into account the way Dominicans have examined and thought about themselves throughout history. And this is why, in order to understand how the economic and social changes which occurred in the Dominican Republic in the twentieth century have affected national self-perception, it is necessary to go back in history in order to attempt to define how the Dominicans viewed themselves during the process of modernization.

The remnants of Spanish influences are also disappearing since Spain is no longer the metropolis for the Dominicans. The metropolis has changed. The standards now come from the United States, and Dominicans have adapted admirably to them with an enthusiasm that can only be compared to that felt by the indigenous people in the days when Columbus and his companions exchanged small mirrors and little bells for gold nuggets.

Perhaps it is on account of all these changes that some sensitive souls speak of the loss of national identity and of the need to examine this phenomenon in seminars and intellectual gatherings.

Notes

Chapter 1

1. *Montones* means heaps literally, and in this case, raised mound agriculture.
2. *Castellano* is a Castilian gold coin.
3. *Peonía* is a traditional unit of land area in Spanish-speaking countries. The size varies from country to country. In the Dominican Republic it is equal to 1200 *tareas* or about 75.4 hectares (186.5 acres).
4. *Casabe* is flour or powder made from the root of the *yuca* (cassava plant).
5. *Catibia* is flour made from fresh *yuca*.
6. *Hacer la yucca* is when a young man stands outside the house of a girl to demonstrate his interest in her.
7. *Chola* is a type of bread.
8. *Jagua* is a wild fruit from which juice is extracted.
9. *Sancocho* is a kind of stew.
10. *Hutía* or *Jutía* is a rat-like mammal.
11. Any of several tropical American plants, as in the genus *Lonchocarpus,* which contain a substance that can stun or paralyze fish.
12. *Mambí* referred to an indigenous person who rebelled.
13. *Maniel* was a maroon settlement.
14. *Opias* were mythical wild women who inhabited the mountains and had magical powers; Cemí OPIYELGUOBIRAN was a Dog God; he was chained up during the day, but at night he was released and roamed the forest.
15. *Bienbienes* are the ghosts of runaway slaves.
16. This was a very sacred ceremony performed by both *caciques* and *behiques* (medicine men), during which they inhaled a hallucinogenic powder called *cohoba.*
17. *Brujería* means lit. "witchcraft," but it is also a term commonly used to refer to popular religious practices.
18. *Huaquero* is an illegal excavator of indigenous artefacts.

Chapter 2

1. *Cajuil* is the fruit of the "anacardium occidental" tree.

Chapter 3

1. The distinguished Dominican scientist, José de Jesús Álvarez Perelló,

applied the study of blood groups to anthropology, and by means of a statistical audit established that Dominicans have an indigenous component of 17%, with 43% from the negroid component and 40% from the white component. Álvarez Perelló, José de Jesús, 'La Mezcla de Razas en Santo Domingo y los Factores Sanguíneos," *Eme-Eme, Estudios Dominicanos*, Vol. II, no. 8, p. 87.

2. See Grousse, Renato, *El Hombre y su Historia*, Paris, Plon, 1954, pp. 70, 93, 144.
3. Jean Laloup and Jean Nelis, *Cultura y Civilización*, Vol. III, Ediciones DINOR, San Sebastián, 1962; pp. 50–51.
4. Frank Moya Pons, "Notas para una Historia de la Iglesia en Santo Domingo," *Revista Eme-Eme*, Vol. 1, No. 6, p. 11.
5. Héctor Incháustegui Cabral, *En Elogio a los Viejos*, UCMM, 3 October 1978.
6. Carlos Esteban Deive, *Revista Eme-Eme, Estudios Dominicanos*, Vol VI, no.16, pp. 33–34.
7. Valentina Peguera and Danilo de los Santos, *Visión General de la Historia Dominicana*, UCMM, Santiago, Dominican Republic, 1977, pp. 82–3.
8. José Ignacio Rasco, *Integración Cultural de América Latina*, Talleres Gráficos de la Edit. Benout, SA, Medellín, Colombia, 1975, p. 49.
9. Valentina Peguera and Danilo de los Santos, *Visión General de la Historia Dominicana*, UCMM, Santiago, Dominican Republic, 1977, pp. 83–4.
10. Juan Bosch, *Composición Social Dominicana*, Col. PC, Santo Domingo, Dominican Republic, 1970, p. 9.
11. José Ignacio Rasco, *Integración Cultural de América Latina*, Talleres Gráficos de la Edit. Bedout, SA, Medellín, Colombia, 1975, p. 48.
12. Ramón González Tablas, *Historia de la Dominación y Ultima Guerra de España en Santo Domingo*, Edit. Santo Domingo, Soc. Dom. De Bibliófilos, Inc., Santo Domingo, Dominican Republic, 1974, p. 27.
13. Ibid.
14. See Federico Van Der Meer, *Atlas de la Civilización Occidental*, Brussels-Paris, Elsevier, 1953, passim.
15. F. R. Herrero Miniño, *Raíces, Motivaciones y Fundamentos de la Raza Dominicana, XIX*, Ultima Hora, 22 March 1979.
16. H. Hoetink, *El Pueblo Dominicano, 1850–1900: Apuntes para su Sociología Histórica*, Ediciones UCMM, Santiago, Dominican Republic, 1971, p. 236.
17. J. E. Jiménez Grullón, *La República Dominicana*, Havana, 1940, p. 56.
18. See H. Hoetink, *El Pueblo Dominicano, 1850–1900: Apuntes para su Sociología Histórica*, Ediciones UCMM, Santiago, Dominican Republic,

1971, p. 23.
19. Evaristo Heres Hernández and Javier López Muñoz, *La Inmigración Cubana, 1866–1908*, Rev. Eme-Eme, Estudios Dominicanos, Vol. V, no. 29, p. 55.
20. F. R. Herrera Miniño, *Raíces, Motivaciones y Fundamentos de la Raza Dominicana, (Evolución el pasado: La República desde 1940 a 1978)*, XVI, Ultima Hora, 9 March 1979.
21. Information provided by Doña María Ugarte.
22 José Ignacio Rasco, *Integración Cultural de América Latina*, Medellín, Colombia, 1975, p. 53.
23. Frank Moya Pons, *Historia Colonial de Santo Domingo*, Colección Estudios, UCMM, Santiago, Dominican Republic, pp. 36–7.
24. Frank Moya Pons, *Historia Colonial de Santo Domingo*, Colección Estudios, UCMM, Santiago, Dominican Republic, pp. 45–6.
25. B. Vega, Wenceslao, *Historia del Derecho Colonial Dominicano*, Colección Ensayo, No. 1, Santo Domingo, Dominican Republic, 1978, p. 47.
26. J. E. Jiménez Grullón, *La República Dominicana: una Ficción*, T Q Universitarios, Mérida, Venezuela, 1965, p. 24.
27. José Igancio Rasco, *Integración Cultural de América Latina*, Talleres Gráficos de la Edit. Ebnout, SA, Medellín, Colombia, 1975, p. 80.
28. Edwin Walter Palm, *Los Monumentos Arquitectónicos de la Española*, Vol. 1, Ciudad Trujillo, Dominican Republic, 1955, p. 39.
29. *Cañafístola* is a tree, the pulp of which is used as a laxative.
30. Manuel A. Machado Báez, *Santiagueses Ilustres de la Colonia*, Ediciones Centurión, C por A, 1955, pp. 7–8.
31. B. Vega, Wenceslao, *Historia del Derecho Colonial Dominicano*, Colección Ensayo, No. 1, Santo Domingo, Dominican Republic, 1978, pp. 14–15.
32. Frank Moya Pons, *La Dominación Haitiana*, 2nd edn., Colección Estudios, UCMM, Santiago, Dominican Republic, 1972, pp. 46–7.
33. Edwin Walter Palm, *Los Moumentos Arquitectónicos de la Española*, Vol. 1, Ciudad Trujillo, Dominican Republic, 1955, p. 42.
34. César Nicolás Penson, *Costumbres Antiguas y Modernas de Santo Domingo*, Edit., Fundación García- Arévalo, Inc., Santo Domingo, Dominican Republic, 1978, p. 6.
35. Rafael Bello Peguero, *Cofradía de Nuestra Señora del Carmen y Jesús Nazareno, 1592–1872*, Documentos Eclesiásticos de Santo Domingo, Santo Domingo, Dominican Republic, 1974, pp. xv–xvii.
36. *Moreno* means mulatto.

37. Rafael Bello Peguero, *Cofradía de Nuestra Señora del Carmen y Jesús Nazareno, 1592–1872*, Documentos Eclesiásticos de Santo Domingo. Santo Domingo, Dominican Republic, 1974, pp. xvi.
38. Martha Ellen Davis, "Antecedentes Africanos en Cofradías Españolas?" *El Caribe*, 12 February 1977, p. 2.
39. Monsignor Hugo E. Polanco Brito, *La Parroquia de San José de los Llanos, (Breves Notas Históricas)*, Ciudad Trujillo, Dominican Republic, 1958, pp. 9–10.
40. Writer of local customs and manners.
41. César Nicolás Penson, *Costumbres Antiguas y Modernas de Santo Domingo*, Edit. Fundación García-Arévalo, Inc., Santo Domingo, Dominican Republic, 1978, p. 14.
42. José Federico Arnaiz, S. J., "Nuestra Señora de la Altagracia en América," *Listín Diario (Suplemento)*, 22 January 1977, p. 18.
43. María Ugarte, "Semblante de la Virgen de las Mercedes cambiaba en las distintas celebraciones de Semana Santa," *El Caribe*, 9 April 1979, p. 12.
44. Monsignor Juan F Pepén, *Dónde Floreció el Na*ranjo, 2nd ed., Ciudad Trujillo, Dominican Republic, January 1958, p. 42.
45. Catalogue of the exhibition of Dominican Santos de Palo, Museo del Hombre Dominicano, Santo Domingo, Dominican Republic, May 1978.
46. Emilio Rodríguez Demorizi, *Lengua y Folklore de Santo Domingo*, Colección Estudios, UCMM, Dominican Republic, Santiago, 1975, pp. 197, 209, 232.
47. Emilio Rodríguez Demorizi, *Lengua y Folklore de Santo Domingo*, Colección Estudios, UCMM, Dominican Republic, Santiago, 1975, pp. 16–17.
48. Marcio Veloz Maggiolo, *Cultura, Teatro y Relatos en Santo Domingo*, Col. Contemporáneos, UCMM, Dominican Republic, 1972, p. 159.
49. Marcio Veloz Maggiolo, *Cultura, Teatro y Relatos en Santo Domingo*, Col. Contemporáneos, UCMM, Dominican Republic, 1972, p. 159.
50. Marcio Veloz Maggiolo, *Cultura, Teatro y Relatos en Santo Domingo*, Col. Contemporáneos, UCMM, Dominican Republic, 1972, p. 163.
51. Marcio Veloz Maggiolo, *Cultura, Teatro y Relatos en Santo Domingo*, Col. Contemporáneos, UCMM, Dominican Republic, 1972, p. 162.
52. Bruno Candelier Rosario, *Lo Popular y lo Culto en la Poesía Dominicana*, Col. Estudios, UCMM, Santiago, Dominican Republic, 1977, p. 123.
53. See *Poesía Dominicana*, Santo Domingo, Edit. La Nacional, vol. 1, p. 14. It deals mainly with the popular poets.

54. Max Henríquez Ureña, *La Cultura y las Letras en Santo Domingo*, Buenos Aires, Edit. Raigal, 1952, p. 88.
55. Tomás Hernández Franco, *Apuntes sobre la Poesía Popular y Poesía Negra en las Antillas*, Soc. Dom. de Bibliófilos, Santo Domingo, Dominican Republic, 1978, p. 28.
56. E. Garrido de Bogg, *Folklore Infantil de Santo Domingo*, Madrid, 1955, pp. 24–5.
57. Tomás Hernández Franco, *Apuntes sobre la Poesía Popular y Poesía Negra en las Antillas*, Soc. Dom. De Bibliófilos, Santo Domingo, Dominican Republic, 1978, p. 45.
58. Tomás Hernández Franco, *Apuntes sobre la Poesía Popular y Poesía Negra en las Antillas*, Soc. Dom. De Bibliófilos, Santo Domingo, Dominican Republic, 1978, p. 45.
59. Tomás Hernández Franco, *Apuntes sobre la Poesía Popular y Poesía Negra en las Antillas*, Soc. Dom. De Bibliófilos, Santo Domingo, Dominican Republic, 1978, pp. 49–50.
60. Tomás Hernández Franco, *Apuntes sobre la Poesía Popular y Poesía Negra en las Antillas*, Soc. Dom. De Bibliófilos, Santo Domingo, Dominican Republic, 1978, pp. 49–50.
61. Emilio Rodríguez Demorizi, *Lengua y Folklore de Santo Domingo*, Col. Estudios, UCMM, Santiago, Dominican Republic, 1975, pp. 79–80.
62. Verse from a Dominican popular song.
63. Tomás Hernández Franco, *Apuntes sobre la Poesía Popular y Poesía Negra en las Antillas*, Soc. Dom. De Bibliófilos, Santo Domingo, Dominican Republic, 1978, p. 28.
64. Carlos Dobal, *Arte y Tradición en Santiago de los Caballeros*, Col. Estudios, UCMM, Santiago, Dominican Republic, 1977, p. 83.
65. Ibidem.
66. José Manuel Andrade, *Folklore de la Rep. Dom.*, Edit. De Santo Domingo, SA, Santo Domingo, Dominican Republic, 1976, pp. 564–5.
67. José Manuel Andrade, *Folklore de la Rep. Dom.*, Edit. De Santo Domingo, SA, Santo Domingo, Dominican Republic, 1976, pp. 45–6.
68. Emilio Rodríguez Demorizi, *Lengua y Folklore de Santo Domingo*, Col. Estudios, UCMM, Santiago, Dominican Republic, 1975, p. 242.
69. Julio C. Campillo Pérez, *Santiago de los Caballeros – Imperecedero legado Hispano-Colombino-*, Impresión Amigo del Hogar, UCMM, Santiago, Dominican Republic, 1977, p. 11.
70. Carlos Larrazabal Blanco, *Toponimia*, Soc. Dom. De Geografía, Editora del

Caribe, Santo Domingo, Dominican Republic, 1972, p. 43.
71. Tomás Hernández Franco, *Apuntes sobre la Poesía Popular y Poesía Negra en las Antillas*, Soc. Dominicana de Bibliófilos, Santo Domingo, Dominican Republic, 1978, p. 30.
72. Emilio Rodríguez Demorizi, *Lengua y Folklore de Santo Domingo*, Col. Estudios, UCMM, Santiago, Dominican Republic, 1975, p. 79.
73. Emilio Rodríguez Demorizi, *Música y Baile en Santo Domingo*, 1971, p. 176.
74. Fradique Lizardo, *Danzas y Bailes Folklóricos*, Col. Investigaciones no. 2, Santo Domingo, Dominican Republic, 1974, p. 257.
75. Programa del Teatro de UCMM, *Ballet Folklórico Dominicano*, Fradique Lizardo, 17 January 1979.
76. Flérida (de) Nolasco, *Vibraciones en el Tiempo*, p. 139–44.
77. Luis Alberti, "De Música y Orquestas Bailables Dominicanas 1910–1959," Edit. Taller, Santo Domingo, Dominican Republic, 1975, p. 71.
78. Fradique Lizardo, *Danzas y Bailes Folklóricos Dominicanos*, Col. Investigaciones, Santo Domingo, Dominican Republic, 1975, p. 71.
79. *Autosacramentales* are religious plays resembling English mystery plays.
80. Fradique Lizardo, *Danzas y Bailes Folklóricos Dominicanos*, Col. Investigaciones, Santo Domingo, Dominican Republic, 1975, p. 144.
81. Ibid.
82. Fradique Lizardo, *Danzas y Bailes Folklóricos Dominicanos*, Col. Investigaciones, Santo Domingo, Dominican Republic, 1975, p. 153.
83. Valentina Peguera and Danilo de los Santos. *Visión General de la Historia Dominicana*, UCMM, Sntiago, Dominican Republic, 1977, pp. 85–6.
84. Holger R. Escoto F., *Historia de la Arquitectura Dominicana*, Santiago, Dominican Republic, 1978, p. 77.
85. Marcio Veloz Maggiolo, *Cultura, Teatro y Relatos en Santo Domingo*, Col. Contemporánea, UCMM, Santiago, Dominican Republic, 1972, p. 158.
86. Roberto Cassá, *Los Taínos de la Española*, Col. Historia y Sociedad, no. 11, Edit. De la UASD, Santo Domingo, Dominican Republic, 1974, pp. 89–91.
87. Luis S. Escobal, *Biografía de la Catedral Primada de las Indias*, Editora Alfa y Omega, Santo Domingo, Dominican Republic, 1977, p. 12.
88. Valentina Peguera and Danilo de los Santos, *Visión General de la Historia Dominicana*, UCMM, Santiago, Dominican Republic, 1977, pp. 89–90.
89. Julio Genaro Campillo Pérez, *La Nueva Torre de Santiago*, Editora del Listín Diario, 28 March 1979, p. 6.
90. Emilio Rodríguez Demorizi, *España y los Comienzos de la Pintura y Escultura en América*, Gráficas Reunidas, SA, Madrid, 1966, pp. 41–51.

91. Valentina Peguera and Danilo de los Santos. *Visión General de la Historia Dominicana*, UCMM, Santiago, Dominican Republic, 1977, pp. 8, 91.

92. Marqués de Lozoya, "Prólogo de la obra de Emilio Rodríguez Demorizi," *España y los Comienzos de la Pintura en América*, Gráficas Reunidas, Madrid, 1966.

93. Carlos Dobal, *Antigüedades, Arte y Tradición en Santiago de los Caballeros*, Col. Estudios, UCMM, Santiago, Dominican Republic, 1977.

94. Emilio Rodriguez Demorizi, *Pintura y Escultura en Santo Domingo*, Col. Pensamiento Dominicano, Santo Domingo, Dominican Republic, 1972, p. 49.

95. Emilio Rodriguez Demorizi, *Pintura y Escultura en Santo Domingo*, Col. Pensamiento Dominicano, Santo Domingo, Dominican Republic, 1972, p. 60.

96. Darío Suro, *Arte Dominicano*, Col. Pensamiento y Cultural, Santo Domingo, Dominican Republic, 1972, p. 60.

97. Ibidem.

98. *Lechones* means devil masks.

99. Carlos Dobal, *Antigüedades, Arte y Tradición en Santiago de los Caballeros*, Col. Estudios, UCMM, Santiago, Dominican Republic, 1977, pp. 198–9.

100. Roberto Cassá, *Los Taínos de la Española*, Editora de la UASD, Col. Historia y Sociedad, no. 11 , Santo Domingo, Dominican Republic, 1974, p. 201.

101. María Ugarte, "Personajes de la Colonia," *El Caribe*, 8 October 1977, p. 12.

102. Fray Vicente Rubio, O. P., *Datos para la Historia de los Orígenes de la Cuidad de Santo Domingo*, Ediciones Fundación García-Arévalo, Inc., Santo Domingo, Dominican Republic, 1978, p. 11.

103. Eugenio Pérez Montas, *Arq. Estudio para la Revalorización de la Zona Histórica y Monumental de la Ciudad de Santo Domingo*, Dominican Republic, 1973, p. 15.

104. Julio G. Campillo Pérez, *Santiago de los Caballeros: Imperecedero legado Hispano-Colombino-*, Impresión Amigo del Hogar, UCMM, Santiago, Dominican Republic, 1977, p. 33.

105. José Ignacio Rasco, *Integración Cultural de América Latina*, Talleres Gráficos de la Edit. Benout, SA, Medellín, Colombia, 1975, p. 53.

106. Ibidem.

107. Francisco de Ayala, *Situación de la Cultura Española en Originalidad de la Culturas*, UNESCO, pp. 255–63.

108. *Fueros* were charters granted to villages, towns and regions by the Spanish monarchs in the Middle Ages and in which rights and obligations established.

109. Joaquín Balaguer, *El Cristo de la Libertad*, Edición Especial, Santo Domingo, Dominican Republic, 1970, p. 38.

110. Gregorio Luperón. *Notas Autobiográficos y Apuntes Históricos. Col. Cultura Dom.*, vol. I, Edit. Santo Domingo, SA, Santo Domingo, Dominican Republic, 1974, pp. 117–8.

111. Ramón González Tablas, *Historia de la Dominación y Ultima Guerra de España en Santo Domingo*, Edit. Santo Domingo Soc. Dom. De Bibliófilos, Inc., Santo Domingo, Dominican Republic, 1974, p. 40.

112. José Ramón López, taken from Joaquín Balaguer, *El gran pesimismo dominicano*, Col. Estudios, UCMM, Santiago, Dominican Republic, 1975, p. 13.

113. Juan Daniel Balcácer, *Diario de Eugenio Perdomo*, Santo Domingo, Dominican Republic, 1978, p. 15.

114. *Morisco* is a Muslim convert to Christianity; *Mudéjar* is a Muslim permitted to live under Christian rule.

115. Frank Moya Pons, *Historia Colonial de Santo Domingo*, Col. Estudios, UCMM, Santiago, Dominican Republic, 1976, pp. 36–7.

116. F. R. Herrera Miniño, *Motivaciones, Raíces y Fundamentos de la Raza Dominicana (Raíces Históricas)*, III, Ultima Hora, 11 January 1979.

117. Marcio Veloz Maggiolo, *Cultura, Teatro y Relatos en Santo Domingo*, Col. Contemporanoes, UCMM, Dominican Republic, 1972, p. 157.

118. Pedro J. Santiago, *El Escudo de Armas de la Ciudad de Santiago*, Santo Domingo, Dominican Republic, 1977, p. 5.

119. David Dixon Porter, *Diario de una Misión Secreta a Santo Domingo*, Edit. Santo Domingo, Santo Domingo, Dominican Republic, 1978, pp. 10–11.

120. Marcio Antonio Mejía Ricart, *Las Clases Sociales en Santo Domingo*, Edit. Librería Dom., Cuidad Trujillo, Dominican Republic, 1953, p. 37.

121. Emilio Rodríguez Demorizi, *Lengua y Folklore de Santo Domingo*, Colección Estudios, UCMM, Santiago, Dominican Republic, 1975, pp. 158–9.

122. F. R. Herrera Miniño, *Raíces, Motivaciones y Fundamentos de la Raza Dominicana, (Evolución en el pasado: La Colonia 1492–1844)*, Ultima Hora, 9 February 1979.

123. F. R. Herrera Miniño, *Raíces, Motivaciones y Fundamentos de la Raza Dominicana, (Evolución en el pasado: La Colonia 1492–1844)*, Ultima

Hora, 4 January 1979.

124. Gregorio Luperón. *Notas Autobiográficas y Apuntes Históricos*, Col. Cultura Dom., vol. I, Edit. Santo Domingo, SA, Santo Domingo, Dominican Republic, 1974, p. 117.

Chapter 4

1. *Maniel* referred to a community of runaway slaves.
2. *Calenda* is a type of stick-fighting dance.
3. Spanish slave legislation was based on thirteenth century law called the *Siete Partidas* of Alfonso X the Wise.
4. *Ladino* is Spanish-speaking Christianized African.
5. *Bozal* was used to refer to recent arrivals from Africa who couldn't speak Spanish. (Derived from *bozal*, the muzzle used to restrain untamed animal.)
6. A *pieza de India* was a male slave with no physical defects.
7. *Yautía* is a tropical American aroid with edible tubers that is cooked and eaten like yams or potatoes, tannia.
8. In Spanish America, the term *carabalí* included a number of ethnicities: Efik, Qua-Ejagham, Efut, Ibibio, Igbo and Ijaw.

Chapter 5

1. *Situado* is a portion of the revenue from mines in New Spain.
2. *Peninsular* is a person born in Spain.
3. *Africa en América Latina*, p. 340.
4. *Etude sur le culture dans les côtes Colombiennes sur la mer Caribe*, p. 15.

Chapter 6

1. Ralph Linton, *Cultura y Personalidad*, Mexico/Buenos Aires: FCE, 1967, p. 43.
2. Ibidem, p. 45.
3. Ibidem, p. 51; see also Ralph Linton, *Estudio del Hombre*, Mexico/Buenos Aires: FCE, 1965; Bronislaw Malinowski, *Una teoría científica de la cultura*, Buenos Aires: Edit. Sudamericana, 1967; C. and Kelly Klickhohn, "The Concept of Culture," in Ralph Linton, *The Science of Man in the World Crisis*, 1945; A. L. Kroeber, *Antropología General*, 1948.
4. José Del Castillo and Walter Cordero, *La Economía Dominicana durante el Primer Cuarto del Siglo XX*, Fundación García Arévalo, Santo Domingo, 1979, p. 12.

5. Ibidem, p. 11.

6. Havana: Editorial de las Ciencias Sociales, 1970.

7. Claude Fohlen and François Bédarida, "La Era de las Revoluciones (1760–1914)," in Parias, Louis-Henri, ed., *Historia General del Trabajo*, vol. III, Mexico/Barcelona: Ediciones Grijalbo, 1965, pp. 283–9.

8. Ibidem, p. 130.

9. Nicholas S. Timasheff, *La teoría sociológica*, Mexico/Buenos Aires, Fondo de Cultura Económica, 1963, pp. 31–48; Armand Cuvilier, *Manual de Sociología*, Buenos Aires: Editorial "El Ateneo," 1963, pp. 28–39.

10. Ibidem, pp. 49–63 and 45–8.

11. See Walter Montenegro, *Introducción a las doctrinas politico-económicas*, Mexico/Buenos Aires: Fondo de Cultura Económica, pp. 23–47.

12. On positivism in Latin America, see Ralph Lee Woodward Jr., ed., *Positivism in Latin America, 1850–1900*, Lexington/Toronto/London: DC Heath and Co., 1971; see also José Luis Romero, *Latinoamérica: las ciudades y las ideas*, Mexico: Siglo XXI, 1976, pp. 307–18; Pedro Henríquez Ureña, *Historia de la Cultura en América Latina*, Mexico: Fondo de Cultura Económica, 1975, pp. 110–127.

13. There is an extensive and ever-growing bibiliography on the regime of Ulises Heureaux, known as Lilís. However, much of it wrongly interprets him and his role within the context of his activities as Head of State. A large number of the traditional authors, unreservedly upholding a view that privileges the role of the individual in historical events, show Lilís as a despot, motivated solely by personal control of power and its rewards. This tendency tends to ignore an analysis of the context in which Lilís was operating. In this way, class analysis, a study of the economy, of international relations and of the range of ideas of the era are absent from these evaluations. This distorts Lilís' image and tarnishes his role. Nevertheless, studies carried out more recently by experts in the social sciences are increasingly making possible an appropriate and dispassionate appreciation of Heureaux's regime. The pioneer of this trend has been Harry Hoetink with his excellent and stimulating *El Pueblo Dominicano: 1850–1900*, UCMM, Santiago, 1971. The space opened up by Hoetink has been explored by many authors, especially young American and Dominican professionals who are too numerous to list here.

Modern Mexican historiography and studies in the social sciences (political science, sociology, and economics) have shed new light on the regime of Díaz. An eloquent example of this line of analysis is the work of Juan Felipe Leal, *La burguesía y el Estado mexicano*, Ediciones "El Caballito," Mexico, 1974, which refers to the matter thus:

The measures that the liberals put forward once they were in power were notably different from the theoretical model. Both the governments of Juarez and Lerdo as well as that of Díaz later on, were characterized by the establishment of a strong, centralized State and by the concentration of power in the hands of the executive. The legislative chambers could not function independently, the judicial power found itself to be impotent, the States were losing their powers and popular suffrage was disabled. The doctrine of free exchange had to adjust to the demands of a taxation system that obtained most of its income from customs duties; to the conditions created by the depreciation of silver which created de facto protectionism; to the sales taxes imposed by the States and the town councils, as well as the direct participation of the State in certain areas of the economy. The dissolution of the ecclesiastical and indigenous land-holdings did not lead to medium-sized commercial agriculture but to the expansion of the large *haciendas* and the prohibition by law of enforced labor. In practice this meant the systems of coercive labor were reinforced. (66)

14. Pedro Henríquez Ureña, "La Antigua sociedad patriarcal de las Antillas. Modalidades arcaicas de la vida en Santo Domingo durante el siglo XIX," in *Obras Completas*, UNDHU, Santo Domingo, 1978, vol. v, 1921–1925.

15. Emilio Rodríguez Demorizi, ed., *Informe de la Comisión de Investigación de los EUA en Santo Domingo en 1871*, Ciudad Trujillo: Edit. Montalvo, 1960, pp. 74–5.

16. Vicente Tolentino Rojas, "Población del Santo Domingo Español," *Ciencia*, 2 (4), Oct–Dec 1975, pp. 128–9.

17. Frank Moya Pons, "Nuevas consideraciones sobre la historia de la población dominicana: curves, tasas y prblemas," *EME EME Estudios Dominicanos*, 15, Nov–Dec 1974, pp. 3–28.

18. See Jean Stephens, "La inmigración de negros norteamericanos en Haiti en 1824," *EME EME Estudios Dominicanos*, 14, Sept–Oct 1974, pp. 40–71; José Augusto Puig, *Emigración de Libertos Norteamericanos a Puerto Plata en la Primera Mitad del Siglo XIX. La Iglesia Metodista Wesleyana*, Santo Domingo: Alfa y Omega, 1978.

19. "Sobre Inmigración," *El Dominicano*, 23 October 1845.

20. See Alonso Rodríguez Demorizi, "Provincia de Puerto Rico," in Emilio Rodríguez Demorizi, *Noticias de Puerto Plata*, Santo Domingo: Editora Educative Dominicana, 1975, p. 92; Del Castillo, José, *La inmigración de braceros azucareros en la República Dominicana, 1900–1930*, Cuadernos de la CENDIA, UASD, Santo Domingo, 1978, pp. 43–9.

21. Joaquín Balaguer, *La Realidad Dominicana*, Buenos Aires: Imp. Ferrari

Hermanos, 1947, pp. 28–39.
22. H. Hoetink, Op. cit., pp. 70–5.
23. *Patente* is an annual tax paid to obtain authorization to run a commercial, industrial or professional enterprise.
24. E. M. Hostos "Inmigración y Colonización" and "Centro de Inmigración y Colonias Agrícolas," in Emilio Rodríguez Demorizi, ed., *Hostos en Santo Domingo*, Ciudad Trujillo: Imp. J. R. Vda García, 1939, vol. 1, pp. 85–95 and 177–82.
25. Although San José de Ocoa appeared, according to the administrative-political division of that period, as a municipality of the province of Azua, it is included in the records relating to foreigners corresponding to the province of Santo Domingo. This latter province included San Cristóbal, Baní, Guerra, Los Llanos, Bayaguana, Monte Plata, Boyá, San Carlos and La Victoria as municipalities, and the cantons of Pajarito, Sabana Grande and Yamasá. See Tolentino, Vicente, *Historia de la division territorial, 1492–1943*. Santiago: Colección Trujillo, Editorial El Diario, 1944, pp. 170–77.
26. *Quintal* is 100 lbs.
27. José del Castillo, unpublished work.
28. *Guarapo* is sugar cane juice.
29. See José del Castillo, "Fichas de Historia Azucarera. La Isabel," *Azúcar y Diversificación*, no. 36, Aug 1977, pp. 13–14.
30. José del Castillo, unpublished work.
31. A *tarea* is a Dominican measure equivalent to 619 square meters.
32. Ibidem.
33. Juan J. Sánchez, *La Caña en Santo Domingo*, Santo Domingo: Editora Taller, 1972, pp. 43–44.
34. The IAD is the public institution for agrarian reform.
35. José del Castillo, unpublished text.
36. Juan J. Sánchez, Op. cit., p. 56.
37. José del Castillo, unpublished text.
38. Ibidem.
39. Ibidem.
40. Ibidem.
41. Ibidem.
42. Ibidem.
43. Ibidem.
44. "Proyecto de Cables i líneas telefónicas. Algunas observaciones," *El Eco de la Opinión*, 22 January 1886.

45. "Directorio del Teléfono," *El Eco de la Opinión*, 1888.
46. Federico García Godoy, "El Ferrocarril del Cibao," *Eco de la Opinión*, 14 May 1887.
47. H. Hoetink, Op. cit., p. 100.
48. "Centro Comerciales," *Eco de la Opinión*, 15 August 1884.
49. Cited from the *Informe de la Comisión de Investigación de los EUA en Santo Domingo en 1871*, p. 286 in Hoetink, H., Op. cit., p. 58.
50. Enrique Deschamps, *La República Dominicana. Directorio y Guía General*, Santo Domingo: Editora de Santo Domingo, 1974.
51. H. Hoetink, Op. cit., pp. 51–2.
52. *Santo Domingo (A Handbook)*. Bureau of the American Republics, Washington, Government Printing Office, 1894.
53. H. Hoetink, Op. cit., p. 68.
54. Compañía Biográfica, *Libro Azul de Santo Domingo*, New York: Klebold Press, 1920, p. 142.
55. H. Hoetink, Op. cit., p. 68.
56. Compañía Biográfica, Op. cit., p. 53. Terk also appeared as a silent partner in the firm Juan Elías & Cía, founded in 1918. See p. 55.
57. See Emilio Rodríguez Demorizi, *Noticias de Puerto Plata*, Santo Domingo: Edit. Educativa Dominicana, 1975; ___ *Sociedades, Cofradías, Escuelas, Gremios y otras corporaciones dominicanas*, Santo Domingo: Edit. Educativa Dominicana, 1975; ___ *Luperón y Hostos*, Santo Domingo: Editora Taller, 1975; Tolentino, Hugo, *Gregorio Luperón (Biografía Política)*, Santo Domingo: Alfa y Omega, 1977.
58. Marcos Martínez Paulino, *Publicaciones Dominicanas desde la Colonia*, Santo Domingo: Editora del Caribe, 1973.
59. Evaristo Heres Hernández and Javier López Muñoz, "La inmigración Cubana y su Influencia en Santiago de los Caballeros en el Siglo XIX (1868–1908)," *EME EME Estudios Dominicanos*, 29, Mar–Apr 1977, pp. 55–104.
60. Joaquín S. Inchaústegui, *Reseña Histórica de Baní*, Valencia: Editorial Guerri, 1930, p. 144.
61. See Emilio Rodríguez Demorizi, *Hostos en Santo Domingo*, Ciudad Trujillo: Imp. J. R. Vda García, 1939, vols I and II; *La influencia de Hostos en la Cultura Dominicana (Respuestas a la encuesta de EL CARIBE)*, Ciudad Trujillo: Editora del Caribe, 1956; Juan Bosch, *Hostos el Sembrador*, Río Piedras: ediciones huracán, 1976; for Hostos' works see *Moral Social*, Buenos Aires: Editorial Losada, 1939 and *Tratado de Sociología*, Buenos

Aires: Edit. EL ATENEO, 1941.

62. Evaristo Heres Hernández and Javier López Muñoz, Op. cit.

63. José del Castillo, *La Inmigración de braceros azucareros en la República Dominicana, 1900–1930*, Cuadernos del CENDIA, UASD, Santo Domingo, 1978, pp. 52–3.

64. Samuel Hazard, *Santo Domingo, Su Pasado y Presente*, Santo Domingo: Editora de Santo Domingo, 1974, p. 181.

65. See Julio César Mota Acosta, *Los cocolos en Santo Domingo*, Santo Domingo: Editorial La Gaviota, 1977; Francisco Richiez Acevedo, *Cocolandia*, mimeo, 1967; Patrick Bryan, *En torno a la recepción de los cocolos en la República Dominicana*, UASD, mimeo, Santo Domingo, 1973.

66. Today Marcus Garvey is considered one of the three founding fathers of Jamaican nationality, along with Sir Alexander Bustamente and Michael Manley Sr. On Garvey and his movement, see Clarke, John Henrik, ed., *Marcus Garvey and the Vision of Africa*, New York: Random House, 1973.

67. José del Castillo, unpublished text.

68. Ibidem.

69. Joaquín Balaguer, Op. cit., pp. 102–5.

70. *Humor y Comercio*, 14 December 1930.

71. *Humor y Comercio*, 3 July 1927.

72. Juan Antonio Alix, *Décimas*, Santo Domingo: Librería Dominicana, 1969, vol. II, pp. 43–5.

73. *Lugarú* is someone who can turn into animals; it is also a word derived from the French *loup-garou* meaning werewolf.

Selected Bibliography

Compiled by Ernesto Sagás

Atkins, G. Pope. 1981. *Arms and Politics in the Dominican Republic.* Boulder, CO: Westview Press.

Atkins, G. Pope, and Larman C. Wilson. 1998. *The Dominican Republic and the United States: From Imperialism to Transnationalism.* Athens, GA: University of Georgia Press.

Austerlitz, Paul. 1997. *Merengue: Dominican Music and Dominican Identity.* Philadelphia, PA: Temple University Press.

Baud, Michiel. 1995. *Peasants and Tobacco in the Dominican Republic, 1870–1930.* Knoxville, TN: University of Tennessee Press.

Betances, Emelio. 1995. *State and Society in the Dominican Republic.* Boulder, CO: Westview Press.

Betances, Emelio, and Hobart A. Spalding, Jr., eds. 1995. *The Dominican Republic Today: Realities and Perspectives.* New York: City University of New York.

Black, Jan K. 1986. *The Dominican Republic: Politics and Development in an Unsovereign State.* Boulder, CO: Westview Press.

Calder, Bruce. 2005 (1984). *The Impact of Intervention: The Dominican Republic During the U.S. Occupation of 1916–1924.* Princeton, NJ: Markus Wiener Publishers.

Gleijeses, Piero. 1979. *The Dominican Crisis: The 1965 Constitutionalist Revolt and American Intervention.* Baltimore, MD: Johns Hopkins University Press.

Hall, Michael R. 2000. *Sugar and Power in the Dominican Republic: Eisenhower, Kennedy and the Trujillos.* Westport, CT: Greenwood.

Hartlyn, Jonathan. 1998. *The Struggle for Democratic Politics in the Dominican Republic, 1961–1996.* Chapel Hill, NC: University of North Carolina Press.

Hoetink, Harry. 1961. *The Dominican People, 1850–1900: Notes for an Historical Sociology.* Baltimore, MD: Johns Hopkins University Press.

Kryzanek, Michael J., and Howard J. Wiarda. 1988. *The Politics of External Influence in the Dominican Republic.* Westport, CT: Greenwood.

Lowenthal, Abraham F. 1972. *Dominican Intervention*. Cambridge, MA: Harvard University Press.

Lundius, Jan, and Mats Lundahl. 1999. *Peasants and Religion: A Socioeconomic Study of Dios Olivorio and the Palma Sola Movement in the Dominican Republic*. Oxford: Routledge.

Martínez-Vergne, Teresita. 2005. *Nation and Citizen in the Dominican Republic, 1880–1916*. Chapel Hill: University of North Carolina Press.

Moya Pons, Frank. 1998. *The Dominican Republic: A National History*. 2nd ed. Princeton, NJ: Markus Wiener Publishers.

Nelson, William J. 1990. *Almost a Territory: America's Attempt to Annex the Dominican Republic*. Newark, DE: University of Delaware Press.

Pacini Hernandez, Deborah. 1995. *Bachata: Social History of a Dominican Popular Music*. Philadelphia: Temple University Press.

Palmer, Bruce, Jr. 1989. *Intervention in the Caribbean: The Dominican Crises of 1965*. Lexington, KT: University Press of Kentucky.

Peguero, Valentina. 2004. *The Militarization of Culture in the Dominican Republic, from the Captains General to General Trujillo*. Lincoln, NE: University of Nebraska Press.

Roorda, Eric. 1998. *The Dictator Next Door: The Good Neighbor Policy and the Trujillo Regime in the Dominican Republic, 1930–1945*. Durham, NC: Duke University Press.

Sagás, Ernesto. 2000. *Race and Politics in the Dominican Republic*. Gainesville, FL: University Press of Florida.

Sagás, Ernesto, and Orlando Inoa, eds. 2003. *The Dominican People: A Documentary History*. Princeton, NJ: Markus Wiener Publishers.

Sharpe, Kenneth E. 1991. *Peasant Politics: Struggle in a Dominican Village*. Baltimore, MD: Johns Hopkins University Press.

Turits, Richard L. 2002. *Foundations of Despotism: Peasants, the Trujillo Regime, and Modernity in Dominican History*. Stanford, CA: Stanford University Press.

Wiarda, Howard J. 1968. *Dictatorship and Development: The Methods of Control in Trujillo's Dominican Republic*. Gainesville: University of Florida Press.

Wiarda, Howard J., and Michael J. Kryzanek. 1981. *The Dominican Republic: A Caribbean Crucible*. Boulder, CO: Westview Press.

Notes on Contributors

José del Castillo Pichardo is a sociologist, historian and essayist. He studied sociology, economic development and international relations at the Universidad de Chile. For the past ten years, he has been Advisor to the Governors of the Central Bank. He was also a lecturer and researcher for thirty-six years, heading the department of Investigaciones Científicas at the Universidad Autónoma de Santo Domingo and the Museo del Hombre Dominicano. He is a national and international consultant. His most recent works are the collection of essays *Agenda de Fin de Siglo* and *El Bolero, Visiones y Perfiles de una Pasión Dominicana*, with Marcio Veloz Maggiolo and Pedro Delgado Malagón.

Carlos Esteban Deive is a well-known Dominican writer and researcher. He was director of the Department of Social Sciences of the Museo del Hombre Dominicano and dean of the humanities faculty at the Universidad Nacional Pedro Henríquez Ureña (UNPHU). He has also been the cultural attaché at the Dominican embassy in Madrid and president of the Feria Internacional del Libro in Santo Domingo. Among his various awards are the Premios de Ensayo y Novela Siboney; the Premio Nacional de Historia (twice); the Premio Nacional de Ensayo; and the Premios Caobo of the Academia de Ciencias y Nacional in recognition of his life's work. He recently received the Premio de Novela "Edilio Rusconi," sponsored by the Italian foundation, for his story "El festín de los generales." He is the author of more than twenty books, among which are *Vodú y Magia en Santo Domingo, La esclavitud del negro en Santo Domingo, La Española y la esclavitud del indio*, and *Heterodoxia e inquisición en Santo Domingo*.

Carlos Dobal studied at the faculties of law and social sciences of the University of Havana, where he obtained his doctorate, and at the Escuela Posgraduada para Profesores de Literatura y Arte in the Humanities Faculty of the Universidad Central de Madrid. He has published many pamphlets, essays and articles, organized courses and given numerous lectures and talks on historical and artistic themes. He received the national awards of the Order of Carlos Manuel de Céspedes in Cuba in 1952 and the Order of Vasco Núñez de Balboa from Panama as well as the Equestrian Order of St. Sylvester the Pope, from the Vatican. Dobal was a professor at the Universidad Católica Santo Tomás de Villanueva in Havana. He also headed the Department of History and Geography and was in charge of the departments of cultural history, art history and the history of political and social ideas at the Pontificia Universidad Católica Madre y Maestra (PUCMM). He was Director of the Diocesan Museum and President of the Comisión Diocesana de Arte Sacro (Diocesan Commission for Sacred Art) in Santiago. In 1986 he was awarded the Premio Nacional de Historia. In 2004 the Santiago Town Council declared him an "Adoptive Son."

Frank Moya Pons is the most widely read Dominican historian. He earned his Ph.D. in Latin American history and economic development at Columbia University. He has taught Dominican history since 1964 and has been a visiting professor of Latin American and Caribbean History at Columbia University (1987–1989), University of Florida (1985, 1989–1992), and the City College of the City University of New York (1993–1999). He was also a professor of Dominican history at the Universidad Católica Madre y Maestra, in Santiago, Dominican Republic (1969–1975). He was the founder and director of the Centro de Estudios Dominicanos, editor of the journal *EME EME*

Estudios Dominicanos, president of the Sociedad Dominicana
de Bibliófilos, secretary of the Academia Dominicana de la
Historia, executive director of the Fondo para el Avance de las
Ciencias Sociales, director of the Museo de las Casas Reales,
and executive secretary of Forum, Inc. More recently, Frank
Moya Pons became the first Minister of the Environment and
Natural Resources of the Dominican Republic (2000–2004). He
has published twenty-seven books and numerous articles,
essays, and studies on Dominican and Caribbean history, and
has edited more than forty volumes on Dominican social and
economic affairs. Among some of his published books are *The
Dominican Republic: A National History* and *Historia Colonial
de Santo Domingo.* He is currently the dean of the Dominican
Academy of History.

Ernesto Sagás is a political science professor at Southern New
Hampshire University and board member of the organization
Vote Now New Hampshire Hispanics. He is the author of *Race
and Politics in the Dominican Republic* and co-editor of *The
Dominican People: A Documentary History.*

Rubén Silié is a graduate of the Department of Sociology of the
Universidad Autónoma de Santo Domingo (UASD). He holds
postgraduate degrees in economic history from the Ecole
Pratique des Hautes Etudes of the University of Paris and the
Instituto Tecnológico de Santo Domingo (INTEC). He has
published several articles on Dominican historiography and is
the author of articles on racial questions as they related to the
colonial period and the current link to the "Haitian problem."
His book, *Economía, esclavitud y población,* won the Juan Pablo
Duarte national prize for history.

Bernardo Vega is a multifaceted author. A full member of the Academia Dominicana de la Historia, he has written twenty-eight books on Dominican history, four of which received the *Premio Nacional de Historia Juan Pablo Duarte*. He was awarded the Premio Nacional Feria del Libro "Don Eduardo León Jimenes" on two occasions. He has also published a novel. In addition, he has published six books on archaeology: *Pictografías, Los metales y los aborigines de la Hispaniola, Los cacicazgos de la Isla Hispaniola* (translated into French by UNESCO), *Santos, shamanes y zemíes, Arte neotaíno* and *La verdadera ubicación del golfo de las Flechas*.

Marcio Veloz Maggiolo is a Dominican writer, archeologist, and diplomat. Awarded numerous national literary prizes, his novels have been translated into several languages. In addition to his well-known poems, short stories, novels, and theater scripts, he has published more than thirty books and hundreds of articles in academic journals, magazines, and newspapers. His publications encompass a wide range of issues, from pre-Columbian Caribbean societies to original cultural studies. Some of his best-known works are *Trujillo, Villa Francisca y otros fantasmas*; *De abril en adelante* (novela); *Ritos de cabaret* (novela); *La Mosca Soldado* (novela); *El hombre acordeón* (novela); *Uña y carne* (novela); *La biografía difusa de Sombra Castañeda* (novela); *La memoria fermentada*; *Cultura, teatro y relatos*; *Judas, el buen ladrón*; *Materia prima* (novela sociológica); *Arqueología prehistórica de Santo Domingo*; *Arqueología de Yuma*; and *Arqueología de la Cueva de Berna*. Marcio Veloz Maggiolo is a Law graduate from Universidad de Santo Domingo and earned a doctoral degree in History at Universidad de Madrid. He has served as the Dominican Republic ambassador to Mexico, Italy, and Peru; the Director of Museo de las Casas Reales; and Undersecretary of Education for Cultural Affairs.

Related Books by Markus Wiener Publishers

The Dominican People: A Documentary History edited by Ernesto Sagás and Orlando Inoa. "Concise and satisfying . . . solid and convincing."
—Hispanic-American Historical Review
HC ISBN 978-1-55876-296-1   PB ISBN 978-1-55876-297-8

The Impact of Intervention: The Dominican Republic during the U.S. Occupation of 1916-1924 by Bruce J. Calder. "A comprehensive and tolerant study, devoid of jargon." *—New York Times Book Review*
PB ISBN 978-1-55876-386-9

The Dominican Republic: A National History by Frank Moya Pons. "Agreeable and clearly written . . . an indispensable reference."
—Hispanic-American Historical Review
HC ISBN 978-1-55876-191-8   PB ISBN 978-1-55876-192-6

History of the Caribbean by Frank Moya Pons. The latest book by this leading historian.   HC ISBN 978-1-55876-414-9   PB ISBN 978-1-55876-415-6

Space and History in the Caribbean by Oruno D. Lara. "Superbly written and ably presented." *—Midwest Book Review*
HC ISBN 978-1-55876-400-2   PB ISBN 978-1-55876-401-9

Caribbean: Sea of the New World by Germán Arciniegas. "A whacking good story." *—San Francisco Chronicle*
PB ISBN 978-1-55876-312-8

Trujillo: The Death of the Dictator by Bernard Diederich. "Superb. . . . A painstaking documentary thriller." *—New Society*
PB ISBN 978-1-55876-206-0

Libète: A Haiti Anthology edited by Charles Arthur and Michael Dash "Indispensable." *—French Review*
PB ISBN 978-1-55876-230-5

History of Puerto Rico: A Panorama of Its People by Fernando Picó. Outstanding Academic Title of the Year. "Excellent . . . inordinately rich."
—Choice
HC ISBN 978-1-55876-370-8   PB ISBN 978-1-55876-371-5

The African Experience in Spanish America by Leslie B. Rout, Jr. "A masterly survey." *—Times Literary Supplement*
PB ISBN 978-1-55876-321-0

The Chinese in the Caribbean edited by Andrew Wilson. "Well documented . . . artfully balanced." *—Caribbean Studies Journal*
HC ISBN 978-1-55876-314-2   PB ISBN 978-1-55876-315-9